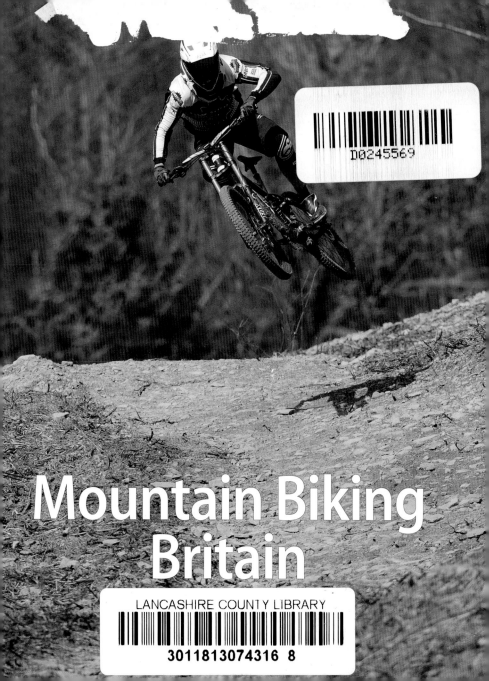

Mountain Biking
Britain

Contents

Title page: Cwmcarn [ANDY LLOYD/PEDAL HOUNDS]

Hello again!

Mountain Biking Britain is back and has had a facelift, something that we felt was necessary as there have been so many changes in the mountain biking world over the last few years – both good and bad. I've made sure that this updated guide will still continue to inspire riders, both young and old, as well as new and experienced, to get out on the trails and push themselves. Here in the UK we are blessed with some of the best riding to be had anywhere in the world, and all within an hour's journey of every major UK city. You'll find some of the best downhill tracks to the most glorious cross country riding (with some breathtaking views) and some of the most gentle, family-friendly, fun rides through our wonderful countryside.

After the 2012 Olympics, there's been a lot of talk about the Olympic legacy and how it will really affect us in the mountain biking community. After a lot research, it's clear to see that we have been affected in a good way. There are several new spots that have made it into the book thanks to being part of the Olympics themselves, the Lee Valley near Stratford is a prime example of this. Not only that, but the popularity of cycling and mountain biking has led to numerous centres being built, as well as inspiring local riders to build new trails and jumps. There's a vast wealth of trails on offer in the UK and it's good to see that mountain bikers are taking full advantage of them. The most prominent feature to the mountain biking scene recently has to go to Bike Park Wales. With plenty of investment in both time and money, you'll find one of the most substantial bike centres in Britain. Built by riders, for riders, it's a centre that's worth a trip to no matter where in the country you live.

With the good must come the bad. When you see a great increase in the amount of trails opening up across the UK, there are inevitably going to be closures. I've seen plenty of trails bulldozed, land being sold off and a few sites in limbo as to whether they will remain in one form or another. Even the iconic Carbisdale Castle has closed, although the trails remain. It's not all doom and gloom though. The additions clearly outweigh the closures, and there are plans to open many more trails. So be assured that there will be plenty of time, and plenty of trails to get your tyres dirty.

Similarly to the last edition of Mountain Biking Britain, I've made sure to add the most useful info to each site – places to stay, facilities, cost (if any), and if there are clubs you can join for those trails. I've tried to make sure it has all the information you'll need for a day, or a holiday on the hills. I do urge you to join any mountain biking forums, or groups for the local trails that you frequent. These groups and associations are the lifeblood of the mountain biking community and regularly help with trail building and fixing.

All that remains is for me to wish you all good luck in finding a great new spot to ride. I've tried to make sure that all information in this book is correct, but if I have got anything wrong (or you wish to recommend somewhere that isn't featured in this book), then please feel free to contact me at mountianbikingbritain@gmail.com.

Get riding!
Chris Moran

How to use the book

Feel free to browse through the book as you see fit of course, but when putting it together, we had in mind that it might be used in the following way:

1 If you already own a bike and know what kind of terrain you prefer, simply check out your local area and comparison chart to find spots you might like. If you fancy a longer trip, or want to get involved with a local riding club, then read up on what's out there in the 'more info' sections in each centre.

2 If you're completely new to mountain biking, and just want to dip your toe into the waters (so to speak), then turn to page 6 to determine which kind of riding you'd like to try out. Then all you have to do is find a nearby trail centre with bikes for hire (see the comparison charts at the back of the book to locate one near you quickly), and then make sure that centre fits in with the kind of riding you can see yourself enjoying.

3 If you're a family and want the perfect day out, simply refer to the beginning of each chapter, where we've starred the best five trail centres for each region. These centres feature bike hire, great visitor facilities, maps, and waymarkers so you're unlikely to get lost on your day out. See the 'Terrain Breakdown' page for more information on what kind of surfaces you might wish to start out on.

4 For each riding spot or trail centre we have tried to give an overall impression – one that will give you a 'snapshot' of what the riding has to offer. We've done this so you can quickly work out whether it's what you want. If you wish to find out more information about any of the places featured in this guide, we've tried to include as many links to further websites, clubs and other links as possible on each relevant page. Please remember, this is not an absolutely definitive guide to the riding spots, it is simply here to give you an overall impression of the best spots near you.

5 Once you've found a good local spot, and met some other riders (and feel like you're part of the brilliant mountain biking scene here in the UK), don't forget to let us know about any more of the amazing – and sometimes underground – spots by emailing Chris at mountainbikingbritain@gmail.com and if you have any photographs, we'd love to see them for possible inclusion in the next edition of Mountain Biking Britain.

Symbols

⊗	Cross-country	⊘	Bikewash
⊙	Downhill	⊘	Uplift
⊕	Freeride	⊙	Map
⊕	4X	⊕	Waymarked
⊕	BMX	⊙	Forestry Commission
⊙	Dirt jump	⊗	Family
Ⓝ	Northshore	⊖	Visitor centre
⊕	Bike hire	⊖	Accommodation
◉	Bikeshop	⊘	Café

What kind of rider am I?

The ultimate mountain bike would be something like this: ludicrously light and stiff, so it's easy to pedal uphill; have loads of gears to help you ascend the most vertical of gradients (and so you can still push hard when you're flying at 50 kph downhill). It would be grippy over mud, rock, wet wood, and sand; and on descents it would have the best ever suspension and geometry to keep you from going over the front of the bike. It would fly over huge jumps, be small enough to take on tight, technical jumps, large enough to attack gaps on downhill courses and be bombproof if you dropped it.

Unfortunately, such a bike doesn't exist, as many of the above requirements completely contradict each other. For example, lightweight rarely (if ever) means strong. And the geometry of a bike that is great going uphill is exactly the opposite to what you want when pointing it downhill. So choosing a bike is a matter of balancing compromises. Our own thinking is that you can break down what kind of rider you are then match the kind of bike or riding that you're after.

What kind of riding do you like?

For those who want to see the countryside, love the aerobic workout from a good ride, enjoy beautiful views and just love being out and about, but aren't too bothered about hard uphill slogs or thrilling descents, a hard-tail XC (cross country) bike is probably a good place to start.

For riders who love pushing themselves aerobically, enjoy (or at least, are not afraid of) uphill climbs, ride a bike because it's a great way of getting out into the countryside, and know that the downhill sections are going to be good fun, then a full-suspension XC bike might be best. If you think you might want to do enduro-style races (or you might want to race your mates!) then you'll want the most lightweight full-suspension XC bike you can afford.

Riders who endure the uphill sections (OK, sometimes they can be a little interesting), love being out in the countryside just so they get to ride the fun, downhill stuff, and like nothing more than to challenge themselves by riding over jumps and over balance-sections (such as northshore), then a strong XC or a Freeride bike will be best. Freeriding can be categorized in many weird and wonderful ways, but we see it as riding pretty much

Foel Gasnach

TOM CALDWELL

everything with the enthusiasm of a kid who wants to jump his or her bike in the air, drop off things, and still loves getting out in the countryside for some rambling action (hunting for jumps!).

For those who love the thrilling downhill sections, jumps and tree roots, and are prepared to either push their bikes uphill (or pay for a lift of some sort), then a downhill bike is brilliant. Note, many people who own a downhill bike might also have an XC bike too.

For those who want to ride their bikes on dirt jumps (a kind of funpark or over-sized BMX track – see the Terrain Breakdown page), and love to be in the air more than anything, then a Dirtjump bike could be perfect.

Note – most riders fit somewhere between riding a full suspension XC and a freeride set up, and generally speaking, they push their bike to its downhill limits. If you can afford two bikes, you'd probably want a downhill bike, and a lightweight XC one.

Now skip to the 'What kind of bike should I be riding?' page…

Terrain breakdown

Many of the trail centres are now as organized as ski resorts, with visitor centres, cafés, hire facilities, changing, showers, car parking and bike washes. They also – like alpine resorts – operate a colour-graded system for each trail so you can make a judgement as to how difficult the riding might be. The colours match the same system as used on alpine ski runs and break down as:

1 **Green trails** are the easiest graded trails, and are suitable for all riders including novices and families. Expect the terrain to be gentle, smooth and with the odd fun challenge along the way (such as a small section of up or downhill riding). Often these runs are on old disused railways, or next to canals and run through areas of outstanding beauty. Please note that some areas in the UK use the colour purple for family-graded or forest road trails.

2 **Blue trails** are more difficult, but should still be fairly easy for athletic, adventurous beginners, and should offer more of a challenge than green trails but be gentle enough for most novices to attempt.

3 **Red trails** are for intermediate riders, and the increase in difficulty over blue trails can be for a variety of reasons. Perhaps the trail is much longer (and therefore, more physically demanding), or it might feature some jumps, drops or steeper down and uphill sections. Red-graded trails may still be attempted by adventurous amateurs, but are best ridden by those who have already got to grips with blue-graded trails and have some bike skills.

4 **Black-graded trails** are for advanced riders, and may feature difficult, technical sections where riding skills are needed. For example, there may be tricky downhill sections over rocks and roots, or there may be drops or jumps on the trail that cannot be avoided.

5 **Orange-graded runs**, which are classified as 'funpark' runs, are usually filled with jumps and various man-made or natural structures to ride over. These can be very, very difficult and should be watched before being attempted.

6 **Diamond** (or double diamond) is another imported symbol from ski resorts and designates a particularly hard section of trail. For example, a jump may be classed as diamond (if there is danger associated with not clearing the entire jump), or double diamond if it's a very large jump.

7 Some trail centres feature 'Skills Areas', where different examples of the likely obstacles to be encountered on the trails is presented in a small area. Skills areas are well worth seeking out, as they will help you brush up on your bike-handling technique, and give you a great idea as to what terrain you prefer riding.

Afan's orange, red and purple trails.

CHRIS MORAN

7

What kind of bike should I be riding?

If you've read the 'What kind of Rider Am I?' page, here is a rough breakdown for each of the bikes.

If you're thinking of buying a bike on a limited budget, please note that the mountain bike magazines websites have fantastic forums for advice and users are always selling their surplus kit. Ebay is a great place to go (once you know exactly what you're after), or you can always go to a bike shop and ask for either a second-hand model or last year's models. The discounts can often be enormous.

Right: Cwmcarn's uplift trailer. Most bikes here will be DH rigs.

Freeride/Downhill

Features   super-sturdy forks (full length usually), plus rear suspension.

Great for   going very fast and riding off large drops.

Pluses   very sturdy great downhill geometry (lots of fork angle forward).

Minuses   very heavy and has wrong geometry to ride uphill.

Travel   at least 7 inches (178 mm) and up to 8 inches (205 mm) on both forks and rear suspension.

Great example   Commencal Supreme DH.

Cost range   £700-3000.

Dirtjump bike

Features   hard tail, suspension on forks, sturdy materials, and only rear gears. Sometimes dirt jump bikes use the smaller 24-inch wheels instead of the regular 26-inch mountain bike wheel diameter.

Great for   riding over large jumps.

Pluses   strong, can take abuse, low maintenance.

Minuses   bouncy downhill, low seat, not made for comfort, few gears.

Travel   4-6 inches (100-150 mm) on the forks.

Great example   DMR Rhythm.

Cost range   £400-900.

Hardtail XC bike

Features suspension forks, but rigid back end (hence the name).

Great for riding gently uphill and along rough terrain, though nothing super technical.

Pluses easier to maintain than a full suspension bike, and simple to ride uphill.

Minuses it will be very shaky when riding fast over bumpy ground (downhill riding in particular), and the geometry will lean you over the front of the bike.

Travel 2.5-4.5 inches (65-110 mm) of up and down movement on the forks.

Great example Specialized RockHopper.

Cost range £300-500

Full suspension, lightweight XC bike

Features suspension forks, plus a suspension system for the back of the bike. Lightweight materials.

Great for going both uphill and downhill.

Pluses lightweight materials mean it'll be breeze up difficult climbs.

Minuses likely to break if ridden hard downhill. It might need lots of maintenance to keep it tuned.

Travel up to 6 inches (150 mm) of movement on both forks and rear suspension.

Great example Santa Cruz Superlight.

Cost range £800-2000.

XC/Freeride bike

Features suspension front and rear, sturdy materials.

Great for riding hard downhill or over jumps and northshore.

Pluses strong, won't break easily if dropped or ridden hard.

Minuses geometry and weight make it more difficult to ride uphill than a pure XC bike.

Travel Around 6 inches (150 mm) of travel on the forks and up to 7.5 inches (190 mm) of rear suspension travel.

Great example Yeti ASX.

Cost range £600-2500.

9

Terrain and terminology

Like any new pursuit (sailing, painting and decorating, car racing), there will be a whole load of words, terms and shortcuts to learn. Mountain biking culture is no different, so here is a list of unfamiliar words that you may come across:

Fire-road/forest road This is simply a dirt road that cuts through many of the UK's forest and are used by forest rangers and loggers for access. They are normally closed to the public with locked gates but easily accessible on a bike (and as such, can be used to get to the top of various hills by the quickest route).

Singletrack This is the terrain best suited for mountain biking (one of the UK magazines is simply named 'Singletrack'). It is a snaking path cutting through the terrain that has been hardened by much cycle use and is a clear marker as to which way other riders have been.

Purpose-built singletrack With the opening of more and more trail centres, purpose-built singletrack is increasingly common. It is usually built by mountain bikers and is like regular singletrack, but with the addition of thoughtful features (jumps, rocks etc), as well as a solid surface that – if possible – drains well and won't clog up with mud. Natural singletrack can be fantastic on its own, but purpose-built singletrack is probably what the majority of riders would prefer.

Double track Double track is basically the mark left by off-road vehicles, or can be overgrown forest road. Again, it can be used to ascend hills or to work out where you are.

Bridleways/horse riding paths The UK is criss-crossed with bridleways and which are wider paths for horses, ramblers or other outdoor users. They are generally not as much fun as singletrack routes (as they are normally quite flat and featureless) but are definitely preferable to forest roads. They are often waymarked too.

Waymarked Waymarked routes are simply areas of singletrack or forest road that have posts at strategic places to show you the direction in which to ride.

Dirt jumps Dirt jumps are areas where local riders have built a network of jumps – normally in close proximity to each other – to pack as many into as short a run as possible.

Berm A berm is a banked turn.

Tabletop If you build a jump with a take off, a middle section that you could walk over, and a landing ramp, you've built a table top.

Gap If you remove the middle section from a tabletop (see above), you've now got a gap jump. Think of it as an Evil Kneivel jump with the buses removed.

Hip A hip jump is one in which the take off and landing are around 45 degrees from each other. So you launch heading straight onwards, and land riding to the left or right.

Rhythm section Dirt jumps come in 'sets' (single lines that can be ridden in one go), also known as 'rhythm sections' which means once you start getting air, you'll go again and again and again.

Chicken line This is an 'opt-out' line on where you might wish ride around a difficult section of trail.

The Track in Portreath's rhythm section in full effect.

Northshore Northshore is purpose-built (normally from planks of wood or felled logs), terrain that can be ridden over in order to test a rider's nerve and balance. The name comes from Vancouver Island's north shore area, where the ground is boggy and the local riders built bridge after bridge over muddy patches on their trails, and noticed they preferred riding the wood structures in the end.

Downhill This is simply singletrack that runs downhill and can feature lots of drops, jumps and tricky rock sections or root sections.

Rock Garden An area of downhill track which is littered with rocks and can be difficult to navigate down. Similar to a mogul field in skiing or snowboarding.

Tracks Tracks are simply trails.

Trails Tracks by another name. The 'path' on which you're riding.

Trials A trial is where potential criminals are put in front of a jury. It's also a style of riding where the idea is to jump your bike from object to object almost always hopping on your back wheel. Not to be confused with a trail (the 'a' and the 'i' are the opposite way around). Trial bikes are basically the 'kick start' of mountain biking.

Essentials Terrain & terminology

Innerleithen (7Stanes).

Enduro, the rise of the all-mountain bike

Enduro has filled a yawning void. As the disciplines of downhill and cross country developed over the last 15 years, they've become more extreme and increasingly specialist. As a result many would-be racers found themselves put off not just by increasingly-technical DH courses and ever more-gruelling XC ones but also the need for specialist bikes.

Enduro has provided that middle ground– a racing equivalent of what the vast majority of riders spend their weekends doing anyway. Riding uphill with their mates and then racing them on the downhills. And vitally - all on the one, all-mountain bike.

And, as the discipline has grown in popularity, so has the market for these do-it-all bikes.

The all-mountain holy grail would be a bike that climbed like a featherweight XC 29er and descended like a slack, low 200mm travel DH beast. In reality the bikes are a compromise, mixing middling geometry and suspension travel with lightweight but strong components.

And the industry hasn't been slow to react to the increase in demand, after all, the type of bikes that cater for the enduro market have always been some of its biggest sellers. The likes of the Orange 5 and the Specialized Enduro are evidence of that.

Carbon frames and components are slashing weights, front mechs and chain guides are being cast aside as 10 and 11-speed transmissions which don't drop chains increasingly become the norm. And, where many early adopters used after-market products to slacken their bikes, factory head angles have plummeted. Just the sheer number of dropper seat posts available now speaks volumes.

Who knows how close we'll get to achieving that elusive perfect compromise but it's fair to say all this investment coupled with advances in material and manufacturing technology mean that it won't be long before very few of us will need more than one bike.

Long live enduro!

How to future-proof your bike: Predictions for the future

Bikes are changing fast as designs progress and strides are made in both manufacturing and materials technology. But which are the must-have upgrades and how can you make sure your bike – and you – don't get left behind? Here are five suggestions to keep you out front:

1 **Fit a dropper seat post** This is probably the most significant after-market upgrade you can make to your bike. Basically a seat post that can be adjusted while you ride. Try fitting one and riding with someone who hasn't. You won't believe the amount of stopping and starting you have to do. And anyone who says they can descend just as fast with their seat up is just lying.

2 **Ditch those fragile inner tubes and go tubeless** You won't only suffer a lot less punctures but your wheels will be lighter and turn quicker. Plus, you'll be able to run them at lower pressures – and have the resulting extra grip – without risking pinch flats. Most tubeless-ready tyres will pop on with a decent track pump and the range is getting bigger all the time.

3 **Ditch your front mech and chain device** With wide-range 10 and 11-speed cassettes plus transmissions that don't drop chains, there's never been a better time to get rid of not only your fiddly front mech and shifter but also your chain device. As well as leaving your bike lighter, there's less to think about. Which - when you're hypoxic – is a revelation.

CHRIS MORAN

4 Widen your bars
It's hard to underestimate the feeling of extra control that wider bars give you. They'll also help you breathe more easily too. The definition of wide depends on your size but is broadly anything from 700 - 800mm. If you ride a lot of tight trees then you'll need to bear this in mind but most people find they soon adjust and that the planted sensation is more than worth it.

5 Shorten your stem
Along with wider bars shortening your stem is one of the cheapest and easiest ways of improving your bike's handling. Putting your weight further behind the hub of your front wheel will give you extra confidence when the going gets steep. It'll also make lofting the front of your bike over obstacles much easier. 50mm would be counted as a short stem.

Southwest England

The Forest of Dean's FODCA Trail in full flow. [TOM CALDWELL]

English Channel

Trails...

1 50 Acre Woods	13 Combe Sydenham	26 Leigh Woods
2 Asham Woods	14 Dartmoor National Park	27 Maddacleave Woods
3 Ashton Court	15 Decoy BMX	28 Mineral Tramways Project
4 Aveton Gifford	16 Forest of Dean	29 Nationwide DJs
5 Bath BMX Track	17 Haldon Forest Park	30 Patchway BMX DJs
6 Blandford UK Bike Park	18 Ferndown DJs	31 Portsdown Hill
7 Brunel Pump Track	19 Hidden Valley DJs	32 Poldice Valley Trails
8 Buckland Rings	20 Hook DJs	33 Portland Bill Quarries
9 Buriton Chalk Pits	21 Hundred Acre Wood	34 Puddletown Woods
10 Bradford Hollow	22 Island Trails	35 Randwick DH
11 Canford Heath and Pit DH	23 JLC Trails	36 Queen Elizabeth Country Park
12 Cann Wood Trails	24 Lanhydrock	
	25 Leckhampton	

37 Red Hill Extreme
38 Rogate
39 Sandford DJs and DH
40 Sheet DJs
41 Stockwood Bike Park
42 Stoke Heights
43 Stoughton Trails
44 Stoke Woods
45 Triscombe DH
46 The Track
47 Watchmoor Wood Bike Park
48 Woodbury Common

The south west of England (at least for the purposes of this book) comprises of Devon, Dorset, Cornwall, Wiltshire, Somerset, and Gloucestershire. Now I'm not sure about you, but heading down in that direction always make me think of boyhood holidays by the coast, and if you are lucky enough to hit one of the Devon or Cornwall spots on a bright sunny day, you will have to agree with me. It is a long way from the cityscape here.

England's south west is a great place to ride a mountain bike, whether you're a local rider in one of the major cities of Bristol, Exeter, Plymouth or Bath, or you are taking a road trip from another part of the country. In fact, for those visiting, there are so many fantastic spots to hit that mountain biking has become an additional attraction to an area that was already beckoning tourists from all corners of the UK. Check out the fantastic Minerals Tramways Project running through Redruth – you will find this bike-specific tourist attraction to have many similarities to the successful 7Stanes areas of Scotland. By using the old railway structures that linked the various mines of the area, Cornwall offers a linked, family friendly area that ticks every box on the mountain biker checklist, like the formidable (and probably best dirt jump site in the UK) TheTrack in Portreath, or the brilliant freeride and downhill paradise of Poldice Valley, it is at the same time a great ride out for the whole family. Impressively, it is also the only place in the UK where you can ride from the north coast to the south coast in a couple of hours. Add in some incredible bike-friendly accommodation, and you can see why a trip to this part of the world is a must for all UK riders.

Geographically, the south west has no actual mountains, but its hills are easily big enough to satisfy the local downhill and freeride enthusiasts. For visitors looking for pure DH thrills, it could be best to re-route over to south Wales, but for lovers of beautiful XC riding, great northshore, and for those who use their bikes to access some lovely remote cafés and wonderful vistas, the south west is a great place to head. The glorious spread-out countryside and scattering of small, picturesque villages has one more advantage too: hit many of the spots mentioned in this book through the off-season, and you're likely to have them all to yourself.

Local scene

Across the eastern edge of the Dorset coast, through the Gloucestershire border, to the very tip of England that is Land's End, there are an untold number of mountain bikers building and shaping their own flawless trails, diligently making the area even better for riders. Just like in the rest of England, the land consists of a mix of un-authorised sites, open access areas, bridleways, national parks, public rights of way, government owned-land, major road and motorway no-man's-land areas, areas of outstanding natural beauty and private land owned by a number of land-management organisations. Perhaps the largest of these – The Forestry Commission – has been very open to the idea of local riders building their own trails on its land, and a forward thinking policy which originated at the start of the 2000s has finally started to reap real rewards in many areas of the country, not least in the southwest. Cann Woods, Hundred Acre Wood, Leigh Woods, Puddletown Forest, Haldon Forest, and Stoke Heights are all very good examples of this partnership in action, and a hearty thanks goes out to the guys and girls at the Forestry Commission for their work. Please respect all signs and closures pointed

❺ Best rides in the southwest

There are plenty of stand-alone spots to head for in the southwest, but we think these are absolute gems and have to be on your list of places to visit in this area:

❶ The Mineral Tramways Project, page 40
(incorporates The Track and Poldice Valley)
If you're looking for a site that ticks every box for every type of rider, look no further. It has beautiful scenery, wonderful pit-stops and cafés, care-free, great bike-friendly accommodation and bike hire, if you need it, at Elm Farm Bike Hire. For those of you that are more proficient at riding, The Track and Poldice Valley make it one of the best kept secrets in the UK.

❷ Haldon Freeride, page 32
This hill to the south of Exeter has everything – free ride, downhill, northshore, and some incredible XC in a wonderfully unspoilt part of the country. It holds a great atmosphere for all abilities and is a great example of riders working in tandem with the Forestry Commission.

❸ Dartmoor National Park, page 29
Who'd have thought that in an area of such outstanding beauty someone would be thoughtful enough to have started an uplift service? Lazy, XC perfection!

❹ Lanhydrock, page 36
Who'd have thought that in an area of such outstanding beauty someone would be thoughtful enough to have started an uplift service? Lazy, XC perfection!

❺ Ashton Court, page 22
This is an MTB site that has been used by riders since 1990, and continues to grow in popularity. There's been a lot of money put into the facilities here (£500,000 to be precise) so make sure it's one you don't miss.

out by the Forestry Commission as they are a very cool organisation and the rangers almost always have your best interests at heart. Some areas, such as the popular downhill routes at Rowberrow Forest have been omitted from this guide because the Forestry Commission doesn't fully own the land used by riders, and we have been asked to not include such sites. We do so obligingly.

Hubs
You will find riders all over the southwest, with groupings mainly coming out of the areas of Exeter and Bristol. They both have amazing scenes, though that is not to say the only scenes. Exeter's Haldon Park is one of the best sites in the region, while Bristol riders have the great spots of Leigh Woods, Asham Woods and Ashton Court to choose from. Add in Woodbury Hill and Stoke Woods all within 30 minutes drive and Bristol is also one of the best cities for riders in the UK. The stand-alone UK Bike Park in Blandford, Dorset, is easily worth a drive from any part of the UK and has something for every type of rider (although at the time of writing, the park's future is still in limbo as it is up for sale), while the fantastic Minerals Tramway Project will see riders of all abilities and ages push Cornwall up the 'must visit' list.

Below: Maddacleave Woods
Bottom: Watchmoor Wood Bike Park
Opposite page: Blandford UK Bike Park

PAUL BLACKBURN

JETHRO LOADER

N1 50 Acre Woods

Train station Clifton Down/Parson Street
Nearest city Bristol
Sat Nav BS8 3TH

Location Leave the M5 at junction 18, take the A4 towards Bristol and continue on towards the Clifton Suspension Bridge. Cross the bridge onto the B3129. When you reach a crossroads, take a right onto the A369 (Abbots Leigh Road) and then take a left onto Beggar Bush Lane. You'll find 50 Acre Woods around 2 km down the road.

Facilities You won't find a shop or cafe in the woods here, it's purely for riding. Nearby Ashton Court has a café that you will be able to buy refreshments from.

Rough round-up Unlike nearby Ashton Court or Leigh Woods, this is a completely volunteer-built section of the surrounding trails. It's only 3 km long but it's an incredibly fun ride that's popular with the locals. There are a couple of technical climbs and a couple of medium-sized drop-offs to give this trail a much more natural feel than its neighbours.

Conditions Can be very prone to mud when the weather has been bad.

ⓘ **More info** Check out Bristol Trails group for trail maps and any info on group build sessions – bristoltrailsgroup.com.

N2 Asham Woods

Train station Frome
Nearest city Bristol
Sat Nav BA11 4NL

Location Asham Woods are about 8 km to the east of Shepton Mallet on the A361. Turn off the road at Nunney, and go through the village taking Castle Hill Road out. After 250 m take another left (signed Leigh On Mendip), and Asham Woods is and 1.5 km along this road on the left. Some signs indicate Torr Works Quarry which the riding is next to to the northeast.

Facilities No facilities but the nearest village is Nunney with local shops.

Rough round-up There are DH trails, a freeride trail, and even some northshore (and more DH tracks in the woods), but it is infrequently maintained and has no official status so don't expect too much! However, if you're in the area it could be a great

place to get involved with and to start building on the already cool jumps and singletrack. Plus the quarry has some brilliant natural terrain and obstacles to take on. MBUK recently shot there with pro freerider Darren Bearclaw so there's definitely some jumps!

Conditions Watch out for mud in winter or when it rains, but the quarry should still have some decent riding.

N3 Ashton Court (The Timberland Trail)

Train station Bedminster Down
Nearest city Bristol
Sat Nav BS41 9JN

Location Leave the M5 at junction 18 and head down the A4 towards Bristol. When you get to Clifton Suspension bridge, cross it and head straight on towards Ashton Court Visitor's Centre which is well signed.

Facilities Ashton Court Estate is a privately-owned manor house and surrounding area. In 2012 it was given a £500,000 new café and bike hire centre. If you feel like heading back over the famous Clifton Suspension Bridge at the eastern corner of the park, you will find plenty of shops in Bristol itself.

Rough round-up An extra 11 km of trails have been built within the last few years which has brought more riders to the area. There is an optional red descent in the middle of the trail which wouldn't look out of place on a DH track but don't let this make you believe it's a Mecca for DH riders. This is mellow, singletrack territory in one of the UK's most spectacular settings, with a little purpose-built wood but generally

natural terrain. Families can make use of the yellow trail (the beginners/family area), a perfect place for kids to get to grips with their bikes.

Despite the extra trails it can still get quite busy. However, the work gone into the new trails will make them rideable all year round, even if there's a wet winter.

Conditions Mud, concerts, and popular weekends are all potential hazards.

ⓘ **More info** The local scene site is bristoltrailsgroup.com, and there's a great page including a map of the trails at – visitbristol.co.uk/things-to-do/avon-timberland-cycling-trail-p1283673.

N4 Aveton Gifford DJs

Train station Ivybridge
Nearest city Plymouth
Sat Nav TQ7

Location About 5 km north of Kingsbridge is the tiny village of Aveton Gifford based in south Devon. Heading south towards Aveton Gifford on the A379, take a left at the village and head to the village of Loddiswell. When you reach Loddiswell, from the corner of Village Cross Road and Fore Street, head north on the B3196 for about 100 m. Take the next right and

as that road bends sharply to the right the dirt jumps are just next to the road on the left.

Facilities There's a shop in Loddiswell which is a less than a minute's ride away.

Rough round-up These dirt jumps are a certainly not worth a long journey, but for local riders this is a one-line of DJs that might provide some fun with a couple of gaps, and some tabletops.

N5 Bath BMX Track

Train station Oldfield Park/Bath Spa
Nearest city Bath
Sat Nav BA2 2PS

Location From the A36 Lower Bristol Road/Rossiter Road, take the A367 south towards Peasedown St John. This road is called Wellsway. After 400 m take a right down Bloomfield Road and Bath BMX is about 200 m down this road. Turn right at the entrance to Chelwood Drive, go to the far end of the car park and follow path to the north.

Facilities The track is virtually in the city centre of Bath, so while there are few direct facilities on site, the nearest shops are minutes ride away.

Rough round-up This ever popular BMX track has benefited from the hard work of local riders in the most recent years. It's a competition-standard BMX track with whoops, berms, tables and gap jumps. Mountain bikers are welcome but to get near the track you will need to wear a helmet, sleeves and leg coverage.

Conditions The track dries out quickly which means that it's open in most conditions. The gate area is tarmacked and the dirt jumps are purpose-built, meaning it's faultless!

ⓘ **More info** Check out one of many Bath BMX groups on Facebook.

N6 Bradford Hollow

Train station Yeovil Pen Mill
Nearest city Bath/Exeter
Sat Nav BA21 5BT

Location Bradford Hollow is 1 km to the southeast of Yeovil. From Yeovil take the A30 in the direction of Sherborne. Cross the railway line, then the river, and take the second right marked Underdown Hollow. The dirt jumps are 100 m up this road on the right.

Facilities With Yeovil so close to the DJs, shops are just a few minutes ride away

Rough round-up The dirt jumps are in the middle of a secluded wood and although most go for the jumps themselves, it would make equally good XC riding. Gaps, tables and step ups with lines for the intermediate to expert, it's a great place for local riders. Probably not worth a long journey.

Conditions Avoid after heavy rain.

ⓘ **More info** Bradford Hollow has a few clips on YouTube and for the GPS nerds, the co-ordinates are 50°56'17"N 2°36'13"W.

☑7 Brunel Pump Track City
🚲

Train station Parson Street
Nearest city Bristol
Sat Nav BS3 1RX

Location The pump track is hidden in the shadow of the A3209 fly-over. When travelling through Bristol city centre, head towards the A38 and drive southwest. When you cross the river, continue on the A38 until you can turn right onto Sheene Lane. Carry on straight onto East Street and take a left onto the B3120 (North Street). Follow North Street until it ends and drive straight over onto Frayne Road; there will be a garden centre at the end of this road so park where you can and ride your bike along the trails, until you reach the pump track which is around 100 m to the northwest.

Facilities No facilities on site but Bristol city centre isn't too far for all amenities and shopping.

Rough round-up It's one of many pump tracks in Bristol but also one of the newest. It's a great place to practice your bike handling skills and join the local scene. There's also plenty of rollers and berms for you to learn how to pick up speed without pedalling.

Conditions Great ride in the summer but can be affected by heavy rain. It also benefits from a lot of light from the fly-over so riders are able to ride long into the night.

ⓘ **More info** Check out Bristol Trails Group for more info on the pump track and any others that can be found in Bristol – bristoltrailsgroup.com.

☑8 Buckland Rings
🚲 🚲 🚲 🚲

Train station Lymington Town/Sway
Nearest city Southampton
Sat Nav SO41 8LJ

Location Buckland Rings is on the southern edge of the New Forest around 30 km to the east of Bournemouth, and 30 km southwest from Southampton. From the M27 exit at junction 1 and take the A337 south through the forest towards Lymington. After about 10-15 km you'll exit the forest and start the approach to Lymington. Before you reach town, take a right onto Sway Road and follow it round to the right. After 200 m take a right and the dirt jumps are near the bottom of this road in the forest to the left next to the railway line.

Facilities Lymington is only a few minutes ride away from the jumps as this public-access forest land has no amenities. There are plenty of shops, including bike shops, that you can get to quickly.

Rough round-up Situated in two disused quarries, the larger of the two is used solely for dirt jumps. The smaller is perfect for freeriders with many drops and cliffs that wouldn't look out of place at Red Bull Rampage. There's a short DH track behind the woods and even a 4X track! It's a neat set up that has benefited from a lot of work from the locals.

Conditions This is mostly clay tracks, all well packed.

☑9 Buriton Chalk Pits
🚲 🚲 🚲

Train station Petersfield
Nearest city Portsmouth
Sat Nav GU31 5SH

Location Buriton Chalk Pits are around 5 km south of Petersfield in Surrey. From the A3, exit at the junction signposted to Buriton and Petersfield on the B2070. Head east off the A road for 100 m before turning right on Greenway Lane heading to Buriton. In Buriton village turn right into Kiln Lane, go uphill to the old signposts where there's a car park on the right and an opening to the left, you'll see where the pits are signed.

Facilities There are no facilities in the chalk pits themselves but nearby Buriton has a corner shop, two pubs (the 5 Bells and Robert Inn) and is a stunningly beautiful Hampshire village.

Rough round-up The real charm lies within the empty woods with a lot of DH trails to ride. There's an obvious ride from the wood entrance back to Buriton village but don't forget that there's the added bonus of a disused chalk quarry which has some dirt jumps built by the locals. We'd suggest a trip to nearby Sheet Dirt Jumps and the brilliant Rogate DH tracks as Buriton alone isn't worth a long journey.

Conditions The forest DH has a well-worn shale track with re-enforced edges in places and chalk clay in the quarry. Avoid after heavy rain.

How to pack your bike for trips
Sam Dale

Sam Dale is already a veteran of UCI World Cup tours. Since the age of 15 he has been travelling to National Point series, Maxxis Cup and one-off events around Europe and the UK. He knows the inside of a Ford Transit better than the guy who designed it. Here are his 10 tips to packing your bike away for travel.

1 Number one has to be: get a bike bag off eBay. It should cost you less than £100 and definitely get one with a hard base and wheels. Some of those airports are massive, and without a bike bag some airlines won't let you on.

2 If you're going to spend money on anything, spend it on a good lightweight pump, a tool kit with good allen keys and some screwdrivers, and get a good pedal spanner.

3 What do I take apart first? I take the wheels off, then the handlebars and brake calipers, then the rear mech (the de-railer), then the pedals off, then I take my chain off to stop it hitting the frame, then I take the brake levers and the gear shifters off the handlebars too. It all goes in the bag.

4 Put the pedals in your normal clothes bag, but wrap them in something first, as they can scratch up anything they come into contact with.

5 Cut some stiff pipe big enough to go in the space where the hubs would go, to prevent your swing arm and your forks getting squashed. Keep your axel on for the same reason. You'll also want some cable ties for all the brake and gear cables. If you've got loads then just cut them when you take the bike apart and put new ones on when you put it back together.

6 Put a bit of plastic in between the brake pads so that if the lever gets accidentally squashed, it won't pull the pads together and the pistons won't get pushed out. They're a nightmare to get back in 'cos if there's no air in the brake system you'll have to re-bleed them.

7 Take your brake rotors off to stop them getting bent, and then put them in a bit of cardboard and tape it up to stop any oil or anything getting in there. If they get contaminated they won't be as effective.

8 Take a small bottle of oil to lube the chain with. Make sure it's got a tight top on it so it doesn't leak. Then chuck all your pads, protection wear and rain gear in with the bike to give it extra padding. Not your main clothes though – my sharp suits and going out wear are kept away from all that grease and oil!

9 Deflate tyres. Then cover your bike with all your pads and wet weather gear to give it some padding.

10 Last thing to do before you leave the house: check you're not overwwieght – 32 kg is the max for any one bike bag. You should be able to take in on pretty much all airlines. Easyjet and Ryan Air sting you for sporting luggage though, but BA are pretty good. That's how they make all their money innit?

Sweet, wondrous allen key.

Blandford UK Bike Park

Train station Gillingham

Nearest city Southampton

Sat Nav DT11 0TF

Opening times The park is run using club memberships so there are no opening times – members ride whenever they feel like it

NOTE: At time of research, Blandford Freeride Park is currently closed as they look to find a buyer.

Location Commonly known as Blanford Freeride Park, now named UK Bike Park, you'll find it at the top of Okeford Hill near Shillingstone in Dorset. If you're looking to have a full day's riding then Shillingstone is the perfect place for an overnight stay with traditional pubs and a couple of corner shops making this small village very quaint. Blandford is on the A350 around 10 km south of Shaftesbury. From Blandford take the A357 northwest in the direction of Sturminster Newton. Just after Shillingstone turn left into Shillingstone Lane towards Okeford Fitzpaine. There, turn left again towards Ibberton, and take the next left towards Turnworth. The UK Bike Park car park is about 1.5 km down this road on the right. The park itself is on the left.

Facilities Plenty – this is a purpose-built mountain bike centre with a permanent uplift (using army-style trucks), although private hire is for a minimum of 10 riders (there are public days – check the website). Expect to pay around £20 for public use or £30 for private hire.

XC This is not an XC venue as it has no cross country trails, however due to its multiple size obstacles, it is well suited to the XC rider looking to develop their downhill or freeride handling.

Downhill This is a 125-metre-high hill, (perfect height to push a bike up) with lines and options to the four main downhill routes – Big Grin, BTNE (Ben Terrace's Natural Extension), Dark Side and Devils Dyke. All the courses end up at Mix It Up – a natural bowl full of freeride obstacles and jumps to finish on. If you manage to book into one of the very popular uplift days you can link up the various different sections and hit a different route each time. The park is ideal for novice to intermediate riders as all the features have chicken lines while building up confidence. Expert or advanced riders may find that there is not much here to challenge them, but the park is constantly evolving new lines of all sizes.

Freeride The park is a popular freeride venue and it heavily leans towards this style of riding. In the park there are various ladder drops, gaps, a mini A line style trail, plenty of small to medium jumps, and balance northshore features. The other routes are alternative DH courses or freeride mini-trails in their own right. Berm Bandit, X up, Ladder Ally, Log Jam, Dirty Bomb; George and Zippy, Drop Three and Abyss can all be found in the flatter, summit area of the park and at the start of the downhill course

Not to Miss The foam pit will see most people practicing their X-games moves.

Remember to Avoid It can get really boggy in the winter months if it's been raining.

Nearest Bike/Hire shop Bikelab (T01202 330011) are found in Poole which is a short drive away from the park, or Torico Performance Bikes in Sturminster Newton (torico.co.uk) have a full range of demo bikes.

Local accommodation
Pennhills Farm (T01258 860491) is actually located at the bottom of the freeride park so you couldn't be in a more convenient location and they are more than used to looking after mountain bikers.

Eating There is a range of hot and cold drinks available most days, with burger-style vans coming on weekends and race days.

ⓘ **More info** UK Bike Park (T07881571069, ukbikepark.com) has jpeg trail maps which are available in hard copies on site.

> Lowdown

😊 Locals do
Book very early to get on the uplift days.

☹ Locals don't
Mind showing you around the trails.

✔ Pros
Good progressive ride venue for novice/ intermediate riders.

Good use of the land area.

Ideal day trip or weekend overnight venue.

✖ Cons
Limited space on the public uplifts (but a group can book VIP lifts).

Would exhaust the riding after a couple of days.

11 Canford Heath and Pit DH

Train station Parkstone/Branksome
Nearest city Bournemouth
Sat Nav BH21 3BA

Location Canford Heath and the Pit are just on the northwest edge of Bournemouth. From the A31 heading into Bournemouth take the B3073 and then the A31 again heading towards Wimborne. Turn south at Oakley on the A341, and after 500 m take a left into Queen Anne Drive. Carry on for about 1 km and Canford Pit is behind the grassland on your right.

Facilities You won't find any facilities at the Heath and pit, but Oakley village is a short ride away to the north and will have all the supplies you'll need.

Rough round-up With plenty of chalky and filthy singletrack, Canford Heath is great for the XC enthusiast to explore, and is generally pretty empty. The bombhole and pit are a huge hole that freeriders have built jumps, drops and evern cliff drops around. It's a huge hit for the locals but the majority agree it's not with a long journey.

Conditions Most routes chalky, but mud can be a problem.

ⓘ **More info** Locals The Dorset Rough Riders regularly ride at Canford – dorsetroughriders.co.uk.

12 Cann Wood Trails

Train station Plymouth
Nearest city Plymouth
Sat Nav PL7 4DP

Location Situated just north of Elfordleigh Golf Club, Can Wood Trails are relatively easy to find. They're north of the town of Plympton/Colebrook which is east of Plymouth on the A38. Exit the A38 onto the B3416 heading to Plympton, and after 1 km take a left into Plymbridge Road, then first right onto Boringdon Road, and follow this to the T-junction. Take a right here, follow the road up to the left (Boringdon Hill), and past the Elfordleigh Hotel Golf and Country Club on your left. Park soon after in the Forestry Commission signed car park and Cann Woods are just to the north.

Facilities The land is looked after by the Forestry Commission but there are few facilities. There is a car park for those who drive there.

Rough round-up The trails are predominantly freeride-based with plenty of short downhill sections and trails and all sorts of jumps and drops hidden about the network of trails. A network roughly consisting of 16 km of land. There are a few easy routes but as it's constantly ridden by the locals who are becoming more and more skilled,

the trails are becoming increasingly challenging. As such, expect plenty of cool drops, interesting features and short but really sweet rides.

Conditions As it's all forest land you should expect plenty of roots and singletrack, much of which is prone to mud in the winter due to the popularity of horse riding. Keep an eye out for the occasional walker as well.

13 Combe Sydenham

Train station Bishop's Lydeard/Taunton
Nearest city Exeter/Bristol
Sat Nav TA4 4JG

Location Combe Sydenham Hall and Country Park can be found by exiting the M5 at junction 25 onto the A358/Toneway. Continue onto the A38 and head towards the A3038 and take a right onto Station Road. After this, take a left into the A358 and continue on until you turn left at the B3224. This will roughly be a 10-km drive until reaching a right turn onto the B3188. The manor house will be on your left with various parking and facilities.

Facilities CSH&CP is a privately-owned manor house and park which has re-invented itself as a historical centre (Sir Francis Drake stayed there), as well as using its grounds as a 4x4 and mountain bike centre. Food and drinks available but only for group tours on admission.

Rough round-up The DH course here is competition-standard as there seems to be at least one race here each year. Put £5 in the box at the entrance for the DH area (to the southwest of the car park), head up the fire-road and

PAUL BLACKBURN

Right: Cann Wood Trails
Opposite page: Combe Sydenham

start the course: the first section is open farmland, dropping into berms and plunging into the forest. The course has lots of features including areas that drop off the fire-road to singletrack through the forest, with great gap jumps – up to 20 ft – (with sneak-round tracks), tabletops, fast – open field sections and plenty of doubles.

Conditions The track can be gravelly and exposed, so avoid in high wind. But the forest sections are well covered, with the only problem being mud and water pipes breaking and flooding the course (it has happened!).

ⓘ **More info** Call before you leave (especially for longer journeys) as they often use the course land for mountain bike and motocross competitions – T01984 656 284 or T01643 702259, or check the Information Britain site page on CSH&CP at information-britain.co.uk.

🚲14 Dartmoor National Park
🚲 🚲 🚲 🚲 🚲 🚲 🚲

Train station Newton Abbot
Nearest city Exeter/Plymouth
Sat Nav TQ13 9JQ

Location The Dartmoor National Park Authority maintains this huge expanse of public-access moorland in Devon with plenty of starting and finishing points for the adventurous XC rider. If you take tips from the locals, they'd tell you that the preferred routes leave from Bovery, Tracey. From the end of the M5, head down the A38 taking the Chudleigh Knighton exit. From there head west on the B3344 (Bradley Road) towards Bovey Tracey, go through the village of Bovey Tracey, cross the A382 and head straight on (the road changes

to the B3387, but is the same road you were on), and the DNPA car park is signed first right off here.

Facilities You'll be spoilt for choice in Dartmoor as mountain biking is open to roads, bridleways and dedicated singletrack. The ride home is predominantly gentle downhill for families and learners. There used to be a dedicated bus service for an uplift but it is no longer running. There's still an opportunity to uplift but you will need your own vehicle to do so.

Rough round-up There are plenty of serious XC routes and long-distance enduro rides, many well-signed. Beginners and families love the area, with the Granite Way (an 11-km scenic route from Okehampton to Lydford) takes in viaducts and areas of spectacular beauty.

Conditions Avoid in the wet, and can be boggy for long periods in winter.

ⓘ **More info** dartmoor-npa.gov.uk has a great routes page. Bikus is a fantastic mountain bike shop in Bovey Tracey – T01626 833 555.

🚲15 Decoy BMX
🚲

Train station Newton Abbot
Nearest city Exeter/Plymouth
Sat Nav TQ12 1EJ

Location Decoy is on Coach Road, to the south of Newton Abbot town centre.

Facilities Decoy is a BMX track that was completed in 1998, and has a couple of tarmac circuits and some dirt jumps.

Rough round-up If you're interested in practising bike control then this is perfect for you. You can hit the surfaced BMX track itself or on the dirt jumps which include tables, hips, double jumps, step-ups and some beginner jumps.

Conditions The dirt jumps are generally fine in most weather (unless it's really muddy), whereas the surfaced track can be ridden no matter what.

ⓘ **More info** Decoy has its own website, decoy-bmx.co.uk.

FORESTRY COMMISSION

Train station Lydney/Gloucester
Nearest city Gloucester
Sat Nav GL16 7EH
Opening times All day, 365 days per year. Free to use

Location The Forest of Dean is west of Gloucester and to the north of the Severn Channel. From Gloucester head west along the A48, turning at Elton towards Littledean on the B4226 (Elton Road). Carry on along this road and take a right after Speech House onto the B4234. Go up about 2 km and the Forest of Dean entrance is on the left and well-signed.

Facilities Cannop Cycle centre is an old Colliery centre and all trails are well marked from here. It also has a café with the Pedalbikeaway Cycle Centre nearby ready to hire out bikes for your day of riding (although they're fairly basic bikes). Parking costs £3 for the day and food and drinks are available from nearby Beechenhurst Lodge. Trail maps can be bought from Pedalbikeaway of the Forest of Dean offices in Coleford for 60p (last check) or downloadable online.

XC A brand new Enduro trail was built in 2013 and is a challenge for any lover of XC. It's not way marked so you will need a GPS just to keep on track. It's filled with singletrack, green track, fast descents and the odd forest road section. As well as the Enduro there's a Family Cycle Trail runs through former railway lines, specially-laid singletrack and well-marked fireroads. It's a very picturesque route perfect for families but as you would imagine – short on challenges for the serious rider.

The Freeminer's Trail (graded Red on the CTC classification) now has 2.5 km of brand new extension with tough climbs, rock garden and a jumps line. It also has the original 4.5-km loop of challenging singletrack with switchback climbs, drops, root sections, hairpins, and some big jumps, all starting from the Cycle Centre.

Downhill Although the downhill course at the Forest of Dean is not officially recognised and waymarked by the forestry, it has been in existence and hosting races since back in 1996 and if you spring forward over 13 years, it is still a great ride. There are at least 10 interestingly-named DH trails and the shuttle allows riders to experience as many as possible in a day's riding. This is perhaps why it has remained a popular place to ride downhill despite the bigger hills of Wales being only one hour away.

Freeride Near the cycle centre you'll find some old coal tips with a range of different sized jumps and steep banks to play with. A short trip up the road and you'll find The Dips – a prime spot with a number of bowls with drops, small jumps and a small set of trails while just north of the Pedalbikeaway Centre there are some dirt jumps with tables and gaps. They're also planning some northshore sections to be built in the near future.

Easy The Family Trail – perfect scenic rides on a hire bike even.

Hard The Freeminer trail is a must, while there new endure trail, mentioned previously, is a welcomed challenge for all good XC riders.

Not to miss A run of the classic downhill which can be ridden on any of today's suspension trail bikes.

Remember to avoid Some of the features and jumps are badly built so check before you ride.

Nearest Bike/Hire shop Cannop Cycle Centre.

Local accommodation
There are many biker friendly places to stay; try The Fountain Inn and Lodge (T01594 562189) or Sarah's Place – a B&B claimed to be specifically for mountain bikers (T01600 860967). Not only that but you can hire cottages, buildings are hire a plot at a local camp site. Try fodmtb.com for useful links.

Eating Cannop Cycle Centre has drinks and snacks, and nearby Coleford has pubs and shops. The Ostrich Inn (T01594 833260) has hearty meals.

ⓘ **More info** The Forest of Dean has its own page on the Forestry Commission website – forestry.gov.uk, the Forest of Dean Cycle Association has its own site – fodca.org.uk, and the Pedalbikeaway Cycle Centre can be found at – pedalabikeaway.com, T01594 860026. Booking your uplift can be done on the FlyUpDownhill site – flyupdownhill.co.uk and the Forest Of Dean MTB site has many useful links – fodmtb.com.

JOHN MACFARLANE/FORESTRY COMMISSION

> **Lowdown**

⊕ **Locals do**
Pre-book the shuttle if they're planning a full day's riding.

Ride up to the dips and play up there before riding one of the many descents back towards the centre.

Use this as a great night-riding spot as there are plenty of trails that are kind to night riders.

⊕ **Locals don't**
Always ride up the hills – you can shuttle it.

Forget to pay and display – the money will benefit the cycle facilities.

✔ **Pros**
Super family riding area, with expansive flat routes.

Fun short trails, lots of good singletrack.

A great place for XC riders to sample downhill as the courses are not too technical.

✘ **Cons**
Lots of roads in the area to cross.

Not perhaps the same variety for expert riders found in some regions.

A lot of cycle events are held each year so parking can be limited on those days.

PAUL HAWKINS/FORESTRY COMMISSION

Tip There is no formal uplift arrangement at the Forest of Dean but public roads run through the wood and it can be shuttled very easily with your own vehicles and is very popular for this reason.

⤵17 Haldon Forest Park

🚲 🚲 🚲 🚲 🚲 🚲 🚲 🚲

Train station Exeter St Thomas
Nearest city Exeter
Sat Nav EX6 7XR

Opening times As the park is Forestry Commission-owned it means that the park is open all year round from 0830, with the only time limit being dusk (from April to October anyway – for October to April it's 0830-1700). However, remember to check the website as it will inform you about essential repairs and building work. There are some night rides to go on throughout the winter but it's best to pre-book through the Forest Cycle Hire shop.

Location Travel on the M5 towards Exeter where the motorway ends and continue on the A38 south towards Plymouth. On the hill, as you exit the city, take the turn off signposted Exeter Race Course (it's a brown sign with pictures of horses). Turn right (going under the A38) and follow the Forest Park Centre signs. Carry along this road (past the Haldon sign), and the car park is on the left.

Please note that the Forestry Commission advise you not to use the postcode in your Sat Nav as it will take you to the FC office and not the visitor car park. When driving there you will need to carry on past the first gateway, which has 'office entrance

only' painted on the road, and you will reach the main entrance about 200 m further down.

Facilities Haldon Forest is one of few places that has influence from riders and the Forestry Commission. It's already one of the best trail centres in the UK with something for everyone, whether you're looking for a family day out with the kids and hoping to get them into the sport, or whether you want to try out some pump track and northshore riding. All done with an ethos of respect for the environment that goes down to the choice of wood used to build obstacles.

XC The XC scene at Haldon, with a mixture of trails to test yourself with, is XC riding at its best. There's been a lot of work and a lot of money gone in to developing the trails over the recent years but this money has resulted in some great trails ranging from absolute beginner to expert rides. All rides are well signposted but if you want a paper version, you can download the map from the Haldon website. The trails will stay open through the majority of weather conditions thanks to good drainage and the amount of bridges.

Downhill Despite not having any specific DH routes, the Ridge Ride Extreme and the Ridge Ride trails would put a smile on any DH rider.

Freeride There used to be a huge freeride area in Haldon, thanks to the locals, but time, storms and the Forestry Commission have made sure that this has been dismantled over the last few years. The money used on developing new trails at the park has also gone into to building a 'skills area' with a pump track. There's a small amount of northshore riding and maybe 1 or 2 dirt jumps but they're nothing to get excited about. Haldon Forest is definitely more for the XC rider than the freerider.

Easy The Discovery Trail is the easier trail and recommended for families. It's also a great place to build up your confidence before moving on to the Challenge Trail.

Hard The Ridge Ride is the trail built for riders wanting a real challenge.

Not to miss Night riding in the winter.

Remember to avoid Check the Forestry Commission website to see if there are any closures before leaving the house.

Nearest Bike/Hire shop Haldon now has its own cycle hire on site that will cater for adults, kids, parents wanting a trailer and disability bikes.

Local accommodation Upcott House is a bike-friendly Edwardian house on the edge of Dartmoor and offers B&B accommodation (T01837 53743, upcotthouse.com).

Eating Haldon has The Ridge Park Café available for all visitors to the park.

ⓘ **More info** Exeter Mountain Bike Club – embc.primitivemedia.co.uk, The Forestry Commission Haldon –.forestry.gov.uk. and the Forest Cycle Hire – forestcyclehire.co.uk.

> **Lowdown**

☺ **Locals do:**
Sign up to the Discovery Pass to get free parking for a year.

Ride amazingly well (as to be expected with this on their doorstep).

Pre-book night rides in the winter.

☹ **Locals don't**
Build anything illegally.

Leave anything behind in the forest.

Camp in the forest grounds

✔ **Pros**
One of UK's great trail centres.

Guided rides and night riding available.

✖ **Cons**
No great DH tracks.

As a co-op organization relying on volunteers, new areas build up slowly.

18 Ferndown DJs

Train station Bournemouth
Nearest city Bournemouth
Sat Nav BH22 9EN

Location When travelling on the A27 towards Bournemouth, the motorway will turn into the A31. Continue on this road until the A31 splits into two different roads – the A31 and the A347. You will need to follow the A347 but only until the next roundabout. Take the second exit onto the B3072 and drive about a mile down the road. Take a left onto Church Road, then right into Cherry Grove. Park your car and the dirt jumps will be just past the football pitches.

Facilities Ferndown itself will have plenty of shops.

Rough round-up The council had recognised that the area needed some developing for bikes and so they worked with the community to build some dirt jumps. As the jumps are built by hand and are regularly changed (with full backing from the council), you never really know what you're going to get. Definitely worth a trip if you're a local but not worth a long trip.

Conditions Best to avoid in and after heavy rain.

CHRIS MORAN

19 Hidden Valley DJs

Train station Hamworthy
Nearest city Bournemouth
Sat Nav BH17 7YR

Location This predominantly freeride area is located on the west side of Bournemouth. Heading out of Bournemouth on the A35 towards Dorchester, make sure you follow this road as it goes underneath the A3049. You'll reach a roundabout with Creekmore Lane on your right; go straight over until you hit the next roundabout and take a right onto Longmeadow Lane. Park at the end of this lane and enter Upton Heath on your left. Hidden Valley is the about 200 m to the east of where you've parked and is a large clay quarry.

Facilities Head into nearby Creekmore for local shops

Rough round-up Otherwise known as the Clay Pits or Canyons, the Hidden Valley DJs are very popular with the local scene due to the brilliant dirt jumps (featuring big jumps, step downs, drops, tables, hips and good berms). Not forgetting the great drop-ins to the bowl, which gives it an almost skatepark feel. There are also some short DH trails and plenty of XC singletrack in the surrounding area. All in all, well worth a visit if you're in the area.

Conditions This is mostly clay. Avoid when wet, but great for shaping!

20 Hook DJs

Train station Swanwick
Nearest city Southampton
Sat Nav SO31 9JH

Location You'll find the Hook DJs to the south of Locks Heath which is roughly 6 km southeast of Southampton. Leave the M27 at junction 9 and head south on the A3051 for about 6 km. When you reach a roundabout take the second exit onto Hunts Pond Road. At the second roundabout on this road turn right onto Abshot Road, follow this road until you reach another roundabout and take a right onto Warsash Road. Follow this road and take a left into Fleet End Road, you'll soon see New Road in front of you. Park after the line of houses and the DJs are just on the other side of the copse to the left.

Facilities Ride into Warsash, the nearby village, for shops and amenities.

Rough round-up As this is council land, the DJs have been built with local permission. They're nothing special and not worth a long haul drive but they are perfect for local Southampton riders.

Conditions This is open grassland next to a copse of trees in a popular dog-walking area. Avoid after rain as it can get muddy.

⛰21 Hundred Acre Wood

Ⓔ Ⓔ Ⓔ Ⓔ

Train station Fareham/Porchester/Botley

Nearest city Portsmouth/Southampton

Sat Nav PO17 6JD

Location You'll find Hundred Acres around 5 km north of Fareham, Hampshire, between Portsmouth and Southampton. Exit the M27 at junction 10 and drive up the A32 (Hoads Hill Road). At Wickham, turn east (right) onto the B2177 Southwick Road and carry on for 1 km then take a left into Hundred Acres Road. Carry on down here for 1 km and park at the Hundred Acre Forestry Commission car park.

Rough round-up This is a beautiful and picturesque tract of of land in the Hampshire countryside, with plenty of fun and gentle XC routes. Many are signed by the FC, and cutting off these family routes are plenty of good trails that might be a little more testing for better riders and extend as

far as you could wish to ride in a day. Recommended for adventurous riders who like to route-find.

Conditions Most routes are fantastic singletrack or bridleways and tend to be gravelly and exposed, so avoid in high wind. As always, mud is a frequent problem.

⛰22 Island Trails

Ⓔ

Train station Havant

Nearest city Portsmouth

Sat Nav PO11 0ED

Location Just off Havant, to the east of Portsmouth, is Hayling Island. From the A27 Havant bypass take the A3023 to Hayling Island. Continue for 3 km past North Hayling on your left, then through Stoke, then before South Hayling take a right into Station Road. Continue for around 400 m and take a right into Furniss Way. Park at the end and the dirt jumps should be right in front of you.

Facilities South Hayling has plenty of shops and amenities for riders.

Rough round-up Havant Council have put a lot of money into developing the Hayling Billy Trail – a trail which has the dirt jumps at the end. As such, the council has put money into the dirt jumps also and they're loved by BMX and MTB riders alike. With plenty of lines, there's enough there to entertain the intermediate and above. These jumps are built by locals with council backing so plenty of scope for volunteers to get involved with building and more.

Conditions This is a well-drained area that has been purpose-built, but will still be off-limits in bad weather.

⛰23 JLC Trails

Ⓔ

Train station Polsloe Bridge

Nearest city Exeter

Sat Nav EX1 3DS

Location Leave the M5 by junction 29 heading towards Exeter on Honiton Road (the B3183) and take a right into Sweetbrier Lane. Sweetbrier then turns into Vaughan Road if you continue straight. Take a left heading onto Whipburn Lane, then immediately right into Georges Close. You'll find the dirt jumps on the left hand side, just past football pitches. Alternatively, find Polsloe Bridge Train station – the park land is directly to the south.

Facilities As you would expect, no facilities are on site as these are hand built trails. However, Exeter has plenty of nearby shops so you won't have to go far to find what you need.

Rough round-up The JLC trails are primarily BMX dirt jumps with lots of gaps, berms and drop in all condensed into a small, level area the size of a five-a-side pitch. The jumps are out in the open, and right next to five football pitches in the middle of a big city, so expect it to be busy if you turn up on a weekend. Expect it to be as pikey as any other inner-city skate park of BMX area. This is no place for learners, and respect must be afforded the locals who have put an enormous effort into building the jumps.

Conditions Rain will ruin any chance of riding so make sure you keep an eye on the weather.

Southwest England JLC Trails

35

⬂24 Lanhydrock Cycle Hub

⊗ ⊛ ⊙ ⊚ ⊘ ⊛ ⨍

Train station Bodmin Parkway
Nearest city Plymouth
Sat Nav PL30 5AD

Location Lanhydrock is just south of Bodmin and not too far away from Newquay. If you're traveling from the northeast, the A30 is the main road that you'll need. Luckily, the cycle hub is signposted from the A30, so finding it couldn't be easier. For those travelling along the A38, drive along the A38 until you can turn onto the A30 and follow the signs.

Facilities As it's a National Trust site, it benefits from having a lot of facilities.

These include bike hire, free parking, café and restaurants, Visitor Centre, toilets and more. It's open 364 days of the year but worth checking on the website before leaving (below). To use the gardens for riding, you will have to pay a fee, which at the moment stands at £7 for adults and £3.50 for children.

Rough round-up This is a brand new site that opened in February 2014 and has a lot to offer. Green, blue and red trails are ready to be ridden by riders of all abilities. It's mostly XC area but there are some quick runs that should excite the downhillers among you. The skills area is there to encourage your bike handling skills and also holds a few

jumps for those of you who visit for this purpose. Not recommended to travel all this way if you're only after dirt jumps. There's bike hire on site that hire out both adult and children's bikes – £12 for an adult (half day) and £10 for a child (half day).

Conditions These are purpose built trails so expect them to be rideable throughout most conditions.

ⓘ **More info** Visit the National Trust website for more info and a downloadable bike map – nationaltrust.org.uk/lanhydrock.

Train station Chelthenham Spa
Nearest city Cheltenham
Sat Nav GL53 9QQ

Location Leckhampton DH is around 2 km south of Cheltenham town centre. From the M5 leave at junction 11 and head along the A40 to Cheltenham town centre. When you get there take the A46 south (the Bath Road); after a few hundred metres, take a left on to Leckhampton Road. Head down here past the rehab hospital on the left and Leckhampton Woods are straight on, just before Daisybank Road on the left.

Facilities As you're in the woods there aren't any shops but Leckhampton and Cheltenham have plenty.

Rough round-up Leckhampton has several DH trails snaking through woods but the majority of them are incredibly short. With plenty of drops, step ups and interesting terrain to ride, they're also as sweet as they are short. There are steep, technical sections on some, with roots and loose ground as well as off-cambers to ride. There's everything here from XC-style riding to some difficult DH. Not forgetting the freeride area which has a nice trail running to the side of it.

Conditions Mostly singletrack through forest land. Avoid after periods of rain.

ⓘ **More info** The local riders are rightly proud of their area, and have built the site thecorrective.com to help get council support and to welcome diggers to maintain and increasing the mountain bike scene at Leckhampton, nearby Cleave Hill and in Cheltenham.

Train station Bedminster Down
Nearest city Bristol
Sat Nav BS41 9JN (for Ashton Court next door)

Location Leigh Woods are next door to Bristol's Ashton Court and just to the north of Clifton Suspension Bridge on the western edge of the River Avon gorge.

Facilities You will normally find burger vans selling refreshments on site but if this isn't to your taste, Leigh Woods are minutes from Clifton which has plenty of shops and amenities.

Rough round-up There are three main trails to Leigh Woods, one moderate, one difficult and one skills park. The skills park has small drops, rock gardens and rollers to progress your ability with an increasing level of difficulty as you move from one challenge to the next. The moderate trail is an engaging ride through the woodland whereas the red grade/difficult trail is much more technical.

There are three entrances – from North Road, from the Forestry Commission entrance 2 km east of Abbots Leigh Village or by the River Avon trail around 3 km north of Clifton Suspension Bridge. This is the steepest section so it might be worth finishing your day by exiting here.

Conditions Avoid in muddy conditions.

ⓘ **More info** Check out the Bristolian local scene – bristoltrailsgroup.com.

FORESTRY COMMISSION

FORESTRY COMMISSION

Forestry Commission
Welcome to Leigh Woods
Part of the Forest of Avon
For enquiries tel: 01594 833057

Southwest England Leigh Woods

◯ ◯ ◯ ◯ ◯ ◯ ◯

Train station Gunnislake
Nearest city Plymouth
Sat Nav PL19 9DP
(for Dartmoor Cycles)

Opening times The trails are private land, hence the membership fees, and can only be ridden on open days, weekends and holidays. Contact Woodland Riders (woodlandriders.com) to join, membership is currently £30 per year for adults, £25 for students and £15 for under 16's, or a day pass costs £5. You can buy all passes online or day passes on the day of riding from Dartmoor Cycles. Uplift fees are £27 for members for the day and slightly more for non-members. There is no trail map available at present although all trails are shown on the information board at the car park.

Location When travelling from Tavistock, take the A390 west towards Gulworthy. Then head south (take a left) on the B3257 towards Morwell where the road forks and you take the right hand road for 500 m. The road will turn sharply to the right but you will need to take a left exit which is the access track to Maddacleave Woods. Be warned though – you must be a member to ride here, so it's best to head to Dartmoor Cycles in Tavistock first or see below.

Facilities The trails benefit from a great view overlooking Cornwall as they're situated on a steep face next to the Tamar river. The woods house some spectacular rock formations that just-out over the severe slope. As the trails are cut into the landscape, it means that many of them are permanent downhill routes; two aimed at experts with the third a more gentle and suitable to ride on an XC bike as well as DH bikes.

XC Some parts of the woods can be classed as XC but it's not the home of XC riding. There are links from this venue out to other general cycle paths in the Tamar Valley that link many of the heritage sites, but they are not designed specifically for mountain bikes. However there is some excellent XC riding on Dartmoor which is an expansive moorland National Park. You should not ride out onto the moor without being prepared though, as the weather can change very quickly and it is easy to lose your way. Take a map and compass or GPS and you'll have a great time.

Downhill You'll soon discover that this is a primarily downhill venue with several trails to test the abilities of all riders. The black routes should only be attempted by expert downhillers, who will love the challenging features on offer from this hill. It is a national standard competition trail, though many have commented on it being

> **Lowdown**

☺ **Locals do**
Make sure they've bought their day pass before heading to the woods.

Pre-book and use the uplift facility to get the most out of a day on the hill.

Ride within their own abilities.

☹ **Locals don't**
Ride here when it's very wet – the rock can be very slippery.

Ride on their own or without a phone.

✔ **Pros**
One of the most technical downhill facilities in the UK.

A well managed facility.

✖ **Cons**
Riders looking to get some miles under their belt will have to look elsewhere.

Members only and with strict rules (although sensible ones).

of international difficulty. The red trail runs down the hill following much gentler gradients and with less technical features, more suitable for riders with less downhill experience. Definitely not a group of trails to miss out on.

Freeride You won't find any stand-alone freeride stunts or trails but you will find that some of the harder lines and bigger jumps on the downhill routes will challenge all but the professional freeriders. Because of this, a day's riding using the uplifts will appeal to all freeriders.

Easy Riding the HSD (the easier of the red trails) a couple of times

should get you used to the obstacles you'll find on the other rides

Hard For expert riders it will probably take more than a full day's riding to master all the lines and options on the two more technical downhill runs.

Not to miss A run down the red route as it flows perfectly.

Remember to avoid It is an old tin mining site so stick to the marked trails at all times.

Nearest Bike/Hire shop Dartmoor Cycles in Tavistock (T01822 618178, dartmoorcycles.co.uk).

Local accommodation
Being a popular tourist area there is no shortage of B&Bs offering somewhere to put your head down either in town or on many of the farmhouses in the area. Try former railway station Tavistock Railway Station (T01822 610136).

Eating For something to keep you going when out at the woods stock up on pasties from the Original Pasty House as they have 13 different flavours to choose from (T01822 616003, pastyhouse.co.uk).

ⓘ **More info** Dartmoor Cycles are the main hub for the centre, although Maddacleave does have its own site at gawtongravityhub.co.uk.

39

Mineral Tramways Project

Train station Redruth
Nearest city Plymouth
Sat Nav TR16 5UF

Location The Mineral Tramways Project is a range of sites in the southwest of Cornwall that make use of the ex-mining railway lines to take in the beautiful countryside. The Coast to Coast trail, the main trail in this range, starts at the Elm Farm Bike Hire, set up on the outskirts of Portreath. To get to Elm Farm, head down the A30 to

Redruth, then head off the A30 onto A3407 before taking a right onto Tolgus Place. This will turn into the B3300 New Portreath Road north. Head in the direction of Portreath/Cambrose, after 1 km take a right into Cambrose and through the village on Chapel Hill. Carry along this road for 1 km and the Bike Barn and Elm Farm Cycle Centre are signposted off to the left.

Facilities Elm Farm Bike Hire is the full set up for anyone visiting with info and maps on the Mineral Tramways

Project incorporating the Coast to Coast Trails, bike hire, campsite, B&B, holiday cottages and more. The MTP has over 60 km of trails, using the disused railway lines that fell into neglect following the dismantling of Cornwall's mining industry. The trails can be ridden on their own, or used to link up with some of the fantastic downhill sites in the area (such as Poldice Valley Trails) or the popular dirt jumping site of The Track in Portreath. Not forgetting the many kilometres of singletrack offshoots.

ROGER KNIGHT

Locals do
Use the tramways to get to some of the UK's best dirt jump and downhill sites.

Locals don't
Have much to worry about in this part of the world!

Pros
60 km of riding means you'll not get bored.

Cons
With separate DH and DJs, there's not much to complain about!.

Rough round-up With substantial investment, this is a fantastic project and it links up several well-known mountain bike sites in the southwest. It's a great location for families to take a trip for a weekend or week-long holidays. The Coast to Coast trail is the main attraction, a 17.5-km ride (or 35 km if you loop it), from the north coast of Cornwall to the south coast town of Devoran (where a stop at The Quay Inn is a must), enables you to brag that you've ridden from the top to the bottom of England. Much of the trail is very pleasant and easy riding, perfect for families, though if you're looking for more adventurous areas they are easily found and the Elm Farm crew will be happy to point out off-shoot areas that suit your ability levels.

ROGER KNIGHT

Terrain The MTP features disused embankment riding, and is mostly level, pleasant family riding. But using the trails to access the singletrack, downhill or dirt jumping facilities nearby will bring you into contact with every grade of terrain from the easiest green trails to the most difficult of black runs.

XC The Coast to Coast trail is the main one here, but the involvement of Cornwall County Council means the project is only going to continue to grow. All trails are waymarked but maps are available if you get lost.

Downhill See the Poldice Valley pages.

Dirtjumps/Freeride The Track in Portreath is one of the UK's best dirt jump sites with every range of jump from beginner, to foam pit, to the most enormous gaps imaginable. See The Track's stand-alone pages for more details.

Not to miss The Coast to Coast trail is still the flagship trail to ride.

Remember to avoid Leaving the camera at home – this is beautiful scenery.

Nearest Bike/Hire shop Elm Farm Bike Hire is the main information hub.

Local accommodation
Elm Farm has a campsite, B&B, and holiday cottages to stay in.

More info For all info on the MTP and the Coast to Coast Trail, please check out the Elm Farm website – elmfarm.biz

Southwest England Mineral Tramways Project

N29 Nationwide DJs

Train station Swindon
Nearest city Bath/Reading/Bristol
Sat Nav SN3 1TX

Location Croft Community Cycle Trail are just to the south of Swindon. Leave the M4 at junction 15, and head north on the A419 Marlborough Road. Take the A4259 – the first left at the roundabout – and then the first left at the next roundabout into the B4006 (also called Marlborough Road). Take the second left off this road (Piper Way), and the DJs are about 100 m down here opposite the Nationwide HQ.

Facilities Swindon is very close to the community trail so access to shops is easy.

Rough round-up There's a 1-km purpose-built XC loop in the woods, put together by a Nationwide employee named Steve Smith, and with help from the building society, local council and a national lottery grant. There's a 5-km advanced trail with some steep, tough singletrack including features such as berms, rocks, roots and drop-offs. The DJs can be found tucked away behind the XC trails opposite the Nationwide Building Society HQ.

Conditions This is purpose-built trail and should work in most weather, but avoid after a period of heavy weather.

N30 Patchway BMX DJs

Train station Patchway
Nearest city Bristol
Sat Nav BS32 4JT

Location You'll find Patchway just off the M5 at the north edge of Bristol. Exit the motorway at junction 16, and head south on the A38 Gloucester Road. After 1 km turn off the A38 to the right, and at the roundabout take a right down Coniston Road. After 400 m, take another right down Waterside Drive. The track is just to the right and clearly visible.

Facilities Patchway has plenty of shops and amenities nearby.

Rough round-up This is a competition-standard track which is home to the Bristol BMX Club. It was re-designed back in 2012 and was the fourth re-design, something that the riders felt only improved the standard. The track features plenty of berms, rollers, gaps, tables and a drop-in start gate.

Conditions Well-maintained but avoid after rain.

ⓘ **More info** Check out the local scene at bristolbmxclub.com.

N31 Portsdown Hill

Train station Cosham/Portchester
Nearest city Portsmouth
Sat Nav PO6 4DQ

Location Portsdown is a small area of land around 3 km north from Portsmouth city centre, sat next to the town of Paulsgrove. Take junction 12 on the M27 and head north on the A3 for 1 km. Turn left onto Allaway Avenue, then right onto Credenhill Road, left onto Ludlow Road, then right onto Leominster Road and finally right into Lime Grove. All the trails are to the north of this area and are easy to spot. Best parking spot is probably on the edge of where Leominster Road meets Lime Grove.

Facilities Paulsgrove has plenty of shops and amenities.

Rough round-up This area of land is narrow – James Callaghan Drive to the north is the border, but it stretches east and west some kilometres with plenty of DH trails that will give some short, but feature-full descents. Despite having views of the industrial park and the M27, the riding itself more than makes up for it. If you're local, head here for some great riding.

Conditions This is chalky, South Downs land, so dries quite quickly but can be lethally slippery when wet.

🔽32 Poldice Valley Trails

ⓀⒷⒻⒹ

Train station Redruth/Perranwell
Nearest city Truro
Sat Nav TR4 8QZ (for bike Chain Bissoe)

Location Poldice Valley can be tricky to find but with enough help it's fairly straightforward. It's in the village of Carnon Downs, which is on the A39 halfway between Falmouth and Truro in Cornwall. This is a disused mine and can be accessed from the Mineral Trailways Project but we recommend call in to Bike Chain Bissoe near the Old Conns Works for directions, maps, bike hire and snacks. Or if you want to head straight to the valley, head south on the A30 towards Redruth, and take the Redruth North exit onto the A3047. At the first roundabout take the first exit almost back on yourself onto the B3298, then take a right off this road (though still following the B3298) after 400 m. Follow this road for 2 km to St Day, then take a left and follow the back roads towards Twelveheads. Poldice Valley is halfway between St Day and Twelveheads, and the backroads are unmarked and unsigned so it's best to ask someone on the village how to get to the entrance.

Facilities As it's a disused mine, there isn't much for the visiting rider at the valley DH tracks, just amazing trails, but nearby Falmouth can provide lots of entertainment (it's a University town after all!), and a night out in St Ives is always something to write home about. If you're just after a break you could join the Mineral Tramways Project and hit either the bike shop or the visitor's centre for a snack.

Rough round-up There's a strong group in the area and it's a very popular downhill scene. It's home-built but well maintained despite being in a classic wrangle with the council over land use and – as it's a disused mine – safety issues. It's an area predominantly used by freeriders with some great dirt jumps and interesting features to ride on. With constant improvements going on, it's challenging for any visitors to the area as well as riders from the SW who have extensively ridden at The Track.

Terrain It's red clay soil, hence the nickname 'Mars'. Other parts can be rocky.

XC You won't find any specific XC routes that start and end here but there are plenty nearby, with the coastal routes proving to be popular.

Downhill There are many short but interesting downhill sections throughout the whole area and, with the amount of work going into the area, you'll always find a new feature to hit.

Dirtjumps It's a predominantly freeride-based area but you're sure to find the odd step-down gap, along with other gaps and lines and other features to challenge the abilities of all types of rider.

Conditions The area is popular with walkers but it's predominantly known as a mountain biking centre so expect to see plenty of bikes. The XC routes are hard-packed dirt singletrack.

ⓘ **More info** To get involved with the great local scene, join their Facebook group under the search 'Cornwall Freeriders'. It's a closed group so you will have to request to join first. Bike Chain Bissoe – cornwallcyclehire.com.

43

⊿33 Portland Bill Quarries

Train station Weymouth
Nearest city Exeter
Sat Nav DT5 2JT (for the Portland Tourist Information Centre)

Location If you were wondering where much of the stone for the UK's finest buildings has come from, look no further than Portland Bill. And as it's the supplier of many buildings, you'll discover that the place is riddled with quarries. From Dorchester, head south on the A354 and this road will take you straight to Portland. Continue to the southern tip where you will find the Portland Lighthouse and the Tourist Information Centre. You'll be able to collect a map with the quarries located.

Facilities There are shops in Portland and plenty of smaller food and refreshment outlets between the spots.

Rough round-up There's the Old Quarry (just to the south of Glacis Road), New Ground (off New Ground Road), The Gore (to the east of where Easton Lane meets Inmosthay), Tout Quarry (200 m to the east of where Weston Road turns into Reforne), and simply, The Quarry (just north of where Weston Road turns into Pennsylvania Road). These are all filled with dirt jumping treasures such as drop ins, tables, berms, gaps and they're great for make-shift 4X tracks. Don't forget that these are all totally illegal but there's a good scene so you're likely to meet others. The coastal road has some great SC riding with about 16 km of trails.

Conditions This is almost all stone quarry, so it's shaley, dusty and exposed.

N34 Puddletown Woods

Ⓚ ⓖ Ⓢ Ⓕ

Train station Dorchester South/
Dorchester West
Nearest city Southampton/
Bath/Exeter
Sat Nav DT2 8QJ

Location Around 5 km to the
northeast of Dorchester is Puddletown
Woods. From there, take the A35
eastwards towards Bournemouth and
turn off to the right at Two Droves; this

is roughly 400 m before Puddletown
itself. Park at Hardy's Cottage just on
Beacon Hill (where the poet Thomas
Hardy was born), and follow the
singletrack from there to all the
good stuff!

Facilities Nearby Puddletown has
shops, and there's Hardy's Cottage
just off Two Droves which is the main
parking area for the forest.

Rough round-up It might be a
sleepy Dorset site but it holds one
fantastic scene. With a lot of natural
singletrack, DH sections and good
XC riding, it has fallen to disrepair
over the last couple of years but it's
still a fantastic place to ride. Trails
constantly change but with so much
natural terrain, you'll always find
something cool to ride. Plus you can
on chalk paths and get to see the
famous Dorset Chalk Man (the one
with the huge club and erect penis),
which is an usual sight on the trails.
The area is highly recommended and
often relatively empty.

Conditions As always, avoid after
periods of rain.

N35 Randwick DH

Ⓚ ⓓ

Train station Stroud
Nearest city Gloucester
Sat Nav GL6 6EX

Location You'll find Randwick around
8 km to the south of Gloucester. Exit the
M5 at junction 13 and head east on the
A419 towards Stroud. Around 2 km from
the motorway there's a roundabout,
you'll need to take the second exit –
B4008 (Ebley Road). Take that road then
turn left at Foxmoor Lane, then another
left on Redhouse Lane, then another left
onto Ash Lane which turns into Robbers
Road. Randwick is down this road on the
left after about 250 m.

Facilities Randwick has a few shops
that are within riding distance.

Rough round-up Don't be put off
by the fact that Randwick is a small
downhill area, it has some fantastic
drops, jumps and berms through the
trees. It has some impressive forest and
cool natural terrain. You'll always find
others riding these trails and they're all
friendly so don't hesitate to say hello.

Conditions Mud is the constant
problem, and some of the drops are
pretty close to the trees! Good soil
surface, if a little loose in places.

ⓘ **More info** Put Randwick Downhill
into Youtube to see plenty of clips.

Southwest England Randwick DH

Local riders
Paul Blackburn

Bike   Commencal Meta 5.5 XT
Local spot   Poldice Valley
Club member   Cornwall Freeriders
Age   36
Type of rider   All Mountain (everything)

Where's the one place you'd recommend above all for those coming to the southwest?

PB   Gawton in Tavistock. There's a mix of double black DH with fast-flowing singletrack descents. It's an amazing place but only for the experienced rider really.

Where has the best XC?

PB   Afan in Wales! No, here we've got everything, from epic coast rides from Portreath to St Ives that are amazing; tight and rocky climbs and miles and miles of singletrack with stunning cliff-top views, the open boggy, grassy, rocky trails through Bodmin Moor and the fun blasts through woods such as Cardinham in Bodmin, Tehidy in Redruth or Idless in Truro. All offer rooty, muddy trails tucked away in the deepest part of the wood, so hours of exploring is to be had.

Where is the best Downhill?

PB   Gawton in Tavistock is amazing, offering a world-class super steep and tech downhill line called super-tavi with berms, switchbacks, huge jumps (with chicken runs), off-camber rooty sections and flat out sections – it's not for the faint hearted. Also there is a lovely fast-flowing track called HSD that weaves through the trees at a great pace where the only thing holding you back is your own brakes; then there is the Egypt trail which defines the word STEEEEP, also off-camber rooty and full of obstacles, the cause of many an off for me.

The best dirt jumps?

PB   The Track at Portreath. We're lucky to have that. Also there's Mount Hawke indoor skate park, perfect for those rainy days.

If you were to take a family out – say a cousin who's visiting with his kids – where would you head?

PB   Probably the Minerals Tramway Project, starting at Bissoe is the best – a fairly easy cycle from Bissoe (Devoran) to Portreath. But there's also the Wadebridge Camel Trail – a family-friendly gravel trail winding its way along the coastline to Padstow where you can grab a cream tea and a pasty. Lovely. And both have cycle hire facilities.

What secret stashes do you know about?

PB   If I told you it wouldn't be secret now would it!? Look up our group 'Cornwall Freeriders' on Facebook and give us a shout and we'll gladly take anyone along to our secret spots! I will give you this though, our homeground of Poldice is well worth finding with a freeride area, DH line, various singletrack lines and a big natural bowl cut into the landscape – perfect for jumps, etc. Head along Bissoe tramway and keep your eyes to the left, and you'll find it…

If you were a huge fan of cake and wanted to find the best trail with a foodie pit stop, where would it be?

PB   I'd say Smokey Joe's in Redruth is a truck stop that serves up a genius full English. Many a rider has sat on its benches and consumed their ballast for a good day's ride. It's halfway along the Bissoe tramway, easy to find, just follow the trucks! Or there is a café at the cycle hire shop at the start of the trail. To be honest, when you ride in Cornwall you're never far away from pubs that serve great food, cafés that dish up glorious cakes or twee little cottages that have all sorts of home-made delights ready to be devoured by a hungry rider.

Where – if anywhere – outside of your area do you often visit with your bike?

PB Afan Forest in Wales is just an amazing place to ride and a trail I try and visit as often as possible. Also Gawton is only an hour away and usually has a Cornwall freerider or two ripping up its tracks; Cwncarn is always a good bet for a mint day's ride too. We're pretty blessed really in that Cornwall has a hugely diverse range of riding for all sorts of cyclists to be kept happy: from the weekend warrior to the road-riding fitness freak, from dirt jumpers to downhillers, from XC whippets to hardtail hackers, we've got it all. And we're always willing to meet new riders and have a laugh, because that's what it's all about.

Which websites have the best info on your local area?

PB Log onto Facebook and hunt out 'Cornwall freeriders' – it has all the info, advice and giggles you'll need. It always surprises me the amount of like-minded bike-obssessed nuts like myself there are on there – bike chat, bike vids, bike photos, bike links, trail info, tech advice, and mum jokes! We've got everything.

Which is the best shop to head to if you're in the southwest?

PB Easy, Clive Mitchell Cycles in Truro (the Capital of Cornwall). A great bunch of lads who are clued up on all riding disciplines and always willing to help and offer advice. They're also the best mechanics in the southwest, which is handy as we're always breaking our bikes. I wouldn't know what we'd do without 'em (there's got to be a free pair of 5.10's in it for me for that glowing praise, ha ha!). Basically, come to Cornwall, ride bikes and eat pasties. What else is there?

⊗ ⊗ ◯ ◯ ◯ ◯ ◯

Train station Petersfield
Nearest city Portsmouth
Sat Nav PO8 0QE

Location You'll find Queen Elizabeth Country Park just to the south of Petersfield, which is around 25 km north of Portsmouth itself. Traveling from the A3 coming south from the M25, carry on towards Portsmouth and the park is clearly signed by brown 'points of interest' signs and has its own turn off from the A3.

Facilities The QECP has a café and Visitor Centre which serves hot and cold drinks, and has toilets, etc. The car park is pay and display (£3 for a day ticket but more for minibuses and coaches) and the area is very popular with walkers, horse riders and other mountain bikers.

Rough round-up Predominantly XC-based, the QECP will keep you entertained for the day. There are two prime XC trails (the Queen Elizabeth and Meon Valley) both 16 km in length and both well marked featuring some lovely singletrack as they take you into the surrounding countryside via the right of way network and some public roads. There's also a novice

track that is around 6 km and is perfect for a family ride. There's nothing too strenuous here, but it is lovely scenery with fantastic singletrack in a beautiful setting. Alongside that is the expert track, also around 6 km with some good climbing, and some technical off-camber and rootsy trails, and if you find it's too difficult, the two loops interact frequently so you can pull out. There is a group of volunteers that maintain the trails and jumps at the QECP, who also put on Enduro competitions at the park. Well worth checking them out online.

Conditions This is well-kept forest and open land, but still prone to muddy areas in bad weather. Expect mud in spots if it's been raining recently or throughout the winter months.

ⓘ **More info** QECP has its own page on the Hampshire County website at – hants.gov.uk/qecp and so do the QECP Trail Build Collective – qecptrailcollective.co.uk.

Train station Gloucester/Lydney
Nearest city Gloucester
Sat Nav GL14 1JU

Location Red Hill Extreme is a purpose-built centre (combined with mountain boarding), near the village of Elton in the Forest of Dean to the east of Gloucester. Take the A48 from Gloucester towards Chepstow, and turn off at Elton on the A4151 towards Cinderford on the Elton Road. Go past the Tudor Racing Stables and Red Hill Extreme is just on the right, as part of Elton Farm.

Facilities Refreshments available from the farm.

Rough round-up Red Hill is a purpose-built 4X and dirt jump site and, understandably, you'll have to pay to use it (full day £9, half day £6 and evenings £4). There are plenty of jumps, berms, step ups and drops on the trail. They're also hosting a stop on the 2014 British 4X series.

Conditions The DJ and 4X trails are open field land so avoid when windy or wet, and it closes when the weather's bad too. Best to call and check, especially in the winter when it is normally closed.

ⓘ **More info** redhillextreme.co.uk or T07877 147 636.

Train station Liss
Nearest city Portsmouth
Sat Nav N/A

Location Just north of Petersfield and off the A3 is Rogate. From the M25 head south on the A3 towards Portsmouth and exit at the B3006 heading towards Liss. Follow signs for the village, turn right onto Hill Brow Road. Go all the way to the the end, then take a right, then immediately left, then go 1.5 km to the next T-junction (marked Rogate right, and Rake left). Take the left towards Rake, then park up after a few hundred metres as the road bends to the right (if you've hit the crossroads you've gone too far). Rogate DH tracks are in the woods on the left of this road.

Facilities There's parking onsite for around 50 cars and if you're in need of refreshment, there's shops nearby and The Jolly Drover pub less than a mile away. The Cycle Works in Petersfield is probably the closest bike shop.

Southwest England Rogate

49

Rough round-up Rogate is kept by the Forestry Commission but the local riders deserve credit for keeping the place clean whilst building some amazing downhill and freeriding trials. You'll be spoilt for choice when it comes to good downhill rides with plenty of drop-offs and dirt-jump-style features for freeriders and hardtailers to keep themselves busy. It's a popular site but surprisingly absent of dog walkers and other users. It's a very impressive set up and highly recommended.

Conditions This works well in most weather, although busy periods such as holidays etc might be best avoided. There's quite a young scene who are keen to ride hard.

ⓘ **More info** Check out the Rogate Downhill Facebook page for the latest news and updates – facebook.com/rogatedownhill.

N39 Sandford DJs and DH

Train station Wareham/Holton Heath
Nearest city Bournemouth
Sat Nav BH20 7AA

Location Around 5 km to the west of Poole in Dorset are the Sandford dirt jumps. Driving away from Poole, head onto the A35 towards Dorchester. Take the A351 towards Wareham (just outside of Poole) and Sandford is about 2 km down this road. As you pass through the village, take a right into the B3075 (Morden Road), the DJs are around 200 m up this road on the left. You can either walk through the woods, or to drive, carry on up Morden Road for 500 m and take the road off to the left, then first left, and finally all the way back down that road and park at the end.

Facilities Nearby Sandford has shops.

Rough round-up It's a treasure of a DJ set up featuring good gaps, tables and drops, and then on the way out there are some great, if a little short – singletrack and DH trails.

N40 Sheet DJs

Train station Petersfield
Nearest city Portsmouth
Sat Nav N/A

Location Sheet DJs are just off the A272 on the north edge of Petersfield in Hampshire. Heading south from the M25, drive towards Portsmouth on the A3 and exit at the junction marked Petersfield on the A272. Take the first exit at the roundabout (London Road – and still the A272), cross the river, and after about 150 m, the road turns off to the right, heading towards Rogate. Take this road and park immediately on the left. The dirt jumps are on the opposite side of this road in the copse of trees.

Facilities Sheet is the nearest village, just back over the river and will have local shops.

Rough round-up For those visiting Queen Elizabeth Country Park, it's worth visiting Sheet DJs as they're an incredible set of jumps with the charm of being nicely hidden off the road. It has some great lines, hips, gaps and table tops; perfect for any rider who loves DJs. There's a heavy BMX scene here, and there are constant builds, but mountain bikes can be seen occasionally. Not for beginners, and you'd definitely need to know how to ride tight transitions to even drop in here.

Conditions This is a red-clay soil with plenty of re-enforced take offs and landings.

N41 Stockwood Bike Park

Train station Parson Street
Nearest city Bristol
Sat Nav BS14 8DQ

Location Stockwood Bike Park is located behind Whittock Road allotments and a short walk from Burnbush Primary School. When travelling south through Bristol Centre, take the A4 before taking the A37 for around 11 miles. Take a left onto the B3119, then take a right at the roundabout onto Sturminster Road, then a left at Hooper Road and the next left onto Whittock Road. About 100 m up the road will be the allotments – ride around the side and you'll see the track in front of you.

Facilities There is nothing here apart from the track itself but there will be local shops nearby for refreshments.

Rough round-up Built by Architrail, they took inspiration from their World Cup 4X tracks and built a mini 4X track here. Alongside this is

a small pump track, all designed to allow young riders to enhance their bike riding skills, but also allowing more experienced riders to have fun. Not worth a long journey but recommended for locals.

Conditions Superb when conditions are right – dry and sunny. Best to stay away when wet.

Train station Eastleigh/Hedge End
Nearest city Southampton
Sat Nav SO50 8GL

Location There's no official place to park so you will have to find somewhere to leave the car before heading into the woods on your bike. To find the trails you'll need to leave the M3 at junction 13 and head east along the A335 towards Bishopstoke. After 1 km you'll hit a roundabout. Take the third exit – Bishopstoke Road (the B3037) and carry on down here for about 2 km, then turn left onto Sandy Lane, then after 400 m another left onto Harding Lane.

Facilities The nearby village of Fair Oak has plenty of shops and amenities.

Rough round-up Stoke Heights is a large tract of Forestry Commission land that has been explored by mountain bikers for years. Alongside the many XC trails that criss-cross the land, there are some great DH trails (although they are short). None of the trails have been officially built but some purpose-built jumps and berms have been strengthened. A local rider will be your best friend as they'll be able to point out the best places to ride.

Conditions The woods have plenty of roots, and good rock gardens. Avoid if it's muddy, and can be dark in winter. Likely to be fairly empty though.

CHRIS MORAN

Train station Nutbourne/Bosham/ Southborne/Rowlands Castle
Nearest city Portsmouth
Sat Nav PO18 9JG

Location Between Havant and Chichester, to the far west of the South Downs is the small village of Stoughton. From the A27 Havant Bypass exit at Westbourne and take the B2147 heading towards Racton. Turn off to the left at Walderton heading for Stoughton, and carry along this road after Stoughton village for around 1.5 km until the road turns sharply to the left. Here turn right (ie: carry straight on) and park immediately to the right. The DH trails are around 250 m to the northeast.

Facilities This is deep country forest so you won't find a shop but Stoughton will have places for you to buy snacks and drinks.

Rough round-up This is a locally built DH track with some good jumps. There's constant care and attention on the area by a group of locals who are always changing trails so make sure you check it out often. It might be relatively small but well worth a ride.

Conditions Heavy rainfall will make it very muddy and often unrideable. However, the summer months should see this spot become very popular.

ⓘ **More info** Join the Stoughton Downhill Facebook group for info and the chance to join in on digs – facebook.com/StoughtonDownhill

↘44 Stoke Woods

⊗ ⊗ ⊗ ⊗ ⊗ ⊗

Train station St James Park
Nearest city Exeter
Sat Nav EX4 7DP

Location If you take the A37 north out of Exeter city centre you'll find a right turning onto the A396 (Stoke Road), which is about 1 km after the city centre and just before the village of Cowley. After a few hundred metres, Stoke Woods will be on your right. Turn right onto Pennsylvania Road and park at the clearing on the right just after making your way through the woods. The main XC and freeride area starts at this car park, while the dirt jumps are at the other end of the woods, just before Stoke Hill Road heads off into farmland.

Facilities With Cowley just down the road and having plenty of corner shops, as well as Exeter only being 2-3 km away, all the facilities and shops you need are within riding distance. On site itself is only the car park and nothing else (it is free though).

Rough round-up For riders out of Exeter not content to settle for just Haldon Freeride Park, Stoke Woods is similarly impressive, just not as official. There's one hell of a good XC riding area and a good dirt jumping spot to entertain every rider. Plenty on offer.

Terrain There's a lot of unofficial singletrack, with some purpose built freeride obstacles. Ground is mostly hard-packed soil with few rocks but the odd exposed tree root.

XC It's a woods that is predominantly XC singletrack, which is also popular with walkers and dog owners, although not especially busy, so keep an eye out. There are loops all over the forest, ranging from super easy to some lovely technical sections. As it's only half an hour's ride from Exeter, it sees plenty of people popping up for a short session and is notoriously quieter than Haldon but don't let this fool you; there is still a lot to ride in terms of drops, kickers, and log rides. With miles of decent riding to be had, you would expect that getting lost is easy but the forest is surrounded by farmland so you will be fine and practically every acre has networks of singletrack criss-crossing it.

Downhill Most trails head north from the top of the hill towards the river and link the XC loops.

Dirtjumps There are several lines through the jumps ranging from medium to difficult with tabletops, gaps and doubles. These aren't necessarily for beginners as they will struggle with the size and speed of the jumps.

Above and opposite page: Stoke Woods.

Train station Bishop's Lydeard/
Bridgwater
Nearest city Bristol/Exeter/Bath
Sat Nav TA5 1HN (for Marsh Mills)

Location From the M5 exit at
junction 23 in the direction of
Bridgewater. Then take the A39 towards
Minehead. Before you hit the village
of Nether Stowey take a left towards
Marsh Mills and carry on through the
village and for 1 km turning at the next
right. Carry on along that road and take
the left-hand fork. Triscombe DH is
about 1 km along after the fork and is
the hill on your right.

Facilities The only thing you'll find out
in Triscombe way is unspoiled views.
The nearest shop can be found in Over
Stowey. There's also uplift available but
recommended that you get in touch via
their Facebook page first.

Rough round-up Fantastic natural
features, off-camber berms and plenty
of roots to take on. Local riders often
build features on the track so you can
never be sure what will await you
when you get there! You will definitely
find plenty of gullies, great jumps and
sometimes some decent gaps.

Conditions When weather is good,
the tracks are incredible. When it's wet,
mud can be a problem and will really
affect whether you ride or not.

ⓘ **More info** Type 'Triscombe'
into YouTube and you'll see a lot of
videos to tease you. Also, check out
the Triscombe Uplifts Facebook page
(facebook.com/pages/triscombe-
uplifts/337212724049).

Southwest England Triscombe DH

53

⌖46 The Track

⊗ ⊗ ⊗ ⊗ ⊗ ⊗ ⊗ ⊗ ⊗ ⊗
⊗ ⊗ ⊗

Train station Redruth
Nearest city Truro
Sat Nav TR16 4HW

Location The Track (sometimes known as The Cornish Extreme Centre) can be found by heading down the A30, turn off at the Redruth heading towards Portreath on the B3300, the turning to The Track is 50 m on the right having just passed Treasure Park. If you reach Portreath, then you've gone too far! For riders travelling from the train station, exit the station and head towards Treasure Park which is well-signed around town.

Facilities Some have called this the dirt jumper's paradise, heavily weighted towards the freeriders. This is also the perfect setting for kids to progress their riding (as well as all ages riders looking to progress) in a safe environment. If you're after some scenic riding there is a coast to coast trail running from Portreath that is only 18 km one way. The dirt at the track is perfect for building and shaping lips and transitions and a full floodlight system, and large PA set up and a viewing platform results in a great atmosphere. There are numerous lines from beginner to pro, a foam pit to learn tricks in, a soft landing area to dial the airs in, and several purpose built obstacles (wallrides etc) as well as a 4X track.

XC Much like DH riding, The Track doesn't offer XC but there are coastal paths and trails in the country parks that can be cycled to from The Track. There are very few marked rides so hiring a guide is recommended – try Mobius trails (T01637 831383 – mobiusonline.co.uk/biketrails). They'll assess your ability and take you on a suitable ride.

Downhill Much like Corwall, The Track does not offer any downhill riding. But any downhiller could do far worse than to spend a few days here on a hardball brushing up on their jumping skills. If you do crave some DH action, it's about an hour's drive to the Maddacleave woods downhill trails.

Freeride The freeriding here is nothing short of amazing. The Track offers so many different ways to

Not to miss Riders trying out some X-Games style tricks in the foam pit.

Remember to avoid Travelling here when it's less than perfect weather conditions.

Nearest Bike/Hire shop KONA mountain bikes can be hired from the track but make sure to call in advance for a price check.

Local accommodation Nearby Elm Farm has B&B and is affiliated with the centre, therefore offers discounts – elm-farm.co.uk.

Eating The Snack Shack Café is the hub of the The Track as everyone from riders to parents will be there. It'll keep you going for the day but if you're after a bigger meal, head into Truro and try out one of the many gastro pubs.

ⓘ **More info** The Track (T01209 211073, the-track.co.uk) and Cornwall Tourist Board (cornwalltouristboard.co.uk).

> ❯ **Lowdown**

☺ **Locals do**
Ride amazingly well (as to be expected with this on their doorstep).

Take full advantage of opening times by spending all day here.

☹ **Locals don't**
Try and ride the jumps when the sea breeze is strong.

Respect the laws of gravity.

✔ **Pros**
UK's top DJ facility.

Great chilled, friendly atmosphere.

✖ **Cons**
Very specific type of riding.

Can be quite exposed to wind and rain.

progress your riding skills with dirt jumps for all abilities. In fact, there are over a mile of jumps! If you're keen on learning harder tricks, they have a 50 sq m foam pit with multiple ramp and transfer lines in to test your tricks before taking them to the dirt jumps. The BMX race track will also help you test your speed and aerial prowess! Also in the area are Mount Hawke indoor skatepark and Wooden Waves outdoor skatepark in Newquay.

Easy Be sure to start out on the beginner jumps! With so much on offer it's good to build up your confidence and skills before trying out anything harder.

Hard There are plenty of hard lines to try if you're an advanced rider. The only limitations in a place like this are your imagination!

55

SW47 Watchmoor Wood Bike Park

Train station Bournemouth
Nearest city Bournemouth
Sat Nav BH24 2ET

Location Watchmoor Wood Bike Park is easy to find and is about 15 km to the northwest of Bournemouth. When travelling from Southampton or the M27, go west to the end of the motorway and carry along the A31 towards Bournemouth. Take the Ashley Heath turning off the A31 just west from Ringwood, where you'll catch brown signs heading to Moors Valley Country Park. Head through Ashley Heath and the park entrance is on the right just as you exit the village.

Facilities The Moor Valley Country Park has a Visitor Centre with café, bike hire, toilets, car parking and a newly introduced bike wash. Maps are also available for family-based XC to be found in the forest. The main attraction for riders is the northshore.

Rough round-up Northshore is the reason a lot of riders visit and it continues to grow. Despite a lot of structures being demolished due to its age and safety concerns, there's still a lot to ride. There's enough here to impress the beginner and the super pro. There are still some gentle XC rides for the family if that's your choice of riding. Well worth a visit for anyone in the southeast.

Conditions Avoid after heavy rain but many of the XC routes are weatherproofed. The northshore lines are brilliantly built and are regularly updated with different woods and rocks to give more grip to the rider.

JETHRO LOADER

① **More info** Moors Valley Country Park has its own website at – moorsvalley.co.uk, while the Forestry Commission website has a page on the park at forestry.gov.uk.

SW48 Woodbury Common

Train station Exton/Lympstone Commando
Nearest city Exeter
Sat Nav EX5 1JJ

Location Head towards Exeter on the M5 and leave at junction 30, taking the A376 to Clyst St George where the B3179 (Woodbury Road) splits towards Woodbury. Continue through the village until you reach a crossroads – roughly 2 miles away. Woodbury Common is the wooded area directly ahead.

Facilities Nothing but XC land with plenty of rambling routes, bridleways and single track to explore. You can park for free in Woodbury itself and ride up to the common, but only recommended for the serious rider.

Rough round-up Clinton Devon Estates owns the land but continues to leave it open for public use, meaning plenty of riders take full advantage of the XC on offer. You will be spoilt for choice in terms of variety as routes range from short, action packed loops to longer enduro rides. The Royal Navy and Royal Marines regularly hold a XC Championship there.

Conditions The winter can make the trails incredibly muddy but there's always something to ride no matter what the weather.

5 tips for trail etiquette
Sam Reynolds

Sam Reynolds is part of the DMR team. He counts Kingswood's Kech Trails as home, but is equally found on various dirt jumping sites across Europe including the Nissan Qashqai tour. Here are Sam's etiquette tips for when turning up to new trails. As Sam says: "follow these simple tips and hopefully you'll be invited back to ride again!"

1 If possible, before going to the new trails for the first time, try to find out who owns or digs the jumps and drop them an email asking if it's ok to come along sometime. If you don't know who that is, just turn up and generally be polite! When you turn up ask the locals if it's ok to ride, and offer to help dig. You can't have all that fun without helping out a little!

2 Wear a helmet! Besides being sensible, most trails have rules in place not allowing you to ride without one.

3 Take the right bike – put on slick dirt/street tyres for most trails, knobbly tyres dont go down too well with the builders 'cos they churn it up. A dirt jump bike or BMX are most suited to trails, so don't expect to be allowed to ride on a downhill bike with chunky tyres.

4 Respect the locals. Probably the most important rule of all is to respect the jumps, riders and the land they are on. Try to skid as little as possible and if you do for whatever reason damage the jumps, get a spade and fix it. Before dropping in to your run, make sure no one else is going, because cutting out in front of someone is not cool. Litter is also a big one: if anyone dropped litter at my trails they certainly wouldn't be invited back. The cleaner the land, the less likely the jumps are to get knocked down, so the happier the locals will be.

5 Lastly – why not dig your own trails? Find a plot of land, preferably ask the land owner if you can use it, and start building. Seeing your own jumps coming to shape is sometimes almost as satisfying as riding them. Also, when you have a few jumps riding you can invite other riders, and they will most likely invite you back to their trails, giving you more and more places to ride. What goes around comes around eh? So get digging!

London & Southeast England

[JUSTIN SULLIVAN PHOTOGRAPHY]

London & Southeast England

Huntingdon
Stret

CAMBRIDGESHIRE

Cambr

Wellingborough

A14

A448
Warwick
Royal Leamington
Spa
Northampton

Redditch
A46
A45
A43

A142

M5
A5
A14

A46
A40
A45
A428
A11 Roxton

Stratford-
on-Avon
A509
Bedford

Farnborough
BEDFORDSHIRE

A46
A421
Biggleswade
A10
Wa

Evesham
A58
A43
Banbury

Vale of Evesham
Milton Keynes
Letchworth
A505

A44
A422
A6

Moreton-
in-Marsh
BUCKINGHAMSHIRE
HERTFORDSHIRE

Cheltenham
A11M
Stevenage
Stans
Airpo

Stow-on-
the-Wold
Bicester
A53
A418
Luton
Knebworth
A2
Bishop's
Stortford

A429
A44
A1
Great
Gaddesden
A602
A3

Gloucester
A41
Tring
Hertford
A414
Harlow

A417
Witney
Oxford
A34
Aylesbury
St Albans
A9
A19

Cotswold Hills
A55
A4010
M10

GLOUCESTERSHIRE
OXFORDSHIRE
High
Wycombe
A413
A26

M40
A18

Tetbury
Cricklade
Abingdon
Chiltern
Hills
Watford
A21

Malmesbury
Didcot
A22
A24
Slough
A25
A3

A429
A419
A420
A404
Maidenhead
LONDON

Swindon
A34
Reading
A35
Windsor
Heathrow
Airport
A49

Lyneham
Theale
Wokingham
Staines
A40
A14

Chippenham
Marlborough
Newbury
M4
Bagshot
Staines
A17
A8

Melksham
A46
Camberley
A16

Devizes
Woking
A10
A52

WILTSHIRE
Pewsey
A339
A33
Camberley
A39
Leatherhead
A217
A22

Salisbury
Plain
Andover
Basingstoke
Fleet
A27
A37
Guildford
SURREY
Dorking
Godstone
Seve

Amesbury
A303
Fleet
A42
Gatwick
Airport
East
Grinstead
A34

Wilton
A31
A28
A32
A24
Crawley
A41

Salisbury
Grayshott
A31
Bucks Green
A39
A264
Crowborou

A36
Winchester
A3
Billingshurst
Horsham
Hig

Twyford
Petworth
A51

Petersfield
WEST
SUSSEX
A23
Low Weald

M27
Clayton
Lewes
Glyn

Southampton
A354
A283
Brighton

Ringwood
A31
Chichester
A27
A280

Brockenhurst
Fareham
Portsmouth
West
Wittering
A56
Worthing

Poole
A338
Gosport
Bognor
Regis
A47
A43
A15
Newhaven
Seaf

Bournemouth
Cowes
Selsey
A57

Swanage
Yarmouth
Newport
ISLE OF
WIGHT
English Channel

Poole Bay

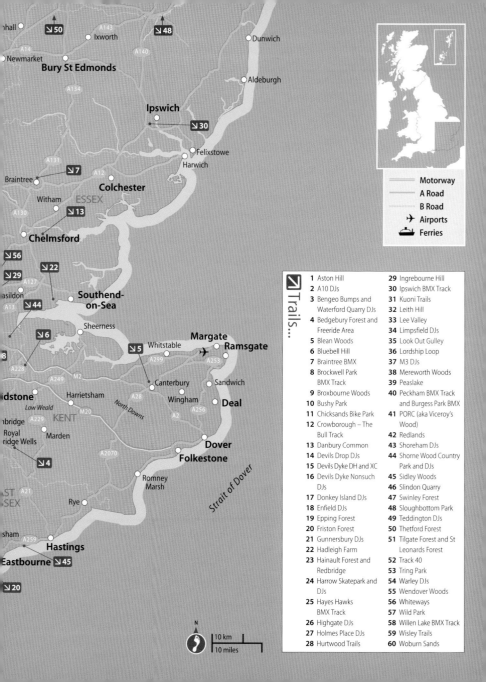

Trails...

1	Aston Hill
2	A10 DJs
3	Bengeo Bumps and Waterford Quarry DJs
4	Bedgebury Forest and Freeride Area
5	Blean Woods
6	Bluebell Hill
7	Braintree BMX
8	Brockwell Park BMX Track
9	Broxbourne Woods
10	Bushy Park
11	Chicksands Bike Park
12	Crowborough – The Bull Track
13	Danbury Common
14	Devils Drop DJs
15	Devils Dyke DH and XC
16	Devils Dyke Nonsuch DJs
17	Donkey Island DJs
18	Enfield DJs
19	Epping Forest
20	Friston Forest
21	Gunnersbury DJs
22	Hadleigh Farm
23	Hainault Forest and Redbridge
24	Harrow Skatepark and DJs
25	Hayes Hawks BMX Track
26	Highgate DJs
27	Holmes Place DJs
28	Hurtwood Trails
29	Ingrebourne Hill
30	Ipswich BMX Track
31	Kuoni Trails
32	Leith Hill
33	Lee Valley
34	Limpsfield DJs
35	Look Out Gulley
36	Lordship Loop
37	M3 DJs
38	Mereworth Woods
39	Peaslake
40	Peckham BMX Track and Burgess Park BMX
41	PORC (aka Viceroy's Wood)
42	Redlands
43	Shoreham DJs
44	Shorne Wood Country Park and DJs
45	Sidley Woods
46	Slindon Quarry
47	Swinley Forest
48	Sloughbottom Park
49	Teddington DJs
50	Thetford Forest
51	Tilgate Forest and St Leonards Forest
52	Track 40
53	Tring Park
54	Warley DJs
55	Wendover Woods
56	Whiteways
57	Wild Park
58	Willen Lake BMX Track
59	Wisley Trails
60	Woburn Sands

Map legend:
— Motorway
— A Road
···· B Road
✈ Airports
⚓ Ferries

10 km
10 miles

While the southeast has little in the way of real mountains, it has one of the strongest mountain bike scenes in the country, with a mass exodus from the cities to the nearby forests, jump spots and secret stashes most weekends. Naturally, because of the amount of riders in this part of the country, and with commercial opportunities to cash in on their outdoor expectations, there are plenty of purpose-built sites already in existence, as well as many planned for the near future.

London is home to hundreds of thousands of bike riders, so it is unsurprising that its nearest riding spots are the most popular. Hence, if you were to head to Swinley Forest or some of the popular Surrey spots on a bank holiday, you're unlikely to have the run of the trails to yourself. This isn't to say the area is crowded, however, and for riders heading to the newly re-named Viceroy's Wood in Kent (originally named PORC), Friston Bedgebury and Thetford Forests, or any of the fabulous trio of centres in Bedfordshire (Woburn Sands, Aston Hill and Chicksands), you're in for a lovely surprise: they're as well kept, open, beautiful and as organized as any trail centre in Wales or Scotland. These are not just for the city dwellers out there, however, make sure you check out these centres if you are passing through, or taking a trip to London – after the obligatory trip to Buckingham Palace, of course.

Local scene

The southeast of England holds the biggest population of riders, but one would presume it has the least facilities for mountain biking. While this is true in terms of real mountains and big descents, there are more than enough world-class trail centres dotted around the counties of West Sussex, East Sussex, Kent, Surrey, Greater London, Berkshire, Oxfordshire, Buckinghamshire, Bedfordshire, Hertfordshire and Essex to keep any rider happy. Like in the southwest, the Forestry Commission plays a huge part in the outdoor experience for many riders here, being behind the fantastic facilities to be found at Bedgebury Forest, Friston Forest and Thetford Forest. But there are also plenty of privately-owned operations here, as well as manor parks, country estates and, in Hampshire, an entire county with a forward-thinking policy on bike riding. Even inside the M25 there are fun places to ride, and naturally the dirt jumping scene here is huge. We've included many BMX tracks in this guide because for many riders, heading to pure dirt jumping

Above: Redlands.
Opposite page: Bedgebury Northshore.

spots can be intimidating, and heading to a BMX or 4X track is a good way to ease into the dirt jumping scene.

Hubs
Where to start? There seem to be three major hubs – those riders in and around Milton Keynes are spoilt for choice with Woburn Sands, Aston Hill and Chicksands on tap, while riders around Tunbridge Wells have The Bull Track, Bedgebury and Viceroy Wood all competing for their attention. Riders in West London, Bracknell and Reading are all within easy reach of the fantastic Swinley Forest, while Surrey and Sussex riders have the incredible South Downs on their doorstep, home to some of the most beautiful XC riding in the country.

❺ Best rides in London and Southeast England

There are plenty of stand-alone spots in the southeast, but riders who are based here should definitely check out:

❶ Thetford Forest, page 97
If you're a lover of XC but you aren't a fan of huge uphill sections, then the trails at Thetford will intrigue you as they run through a stunningly beautiful tract of land, and also have the facilities of a bike shop and a visitor centre. You'll also find plenty of races each year to test out your lung capacity!

❷ Viceroy's Wood, page 90
Not one to miss, the downhill riding here is exceptional, and takes in some stunning views. It's an eco-centric mountain bike spot with great food and a brilliant visitor centre.

❸ Bedgebury Forest and Freeride Park, page 67
With a lot of work by the locals, in conjunction with The Forestry Commission, the freeride area has come along leaps and bounds. There are some very fun obstacles surrounded by beautiful XC riding, with a full visitor centre set-up. A great Kentish rival for Viceroy's Wood.

❹ Swinley Forest, page 95
Despite the Crown Estates levelling many of the trails at Swinley Forsest, they have also opened a few other trails to take on. The purpose built trails take in some of the best woodland in the country.

❺ Leith Hill, page 85
This is one location that's had a lot of work recently, and it's thanks to the local riders and the National Trust. It holds some great downhill trails with berms, rollers, dirt jumps and more. Well worth checking out.

⌐🔽1⌐ Aston Hill

🅺 🆀 🆁 🅺 🅼 🅶 🅵 🅾

Train station Wendover/Tring
Nearest city London
Sat Nav HP22 5NQ

Opening times Aston Hill is open 364 days of the year (they give themselves Christmas Day off). It opens at 0830 and shuts at 1730 (1830 from Sunday 30 March). It's best to check the website before visiting just to make sure.

Location Aston Hill is around 5 km east of Aylesbury and 10 km northwest from Hemel Hempstead. When travelling from the south, leave the M25 at junction 20 heading north to Aylesbury on the A41. After about 16 miles, take the second Tring exit (signposted Tring, Aston Clinton, Wendover and Whipsnade Zoo), take

the first exit at the roundabout at the top of the slip road, signposted Aston Clinton and follow the road. After about 400 m take a left, this will be signposted Wendover. As the road winds up a hill you'll need to take a left, drive up the hill past the golf club, and Aston Hill will be on your left.

Facilities For years Aston Hill has been one of the only venues to provide for downhill and 4X in the south east. The soil at Aston is quite chalky and is littered with flint which can make for interesting riding when wet, but the tracks are well maintained if not manicured and will test the most proficient of riders. In addition, there are 5 DH trails, a 4X track and a combined 5-mile XC loop. As per

usual with big centres like this, there is parking on site (you have to pre-pay on the CTC site – ctc.org.uk/astonhill – but this covers your day's riding as well). You can find B&Bs in Wendover and Tring as well as a fair few pubs for an evening ale.

XC The XC loop at Aston Hill is split into two runs, the first being an almost completely singletrack route that runs along the outside edge of the wood. The second trail starts following the Black, Red and Surface to Air runs. Don't worry, though, if you're not a seasoned downhill rider; the Black and Surface runs veer off leaving you on the Red Run, with steep sections and roots galore.

Downhill There are 5 downhill tracks at Aston Hill, with Surface to Air being the newest. It's a different ride compared to the other natural, rooty trails that Aston Hill is used to as Surface to Air has an all-weather surface. It's berms, jumps and drops from top to bottom so well worth a look. The oldest trail, the Black Run, is still there and is still loved. It's still as steep as ever, filled with roots, drops and off camber sections. The other three rides (Root Canal, Ricochet and Red Run) are all still incredible and well worth a look for the downhill lover.

Freeride The 4X track here features the usual doubles, rollers and tables as well a road gap and a 35 ft end jump.

When it's dry it's insanely quick and a lot of fun but it's a different story in the wet – it's almost unrideable. It's very popular with the locals.

Easy The XC trails are great for beginners as they'll get you used to the steeper, tighter riding of Aston Hill.

Hard The Black Run (DH) is the steepest you'll find but all DH trails are top class.

Not to miss Classed as the best downhill in the southeast.

Remember to avoid Travelling here in less than perfect weather conditions. Call before you leave.

Nearest Bike/Hire shop Mountain Mania in Tring is a 10-minute drive away and offers priority repairs to Aston Hill riders. Dees Cycles in Amersham also offer a 12.5% discount for Aston Hill Members.

Local accommodation
While the majority of visitors just come for the day, there are a large number of B&Bs, hotels and guest houses within a 10-minute drive. For local tourist information you can call Wendover tourist info on T01296 696759.

Eating The well-named Café in the Woods can be found in the neighbouring Wendover Woods but if you're looking for more, Wendover and Tring has plenty to offer.

ⓘ **More info** Bike park contact rideastonhill.co.uk or call the tourist Office (T01296 696759). Also check out the Aston Hill Facebook page (facebook.com/AstonHillBikePark).

> **Lowdown**

⊕ Locals do
Session the road gap on the 4X.

Pre-book their parking and day passes.

⊗ Locals don't
Ride without protection. The flint here is very sharp and can slice your knees and elbows open.

Bite off more than they can chew. It's better to build up confidence first and hit bigger runs.

✔ Pros
Good transport links.

Technical trails.

Quality coaching program.

✖ Cons
Difficult to ride in the wet.

No uplift.

⊠2 A10 DJs
⊘

Train station St Margaret
Nearest city Welwyn Garden City
Sat Nav N/A

Location The A10 dirt jumps are in a traffic island off the A10 near Hertford. Take junction 25 from the M25 and head north on the A10 for around 10 km, then take the exit signposted Great Amwell. At the roundabout, take the first exit onto the B1502 (Standstead Road) and go back under the A10. The dirt jumps are in the copse of woods immediately to the right of this road just after you've passed under the A10 bridge.

Facilities Great Amwell has some shops and facilities.

Rough round-up These dirt jumps are right next to the A10, but otherwise are on land used for little else, so expect few visitors other than riders. There are quite a few lines, ranging from some easier lines to pro-standard. This is no place for beginners however. They would be better off heading to Hertford to ride the Bengeo Bumps.

Conditions This is council land on a traffic island between the busy lanes of the A10. It's a copse with few visitors apart from riders. Respect the building that has gone into the trails and fix any casings.

⊠3 Bengeo Bumps and Waterford Quarry DJs
⊘

Train station Hertford East
Nearest city Hertford/ Welwyn Garden City
Sat Nav SG14 3JS

Location Bengeo Bumps are in Hartford – between Harlow and Welwyn Garden City. When traveling from the A10 heading north from junction 25 of the M25, take the A414 – the Hertford exit. When you reach town, turn right onto the B158 (Port Hill), and drive on this road for around 1 km. Turn right into New Road, then left in Ware Park Road, then left again into Rib Vale. Park at the end of the road where it loops back on itself. The dirt jumps are in a small area of common land behind the houses on the left.

Facilities Bengeo Street has plenty of shops and amenities and is a few hundred metres ride away.

Rough round-up This is a very low budget dirt jump spot between houses that no-one should take a long journey to. But if the A10 dirt jumps are too busy or scary, this might make learners salvage something from the trip. 1 km further north are Waterford Quarry DJs (the quarry is sign posted), which has a sand landing similar to a foam pit!

Conditions This is a small clearing of land between houses. The quarry is a disused pit area.

ⓧ ⓘ ⓝ ⓓ ⓕ ⓖ ⓣ ⓐ ⓖ ⓞ

Train station Wadhurst/Frant
Nearest city London
Sat Nav TN17 2SJ

Location Bedgebury Forest is approximately 15 km southeast of Tonbridge in Kent. From the M25 exit at junction 5 and join the A21 southbound towards Hastings. Bedgebury is signposted off the A21 on the B2079.

Facilities Bedgebury Forest is, understandably, a very popular area, and benefits from the full Forestry Commission deal – Visitor Centre, café, toilets (and showers), bike shop (Quench Cycles – T01580 879694, quenchuk.co.uk, they have suspension bikes, as well as disabled or learning difficulty bikes), car parking (expensive at £9.50 for the day) and a museum.

Rough round-up Bedgebury is a fantastic XC venue with loops heading all over the 800 hectares of rideable land. The local riders banded together to form the 'Boars on Bikes' Bedgebury Forest Cycle Club (boarsonbikes.co.uk, membership gives free parking and

showers etc), and they have created some incredible XC and freeride trails throughout the forest. Well worth a visit if you're in the southeast.

Terrain Virtually all singletrack, with some great armoured bridges, jumps and work put in to add features and obstacles to the trails.

XC Plenty of dedicated, purpose-built trails alongside plenty of family trails for the less experienced or those with kids.

Downhill There are no purpose built DH trails but there are some sections of DH within the XC rides.

Freeride Thanks to a lot of building from the locals, the freeride area has come along in leaps and bounds, with elevated ladders, skinny log rides, drops, see-saws, kickers, berms and a three-way 'combobulator'. The locals are definitely into building, and use sustainable, locally sourced wood to build their park. A good sign for the future. There's also a set of dirt jumps in use but the northshore riding has since been dismantled.

Conditions The XC routes are hard-packed dirt singletrack, prone to bouts of serious mud in the winter. However, where the problem area render the trails unrideable, the locals are hitting back with bridges and reinforced wood.

More info Bedgebury Forest, forestry. gov.uk/bedgebury. Bedgebury Forest Cycle Club, boarsonbikes.co.uk. Mudtrail.co.uk/where-to-ride.php, also has page dedicated to Bedgebury.

PETER D'AGUILAR/FORESTRY COMMISSION

Southeast England Bedgebury Forest & Freeride Area

⬂5 Blean Woods

Train station Canterbury West/
Canterbury East
Nearest city Canterbury
Sat Nav CT2 9DD

Location From the M2 (which
finishes at junction 7) carry along the
A2 towards Canterbury. Leave the A
road after 6 km at Upper Harbledown/
the A2050. After 500 m turn left onto
Palmers Cross Hill, and head towards
Rough Common. In the centre of the
village turn left up New Road, and

Blean Woods is 300 m up this road to
the right after the playing fields on
the right.

Facilities Rough Common has a
corner shop and amenities.

Rough round-up This enormous
stretch of forest is perfect for the
XC rider and there's nothing too
demanding here either. There are
three connected woods offering some
lovely views, with the occasional bit of
technical riding. If you're in the Kent

area then it's good to get this under
your belt but not worth a long drive.
You won't be able to get a map but
the trails are obvious as they've been
ridden a lot. There's local bike hire
(kentcyclehire.com) if you're without a
bike, and reasonably priced too.

Conditions This is relatively wild
country, so mud can shut down the
trails in winter, but if it's been dry for a
while the whole network opens up.

J6 Bluebell Hill

Train station Aylesford/New Hythe
Nearest city Chatham
Sat Nav ME5 9SE

Location Bluebell Hill is around 5 km south of Rochester, Kent. From the M25, exit at junction 2 onto the A2 heading into Rochester. This road will turn into the M2, so exit at junction 3 – the A229. Head towards this A road (which looks like another motorway), but before the entry slip, turn off to the left after 100 m into Maidstone Road. Head down here for 500 m, then turn right onto Common Road. This road crosses the A229. Just after, turn left into the Bluebell Hill car park.

Facilities Nearby Boxley and Walderslade are full of shops and amenities. Bluebell Hill has its own car parking area and dedicated picnic site.

Rough round-up Bluebell Hill is connected to and part of the North Downs Way, and the area is hugely popular with walkers, horse riders and mountain bikers. There is some fabulous XC riding – although not particularly challenging – with great views to the south. There are also some short but interesting DH trails dotted around, with natural banks, berms and drops. Riders often head off to the east or west for sections of the North Downs Way.

Conditions This is chalky, flint-based riding, so works well in most conditions, but still avoid after heavy rainfall.

J7 Braintree BMX

Train station Braintree
Nearest city Braintree
Sat Nav CM7 5BL

Location Braintree BMX Track is on the outskirts of Braintree in Essex. From the A131, exit at Braintree and head for the town centre, and take the B1256. Continue driving until Panfield Lane is on your left, and follow this road until you get to a car park (the golf course will be on your left and the BMX track will be on your right behind a line of trees. If you end up on Deanery Hill, you've gone too far.

Facilities Braintree has shops and amenities.

Rough round-up This is a fantastic BMX track with regular club meets and a decent course for those looking to brush up their freeride and freestyle skills on some doubles, berms, and table tops before taking them to some more serious dirt jumps and DH trails.

Conditions This is a well maintained, pro BMX track with drainage, but still avoid during rainy periods.

More info See Braintree BMX's website (braintreebmx.co.uk).

S8 Brockwell Park BMX Track

Train station Herne Hill
Nearest city London
Sat Nav SE24 0PB

Location Brockwell Park is situated in south east London, just next to Brixton. From the A23 in the centre of Brixton loop around the main church and head south on the A204 Effra Road in the direction of Tulse Hill. Carry on down this road for 1 km and turn left into Bascombe Street. Brockwell Park is just in front of you, and the BMX track is in the north end.

Facilities Nearby Brixton has plenty of shops and amenities, while Brockwell park has a café, a fantastic open air swimming pool, tennis and football areas, and a mini train.

Rough round-up This is a competition-standard BMX track with well-maintained berms, jumps, drop ins and features. It's had some investment to build up the jumps and reinforce the big berms – something that has made the locals smile. Being central London, it is often busy, and probably best avoided at super busy times. Not worth a huge journey, but worth a shot if you're in the area.

Conditions This is a tarmac/soil track with drainage built in, but still avoid if muddy.

ⓘ **More info** brixtonbmxclub.com – The local club: they offer training days.

S9 Broxbourne Woods

Train station Bayford
Nearest city Hertford
Sat Nav IG10 4AD

Location Broxbourne Woods is just north of Enfield and around a 15-minute drive from the M25. Exit the motorway at junction 25 and head north on the A10. Drive for around 5 km until you reach a left turn onto Church Lane. When you reach the roundabout take the third exit onto the B156, go straight over the next roundabout and then take a right onto Park Lane. Continue onto Appleby Street, then right into Park Lane Paradise (this road will turn into Holy Cross Hill), then left onto W End Road. When you reach a T junction (both roads will have the same name) take a right, then left onto White Stubbs Lane and follow the signs.

Facilities There are plenty of shops in the nearby town or a pub just down the road.

Rough round-up These aren't the best trails in the world but if you're looking for a nice XC ride, then Broxbourne will be able to deliver. There are some great singletrack runs in the woods, but you have to find it as they're not waymarked. Broxbourne is a nature reserve as well so there is plenty to see and do.

Conditions When it rains it can become very slippery but it has much better drainage than Epping Forest and is therefore quite popular.

S10 Bushy Park

Train station Teddington
Nearest city London
Sat Nav TW12 2EJ

Location Bushy Park is in Teddington, south of Twickenham and Teddington. From the centre of London, take the A308 through Roehampton and Kingston Vale, and head through Hampton on the Hampton Court Road (still the A308). Just after Hampton, the road cuts straight between Hampton Court Palace Gold Club on the left, and Bushy Park on the right. Park at the park entrance on Chestnut Avenue.

Facilities Teddington has plenty of shops and amenities, and the park has Hampton Court Palace with a variety of museum and café facilities (for a price).

Rough round-up As Bushy Park is a Royal Park, it's open to all but you will have to pay a small fee for parking. Cycling is permitted on the roads, and XC rambling is frequent but unofficial, although you're likely to see plenty of riders. To the east of Chestnut Avenue is the Heron Pond, and to the northeast of this is a dirt jumping spot with two lines of small to average size jumps, although not well-maintained. Not worth a long journey, but if you're in the area...

Conditions This is open grassland park area which can get very busy in good weather and be empty and muddy in bad.

ⓘ **More info** royalparks.org.uk/parks/bushy_park/about.cfm.

↘11 Chicksands Bike Park

⓿ ⓫ ⓬ ⓭ ⓮ ⓯ ⓰ ⓱ ⓲

Train station Arlesey/Millbrook (Beds)/
Stewartby

Nearest city London

Sat Nav SG17 5QB

Opening times You'll only find the
doors to Chicksands shut when it's a
trail-building day or there's a one-off
event. Day tickets can be bought
for £5, regardless of age, and annual
memberships are £60 for seniors (16 years
old and over), juniors are £40 (15 years
old and under) and family memberships
are £120.

Location Just north of Shefford and
around 15 km to the east of Milton
Keynes, you'll find Chicksands Bike Park
(located in Rowney Warren). From the
M1 leave at junction 13 and take the
A507 past Ampthill towards Shefford. At
the roundabout with the A600 take the
first exit to Bedford, carry on over the
next roundabout, and take a left down
Sandy Lane; the car park is signposted.

Facilities Chicksands is a small
village in the area that contains some
great freeride trails on a block of
Forestry Commission land where a

hugely popular freeride area has been
developed. As trail builds are regular,
the runs at Chicksands will change and
will constantly challenge the riders
that visit, no matter if you're a one-
time visitor or a daily regular. The soil
in this area is perfect for riding bikes
all year round – a mix of sand and clay
that drains well and sticks together
to shape transitions and landings.
Branded a Bike Park, this is fantastic
jumping and technical skills territory
with purpose-built trails, berms and
drops, and feature after feature on
every bit of singletrack.

XC Chicksands are working with the
Forestry Commission to rebuild these
trails; as such, they're currently a bit
beaten up, although still rideable.
They're situated outside the confines
of the park so are free to ride. Don't
go purely to ride SC though; sample
everything else too.

Downhill There are two DH tracks
but both are short. They're both also
graded severe so if you're thinking
about having a go, make sure you're
competent on your bike as there are
no chicken runs. These trails have to
be ridden to the full extent – features
and all.

Freeride You'll find that this is a
predominantly a freeride hotspot.
There's something for everyone with
tabletops, dirt jumps, ladderdrops, step
ups and much more. The northshore
that was a fan favourite has now been
taken down due to insurance fears, but
there's still plenty to ride.

4X The 4X course at Chicksands has
recently been remodelled to make for

even closer racing and to make the track much more technical.

Not to miss Racing your mates down the dual slalom and 4 x tracks a bit of friendly competition never hurt anyone.

Remember to Avoid Casing a landing and not fixing it up. You may have paid your £5 but trail etiquette costs nothing.

Nearest Bike/Hire shop Pedals of Biggleswade (T01767 313418) is the closest shop and will be able to repair most problems.

Local accommodation
Try the Embankment Hotel in Bedford (T01234 261332) situated on the banks of the river Ouse and overlooking the Victorian suspension bridge. Also De Pary's Guest House (T01234 261982) with an area for bikes and just a couple of minutes walk from the town centre.

Eating There are some snacks on site, or for great Italian food try Villa Rosa (T01234 269259) in Bedford. The local Dew Drop Inn (T01525 840096) has pub grub.

ⓘ **More info**
chicksandsbikepark.co.uk.

⊻12 Crowborough – The Bull Track

XC GR FR N F

Train station Crowborough/Brighton/ Jarvis Brook

Nearest city London

Sat Nav N/A

Location Crowborough is a town around 10 km southwest from Royal Tunbridge Wells, and you'll find The Bull Track just to the east side of Crowborough. From Tunbridge Wells, take the A267 south towards Heathfield. At Mark Cross (about 5 km down this road), take a left onto Catt's Hill in the direction of Rotherfield onto the B2100. Head down this road keeping to the right in Rotherfield (stay on the B2100), and keep going until you go under the railway tracks as you enter Crowborough. Take the second road on the left after this crossing, then through a water-splash and over a railway bridge then next right. The Bull Track is on the right. Please remember that unauthorised riders run the possibility of having everyone banned – call Alvar for permission to ride first (T07789372352).

Facilities There are hot and cold drinks available on site but only when vans arrive. Nearby Crowborough will have all shops and amenities that you'll need. Normal summer opening hours should be weekends 1000-1800, Thursdays 1800-dark but, again, check when you ring Alvar. The Bull Track often holds race days so make sure to check for these before travelling.

Rough round-up This is a purpose-built DH and freeride area and therefore one of the thriving North Downs mountain biking scene's regular haunts, a haunt that regularly holds races. There is plenty of northshore here, some good jumps and obstacles to ride, and a bit of DH.

Terrain There's plenty of singletrack, with lots of wood scattered around to help out on the boggy sections.

XC There's not a lot here for the XC rider, although some loops on the DH track would be testing!

Downhill The DH track is mostly grassland, and not as technical as those found elsewhere, but it is still fun to ride and the site of many races. There are plenty of YouTube videos of the trail online.

Freeride The freeride trails, impressive northshore (with a 3-m drop) and a load of doubles and gaps are what the majority of people are here for. There are some lines for less experienced

riders but all riding is highly recommended. Let's not forget the road gap which is worth hitting!

Conditions The singletrack here is prone to mud, but the problem areas have been worked on. Rideable in most conditions thanks to extensive drainage work.

ⓘ **More info** jab-ride.co.uk has info and a forum for those who regularly ride and race at The Bull Track, while mudtrail.co.uk has tonnes of info on the local Surrey and North Downs mountain biking scene.

Train station Hatfield Peverel/
Chelmsford

Nearest city Chelmsford

Sat Nav CM3 4NN

Location From the M25, exit
at junction 28 heading towards
Chelmsford on the A12. Exit the A12 at
junction 18 and head east along the
A424 for 3 km to Danbury. When in the
village, turn right into Copt Hill, drive
100 m and there will be a track to your
left that heads into the forest. Park

where you can and follow this track on
your bike. The common comprises of
all land to the south.

Facilities Danbury has plenty of
shops, pubs and amenities.

Rough round-up The freeride area is
looked after by a community of local
riders and features some tight, flowing
DH runs with some one-off features –
a hip, river gaps, kickers etc. There are
no main XC trails but there's a lot in
this wood to allow you a nice XC ride.
Definitely not worth a long journey,

but for those that are in the area, it's
well worth checking out. Local riders
are friendly and should be able to tell
you when build days are on.

Conditions This is forested dirt jumping
and natural trail riding with some added,
man-made obstacles to compliment the
trails, but fairly low-budget.

Train station Hayes

Nearest city London

Sat Nav BR4 9HZ

Location The DJs are relatively easy
to find if you take junction 4 from the
M25 and head towards central London
on the A21 past Farnborough. This the
Croydon Road, and West Wickham
Common is to the north (on the right
heading from Farnborough). Park at the
Croydon Road/West Common Road
entrance and ride through. These dirt
jumps are on the north edge of West
Wickham Common, around 3 km to the
east of Farnborough.

Facilities Hayes – on the north side of
the wooded common – has plenty of
shops and amenities.

Rough round-up There's some XC
riding to be had around the common,
and at the north end there are some
low-budget dirt jumps that contain a
few gaps and tables. Not worth a huge
detour, but for those in the area it's
worth checking out.

Conditions The common can get
boggy in the winter, but otherwise it's
a fairly decent stretch of wooded area,
with some open patches of grass here
and there.

Southeast England Devils Drop DJs

Local riders
Ben Wain

Bike Giant STP Zero and Norco Atomic
Local spot Private trails, I build more than I ride these days!
Club member The Bull Track, helped a bit with Bedgebury too.
Age 29
Type of rider Prefer full on Downhill and shore.
Ride all types though!

Where's the one place you'd recommend above all, for those coming to the southeast?

BW   It would have to be Chicksands for the scale of the park and build quality of the trails. It doesn't have 'real' Downhill or XC but it's a great day out any time of year.

Where has the best XC?

BW   Last one I enjoyed was Friston Forest. There are some excellent trails around the North Downs too.

Where is the best Downhill?

BW   They're all quite short around here, best commercial spot would be PORC (best to go on a race weekend when a track's marked out). There are a few decent secret trails but can't say much about those! Aston Hill is also well worth a look.

The best dirt jumps?

BW   Again I would rate Chicksands for excellent build quality. Wisley's good but has limited access! If you want less steep stuff (more full suss friendly) then The Bull Track's your call.

If you were to take a family out – say a cousin who's visiting with his kids – where would you head?

BW   It would probably be Bedgebury if you've got the cash to spend (expensive parking!); the two grades of trails cross over at various points so you can sample a bit of both and see who likes what.

What secret stashes do you know about?

BW   There's a quite few around that I can't really mention. There are some nice natural drops and rock lines around Tunbridge Wells – worth a look if you're in the area!

If you were a huge fan of cake and wanted to find the best trail with a foodie pit stop, where would it be?

BW   Leith Hill and surroundings have some good bike-friendly stop offs. I have been recommended to try Stephan Langton Inn at some point!

Where – if anywhere – outside of your area do you often visit with your bike?

BW   I have visited the French/Swiss Alps a few times and love it there. The atmosphere and everything is spot on. Am considering maybe Italy next!

Which websites have the best info on your local area?

BW   jab-ride.co.uk for what's happening in the area and photos etc or moredirt.co.uk or mudtrail.co.uk for general info on spots.

Which is the best shop to head to if you're in the southeast?

BW   My personal favorite is Wildside in Tunbridge Wells.

▶15 Devils Dyke DH and XC

🄺 🄶 🄾 🄵

Train station Brighton
Nearest city Brighton and Hove
Sat Nav BN1 8YJ

Location Only 3 km north of Brighton town centre is Devils Dyke, which has its own exit sign off the A27. 200 m before, on the road in, you'll pass some fantastic downhill tracks through the valley to the right of the road – impossible to miss. From the pub, DH routes go off in all directions, with the best being down towards Steyning.

Facilities The Dyke Inn serves food and drinks with stunning views of the South Downs. If you're parking here, you may have to pay & display, so make sure you check before parking. The nearest bike shop would be Baker Street Bikes (bakerstbikes.co.uk) or Evans Cycles (evanscycles.com) in nearby Brighton.

Rough round-up DD is the name given to the end of the road pub, and the views from the top stretch to London to the north, the Isle of Wight to west and Eastbourne to the east. The whole area is criss-crossed by paths that are part of the South Downs Way, and the area near the pub teems with walkers, kite-flyers, parapenters and outdoor types. Head out in any direction and the crowds clear. The XC is fantastic due to the views, and ranges from easy to fairly challenging,

mainly owing to the variety of routes and the potential distances for those looking to do long stretches through quaint Sussex villages. Plenty of one-way routes exist (taking the train out to Hassocks and riding back to Brighton is a popular 12-mile run). Not to be confused with the Devils Dyke dirt jumps in Surrey.

Conditions Most routes are singletrack or bridleways and tend to be gravelly and exposed, so avoid in high wind. Mud is a frequent problem.

ⓘ **More info** Check out the Brighton local scene – brightonmtb.org.

▶16 Devils Dyke Nonsuch DJs

🄳🄹

Train station Stoneleigh/Cheam/Ewell/Ewell East
Nearest city London
Sat Nav KT17 2DE

Location From the M25 exit at junction 8 and head north towards central London on the A24. From central London head south to Ewell on the A24. At Ewell, the A24 goes directly

Above and left: Devils Dyke DH and XC
Opposite page: Devils Dyke Nonsuch DJs.

CHRIS MORAN

past Nonsuch Park. Enter the park, and head to the southwest entrance. 100 m along the park perimeter road there's an entrance into the woods. The DJs are inside here, to the southwest edge of Nonsuch Park.

Facilities Ewell town centre (200 m away) has plenty of shops and amenities.

Rough round-up These are some of the best dirt jumps in the greater London area, with tight transitions, short ready-times, and good sections. There are some huge gaps, and reinforced landings. Not for beginners. The local BMX riders share them with mountain bikers but respect and helping to build is strongly recommended.

Conditions These are clay jumps with logs to reinforce the landings, all set in a tight copse of public trees.

⛰17 Donkey Island DJs
⛰

Train station Shepperton/Upper Halliford/Sunbury
Nearest city London
Sat Nav KT12 2JB

Location Sunbury on Thames is just to the south of the M3 inside the M25. From the M3 exit at junction 1, and head south in the direction of Sunbury on Thames on Green Street. Turn right after 300 m onto Nursery Road, then left on the A244 Upper Halliford Road for 3 km. Cross the river, and turn left into Hepworth Way on the A3050 towards West Molesey. After 1 km turn left into Waterside Drive, and go all the way to the end. Then ride along the water's edge, cross the bridge onto Donkey Island, and go left into the copse.

Facilities Sunbury – just over the river – has plenty of shops and amenities, but the nearest town is Walton-on-Thames.

Rough round-up There's a ditch with berms, drops and some dirt jumps. Not worth a long journey but for those in the area this is worth a look.

Conditions This is a small, wooded area with fairly decent drainage but still prone to bouts of mud after heavy rain.

⛰18 Enfield DJs
⛰ ⛰

Train station Gordon Hill
Nearest city London
Sat Nav EN2 8JL

Location Leave the M25 at junction 25 and head south on the A10. Drive for about 2 miles until you reach a right turn leading into Carterhatch Lane – this will lead into Myddleton Avenue. Take a left into Baker Street, then the fourth right into Lancaster Road. Keep driving straight into Lavender Hill and follow the signs to the Chase Farm Hospital. The dirt jumps are behind the hospital itself.

Facilities Nothing on site as it is only a set of dirt jumps but local shops and amenities are a short bike ride away.

Rough round-up These are a selection of dirt jumps that have been built, maintained and repaired by the local riders for years. There are plenty of big jumps to try your hand at but there's also a smaller jump section for riders who are not so confident. There's also a short section of northshore to try out! Make sure you repair any bad landings and show respect to the jumps.

Conditions Avoid after heavy rainfall.

CHRIS MORAN

⬇19 Epping Forest

❌ ❌ ⭕ ⭕ ❌ ⭕

Train station Chingford (train)/
Loughton (tube)
Nearest city London
Sat Nav E4 7QL

Location You can't miss Epping Forest
– it's the largest open and wooded area
within the M25. From central London
head for the M11 in the direction of
Cambridge. From the motorway, exit
at junction 5 and head in the direction
of Loughton. Go left at Loughton onto
the A121 (heading towards Buckhurst
Hill) and, after 2 km, take a right on
Manor Road, then a right onto the A104
(Epping New Road). Then an almost
immediate left into Ranger's Road (the
A1069). This is the forest boundry road.
Head down here for 1 km then take a
right into Bury Road. Park at the West
Essex Golf Club.

Facilities There is a small tea
room in Epping Forest that will sell
refreshments as well as a Visitor
Centre. They should have route maps
but if not, they're available online.
Chingford itself will have plenty of
shops. GoFurtherCycling is the nearest
bike shop/hire to Epping Forest
(gofurthercycling.co.uk).

Rough round-up As this forest and
open land are common land, they're
also very popular with a variety of
forest users. There's also a huge
amount of fire-road and bridleways
criss-crossing the area. If you're
someone who likes un-congested
riding, there's a lot of singletrack to be
had too. It's a great place to meander
your way around the gentle XC venue
taking off on one of the many diverse
routes that you come across.

Conditions Mud is particularly a
problem here due to the clay base
which prevents proper drainage. Avoid
in mid-winter.

ⓘ **More info** There's a dedicated
website for Epping Forest offering
guided rides and a youth club
(eppingforestmtb.co.uk). Alternatively,
visit essexhertsmtb.co.uk.

JARVIS GOODYEAR

Friston Forest

🌲 🚲 🏔 ⛺ 🔵

Train station Polegate/Hampden Park/
Seaford
Nearest city Eastbourne
Sat Nav BN26 5QF

Location Friston Forest is just to the northwest of Eastbourne, and a very easy drive. Exit the M25 at junction 6 and take the A22 all the way south to Eastbourne. Keep heading into the town centre on the A2270, then turn west towards Newhaven on the A259. Just after the village of Friston – itself around 2 km from Eastbourne – turn north on the B2105 Jevington Road and follow this road for around 1 km. Friston Forest is signed to the left of this road.

Facilities The forest is deep countryside, but nearby Friston has shops and amenities. There's local bike hire in Cuckmere (cuckmere-cycle.co.uk/) that also provide group activities, bike courses and more.

Rough round-up Friston is one of the most popular sites for the dwellers of Brighton and Eastbourne and is a very popular horse riding destination, as well as being maintained by the Forestry Commission. There are several waymarked trails throughout the forest and some unmarked, with plenty for both the adventurous XC rider and families.

Terrain Loads of both unofficial and waymarked singletrack, as well as lots of bridleways.

XC There are plenty of trails to suit most abilities here with the 13-km

XC route being the favourite. Most routes are well-signed, and are a range of difficulties although serious riders might be left wanting. The scenery, and that of nearby Seven Sisters and Beachy Head, is utterly British, with fantastic forest land opening out into rolling hills and huge, chalk cliffs.

Downhill Not many DH trails here as the ones that exist are short. Proclaimed to be of an 'old school' fashion though.

Freeride There's a strong local scene who build armoured bridges, jumps, drops and some random northshore-style wood around the forest, with scope to develop.

Conditions The XC routes are hard-packed chalk and flint singletrack so work in most weather conditions.

ⓘ **More info** Local bike shop Cuckmere Cycle Company in Seven Sisters have a wealth of knowledge on the Forest while mudtrail.co.uk/where-to-ride.php has a page on Friston.

SE21 Gunnersbury DJs

Train station Kew Bridge (rail),
Acton Town (tube)
Nearest city London
Sat Nav W3 8LQ

Location Just north of the M4 in
Gunnersbury Park, Brentford, are the
Gunnerbury dirt jumps. Leave the M4
at junction 2 and head north on Lionel
Road North. Take a right east onto
Pope's Lane (around the edge of the
park), then park at the Gunnersbury
Park Museum. You'll find the DJs in the
southwest corner of the park, just after
the lake.

Facilities The museum has a café,
and there are plenty of shops and
amenities in nearby Brentford.

Rough round-up This is a small area
of dirt jumps with a few small lines
and one section which might appeal
to average riders. Local riders regularly
shape and if you do turn up to ride
they would definitely appreciate some
help in maintaining the jumps.

Conditions Good solid dirt to
work with in a secluded corner of
private land.

SE22 Hadleigh Farm

Train station Benfleet/Leigh-on-Sea
Nearest city Basildon
Sat Nav SS7 2AP

Location Hadleigh Farm can be
found in Essex, just east of Dartford.
When travelling north on the M25,
drive through Dartford and take
a right onto the A13. This is the
main road you will need to follow
so continue driving on the A13 for
roughly 18 miles until you reach a
right turn that leads you onto Castle
Lane. The trail will be found at the
end of this road.

Facilities As it's a Salvation Army
location, there's a tea room for riders
to buy refreshments. Work has begun
on a new Visitor Centre, called The
Hub, which should be finished some
time in the middle of 2015.

Rough round-up Hadleigh Farm
is a XC trail that takes full use of the
Olympic Legacy that has been left to
the country. It's part of the mountain
biking trail that you would have seen
in the Olympics, just with a few minor
changes. It's a 5 km course with two
new technical sections and an extensive
main climb. There's also ongoing work
to make the trail more family friendly.

Conditions As it's Olympic standard,
it's rideable in all weathers.

N23 Hainault Forest & Redbridge

Train station Chadwell Heath (train)/ Hainault (tube)
Nearest city London
Sat Nav IG6 3HP (For Redbridge Cycling Centre)

Location You'll find Hainault Forest just southeast of Chigwell in London. It's an easy drive from the motorway as well. Leave the M25 at junction 28 and head west on the A12. Take a right onto the B175 and continue until you join the B174 and take a left onto Collier Row Road. Take a right into Hog Hill Road, which will then turn into Romford Road. Carry on this road until you see signs for the Country Park.

Facilities It's a well-stocked country park with a Visitor Centre, café, toilets and car park. If you're driving there, parking will cost you £1 for an hour or £3 for the full day. It's open from 0700 each morning but closes its doors at dusk, so make sure you don't get locked in!

Rough round-up Drier than Epping Forest, Hainault is a great place to ride for the XC lover, and it's easy to get to from Central Line for those of you living in London. There are some great hills and singletrack here but for the good trails, you have to be adventurous and head off the beaten track. Redbridge Cycling Centre, which is next door, is a traffic free facility for cyclists with trails for families and competitive riders. It's waymarked so you don't get lost!

Conditions When it's rained heavily it's not the easiest ride in the world but dries quickly so always worth a ride.

ⓘ **More info** Check out redbridge. gov.uk for all the info you need or call the Country Park Office for details on rights of way on T0208 500 7353. You'll be able to pick up a map from the Park Office.

N24 Harrow Skatepark and DJs

Train station Harrow and Wealdstone
Nearest city London
Sat Nav HA3 5BD

Location The skatepark and dirt jumps are two separate locations, both in Harrow. From Harrow town centre, head north on the A409 (Station Road) for 1 km passing Harrow and Wealdstone underground and train station. Take a right at the next roundabout and the skatepark is well signed off to the right. For the DJs, head back to the roundabout on the A409, head south and take a left onto The Bridge, then first left onto Ellen Webb Drive – this will turn into Headstone Drive (and this then turns into Headstone Gardens), for 1 km, then take a right into Pinner View. The DJs are around 200 m up this road, just behind the copse of trees on your left.

Facilities Headstone Gardens has shops and amenities.

Rough round-up Harrow is one of the only 1970s concrete wave skateparks left in the UK, and has a strong skate, BMX and mountain bike scene. The dirt jumps are high-quality with plenty of lines ranging from small to fairly big. The scene here is also large, so be prepared to dig if you wish to ride. Worth a visit for locals or those in this general area.

Conditions The skatepark is well drained and the DJs are well maintained, but as always, avoid in bad weather and always fix any cased landings.

ⓘ **More info** Harrow Skatepark has its own wikipedia page at wikipedia.org/ wiki/Harrow_Skate_Park and website at harrowskatepark.co.uk, although the Facebook page is updated more regularly – facebook.com/harrow. skatepark.

N25 Hayes Hawks BMX Track

Train station Hayes and Harlington
Nearest city London
Sat Nav UB3 1JD

Location From the M4, leave at junction 3 and head north into Hayes on the A312. Take a left at the first roundabout onto North Hyde Road (the A437) and carry on for 1.5 km crossing the railway bridge. Hayes Hawks is about 400 m after the railway bridge and to your right.

Facilities Hayes is full of shops and amenities.

Rough round-up This is an old-school BMX track that is well-maintained and good for some freeride and dirt jumping practice for those learning or progressing. These aren't classic dirt jumps but whoops, berms, and doubles. Not worth a long journey but for locals it could be worth checking out.

Conditions This area is prone to flooding, so avoid if it's been raining.

ⓘ **More info** Hayes Hawks website (hawksbmx.co.uk). Also see Facebook – search for Hayes Hawks BMX.

N26 Highgate DJs

Train station Upper Holloway (train),
Highgate (tube)
Nearest city London
Sat Nav N6 4JH

Location These are a little site right
next to the Highgate tube station in
North London. The tube station sits
on the A1 – Archway Road – so head
southeast towards central London and
turn left after 200 m into Shepherd's
Hill and park where you can. The DJs
are in the copse in the corner.

Facilities Archway Road is full of
shops and amenities.

Rough round-up Not the biggest
set-up in the world but as dirt jumps
in central and north London are hard
to come by, it's perfect for locals. It's
a locally-maintained, semi-legal area
for BMXers and mountain bikers.
All are welcome and there's a small
community of riders who try to
organise build days etc.

Conditions This is central London
parkland. Expect nearby Queens Wood
to be busy with dog walkers but this
area should remain fairly undisturbed.

N27 Holmes Place DJs

Train station Farnborough/Fleet
Nearest city London
Sat Nav GU14 0NY

Location Southwood is to the west of
Farnborough, which is to the south of
the M3 in Surrey and that's where you'll
find the Holmes Place Dirt Jumps. Exit
the motorway at junction 4a heading
south on the A327. After 1 km take a left

at the roundabout and head over the
bridge to the next roundabout. Take a
left here, and head towards Southwood
with the common on your right. Park
where you can and head directly south
into the woods.

Facilities Nearby Southwood has
plenty of shops and amenities.

Rough round-up This is a locals dirt
jump with 3 sets – a 4 pack, a medium-
sized 12 pack, and a rhythm section with
plenty of speed-building pumps etc.
There's a decent local scene with both
BMXers and mountain bikers. Not worth
a long journey but for those in the area it
might be worth improving a few skills on
the jumps. Please respect the work and
effort that have gone into building them.

Conditions This is classic local woods
set up which is popular with dog
walkers. Expect it to be very muddy in
winter and after heavy rain.

N28 Hurtwood Trails

Train station Gomshall
Nearest city Guildford
Sat nav postcode GU5 9RR

Location The Hurtwood Trails are
deep in the Surrey countryside near
the Peaslake trails, roughly 15 km from
Guildford. When travelling north on
the A24, you will reach a roundabout
that leads you to a left hand turn onto
the A2003 (Flint Hill which turns into
Horsham Road), get to the end of this
road and turn left and follow the road as
it curves right onto Vincent Lane. At the
end of the road turn left onto Westcott
Road (A25), continue on the A25 for
7 km and turn left onto the B2126. When
you reach Abinger Hammer.head south

towards Sutton Abinger but take a right
onto Hoe Lane before you reach the
village. Follow this road down and you
will reach Hurt Wood.

Facilities No facilities in the woods
or at Hurtwood Estate as it's privately
owned land.

Rough round-up Despite being
privately owned land, the owners are
more than happy for mountain bikers to
use the forest. The relationship between
bikers and owners is so good that there
are dedicated dig days – check out
hurtwoodtrails.co.uk for all the info.
There is some short XC runs throughout
the forest (not waymarked) but the
locals head in for the dirt jumps. Not
worth a long drive but if you're in the
area it's definitely an area to check out.

Conditions Can get very muddy after
heavy rainfall.

ⓘ **More info** Friends of Hurtwood is
a great site with lots of local knowledge
(friendsofthehurtwood.co.uk); or get in
touch with the guys at Hurtwood trails
for any info (hurtwoodtrails.co.uk).

N29 Ingrebourne Hill

Train station Rainham (train) / Elm Park
(tube)
Nearest city London
Sat Nav RM13 7QT

Location Ingrebourne Hill is situated
in a small wood in South Hornchurch.
Driving north on the M25 past Dartford,
take a left turn onto the A13 and
continue until you reach a turning off the
A13 – this will lead you to a roundabout.
Take a right at the roundabout onto Ferry
Lane, then take a left onto Lamson Road.

When you hit the roundabout take the first exit onto Bridge Road and continue straight over at the next roundabout onto Rainham Road. Take a right onto Victory Road and park where you can. The trail is about 50 m northeast.

Facilities Nearby Rainham has shops and facilities.

Rough round-up It's a small, purpose-built trail with some nice added extras. The newest loop is a switchbacked climb that leads you alongside the Thames. The downhill section has two options for riders – a wide, twisty drop for beginners or a bermed, twisting downhill trail with several jumps. They'll lead you into nice singletrack taking in a double rhythm section, but not before taking you through a pump track.

Conditions Although newly built, probably best to wait for dry weather.

▶30 Ipswich BMX Track
ⓓ

Train station Derby Road
Nearest city Ipswich
Sat Nav IP3 0HB

Location Ipswich BMX is in a park to the southeast of the Suffolk city. Take the A1156 (Fore Street) from the city centre and travel eastwards, in the direction of Warren Heath. After 1 km, take a right into Nacton Road, then when it forks, take another right into Clapgate Lane. After 500 m you'll come to Landseer Park on your right, the BMX track is here.

Facilities There are shops and facilities surrounding Landseer Park.

Rough round-up This is the oldest BMX track in the country and still

holds a few thrills for those looking to improve their bike handling skills before heading to some more serious dirt jumps or DH trails.

Conditions Averagely maintained, this gets muddy in bad conditions and is on open parkland in a city suburb. It does have drainage though.

ⓘ **More info** Ipswich BMX club has its own website, ipswichbmx.co.uk.

▶31 Kuoni Trails
ⓓ

Train station Dorking Deepdene
Nearest city Dorking
Sat Nav RH5 4AT

Location The east side of Dorking in Surrey plays host to the popular Kuoni Trails. If you leave the M25 at junction 9 (exit at Leatherhead) and head south towards Dorking on the A24. As you pass Dorking, on Deepdene Avenue, turn left into South Drive and park, or carry on for 200 m and turn off left into a lay-by. The DJs are just in the woods to your left.

Facilities Dorking has plenty of shops and amenities.

Rough round-up There are two lines at Kuoni – the hard or easy lines. The easy line is perfect for those with a little skill who wish to improve, while the hard line is definitely for more experienced riders, but won't be too testing for those who can take lines at places like Devils Dyke Nonsuch DJs.

Conditions These are clay-soil dirt jumps built in the forest. Avoid when muddy.

▶32 Leith Hill
ⓧⓒ ⓓⒽ ⓓⒿ

Train station Gomshall/Ockley
Nearest city London
Sat Nav RH5 6JH

Location Leith Hill Dirt Jumps are essentially part of the Redlands and Surrey North Downs mountain biking scene, and are to be found just west of the Redlands/Leith Hill XC and DH trails. Head south from Dorking on the A24 and take a right at Beare Green onto the A29 towards Ockley. Take a right onto the B2126 and continue for 1.5 km, then right into Abinger Road heading to Leith Hill. This will turn into Leith Hill Road after the village, carry on straight for 1 km and park where Sheephouse Lane splits off to the right. Just to the southeast of this junction is a quarry.

Facilities Leith Hill has a shop, but for supplies stock up in Dorking.

Rough round-up There has been a lot of work on the trails recently with a brand new trail being built with berms, rollers and new jumps. It's thanks to work by the National Trust and local riders that this has been built so have fun and respect the trails. There are also some DH trails over to the east of the hill, with some drops, wallrides and dirt jumps available. Worth a look in if you've come to ride Redlands.

Conditions This is chalky, flinty land, common to the North Downs, and drains well but is best avoided after heavy rain.

ⓘ **More info** mudtrail.co.uk is a website dedicated to riders looking for XC, freeride and DH challenges in the North Downs.

⬂33 Lee Valley Velo Park

🚲 🅿 🚻 ☕ 🅓

Train station Stratford
Nearest city London
Sat Nav E20 3EL

Location Located to the northeast of London, the Lee Valley Velo Park is easy to find. When travelling north on the M25, take a left onto the A2 just before reaching Dartford and continue for roughly 30 km. You will reach a roundabout where the A2 splits off to the left but you will need to continue straight on to the A102. Drive over the Thames and the road will turn into the A12; the Velo Park will be signposted when you approach Lee Valley Park. Just in case, before crossing the River Lea, you will take a right that goes under the A12, then a left turn onto Quartermile Lane. Follow this road and you'll see the Velo Park on your right.

Facilities The Lee Valley Velo Park has a lot going on as part of the London 2012 Olympic Legacy. If travelling there by car, be aware that there are limited spaces available to park in so it's recommended that you travel via train. There's a café on site that serves hot and cold drinks as well as some snacks. The centre also offers bike lessons to get you used to riding a mountain bike on the different levels of trails as well as the skills track.

Rough round-up You'll be spoilt for choice at this Legacy Park, and the fact that it's in London is great for mountain bikers wanting to find something on their doorstep. The Velo Park has undergone some major work since the Olympics but holds 8 km of

mountain bike trails and a re-vamped BMX track, as well as a road track for those that way inclined. There's also a skills area that is set to be open, and should be by the time this goes to print (summer 2014) for all you riders looking to get airborne.

Terrain The soil here has been imported and the track builders have laced it with plant seeds to really bind the trails together. Once it's all bedded in, it should hold some pretty special riding.

XC With 8 km of purpose-built trails, it's a great place to go riding when in the main bustle of the big smoke. The trails here are graded blue, red and black and are perfect for beginners looking to hone their skills as well as riders looking for a bit of a challenge. For the more hardcore riders of you out there, it's worth a look but not worth spending the whole day here.

Downhill You won't find any DH trails here as it's very cross-country-centric.

Dirtjumps/Freeride There's a purpose-built skills area that's set to test your bike handling skills, but it's not really built for dirt jumpers in mind. It's a nice bit of fun but built to be a taster session for the trails (and to show what kind of terrain you're likely to encounter) rather than as a serious jump area.

4X The Olympic BMX track is perfect for testing your 4X skills and is of an incredibly high standard.

Conditions As the trails are purpose-built, expect it to be ridable all year round. However, it's not sheltered so expect to be hit by the elements if it's particularly bad weather.

ⓘ **More info** For all info, prices and updates on the trails, visit visitleevalley.org.uk.

N34 Limpsfield DJs

⬤ ⬤ ⬤

Train station Oxted/Hurst Green
Nearest city London
Sat Nav RH8 0EB

Location Leave the motorway at junction 6 of the M25 and head south on the A22, take a right at the first roundabout and head down the A25 towards Oxted – roughly 3 km away. Pass through Oxted and cross the train tracks, and carry on for 1 km. Just before Limpsfield Common, turn right into Wolf's Road, then right again after 400 m as the road forks. Park soon after and head direction north into the woods. The jumps are in this copse.

Facilities Hurst Green or Oxted have plenty of shops and amenities.

Rough round-up These dirt jumps are effectively the remains of an unofficial BMX track built in the 1980s and are quite low-budget, but they

are still maintained by local riders. They're good fun and offer some good riding and tests for beginners and intermediates but not worth a long journey. There's some great twisty singletrack through the woods and well worth a look.

Conditions This area is wooded common land and popular with dog walkers etc. Nearby Limpsfield Common has a few XC trails and some open land.

N35 Look Out Gulley

⬤ ⬤ ⬤

Train station Bagshot/Ascot
Nearest city London
Sat Nav SL5 8AY

Location The popular Look Out Gulley can be found around 2 km north west of Bagshot, at junction 3 of the M3. Take the exit and head north towards Easthampstead on the A322. Park opposite the Berkshire Golf Club and head directly west into the forest.

Facilities The nearest decent pub and shops are in Bagshot. This area is largely unpopulated, although popular with horse riders and dog walkers.

Rough round-up There are XC trails looping all over these woods, with some short but interesting downhill to be had, while in the middle is Look Out Gulley, a popular freeride spot with drops, some dirt jumps and gaps. Most of it is natural, with a little bit of building starting to make an appearance.

Conditions These woods are prone to boggy conditions during winter, so avoid after rainfall.

N36 Lordship Loop

⬤

Train station Bruce Grove (train) / Turnpike Lane (tube)
Nearest City London
Sat Nav N17 6LP

Location The Lordship Loop pump track is close to the stadium of Tottenham Hotspur FC and has great transport links. Leave the M25 at junction 25 and drive south on the A10. Follow this road for about 7 miles until you reach Lordship Lane. Take a right, then take your first left into Mt. Pleasant Road. Take a right onto Adams Road and the park will be directly in front of you.

Facilities There are no facilities on site but this park is in the centre of town so shops and amenities aren't too far away.

Rough round-up Haringey Council commissioned this track for the community and it's certainly proven popular. It's full of rollers, berms, double rollers and step-ups. It's perfect for all abilities, with the more experienced riders using the jumps instead of rollers. Not worth a long trip but great for locals.

Conditions Has good drainage and is a quick drying track but not worth riding when wet.

N37 M3 DJs

⬤ ⬤

Train station Camberley/Bagshot
Nearest city Reading/London
Sat Nav GU15 1PJ (for Sovereign Drive)

Location As you could probably guess by the name, the M3 dirt jumps are found next to the M3, just on the north side of the motorway, around 1 km west from Bagshot at junction 3. Exit at the junction and head towards Bagshot, carry on for 1 km until you can turn left onto the A30 (London Road) in the direction of Camberly. Head down this road for 2 km then turn left into the B3015 (The Maultway). Head down here and park before you cross the M3. Head northeast into this grassland (there's an entrance opposite Sovereign Drive), and the DJs are just next to the motorway around 500 m ride away.

Facilities Camberly has corner shops and amenities.

Rough round-up This is a low-budget area of dirt jumps with a few small lines and one section which might appeal to average riders. Not hugely worth a journey but fine for locals to explore. Plus the local area has some half decent XC rambling to be had, although the presence of the motorway isn't good for views etc.

Conditions There is little here to hold off the bad weather, so only take a journey if it's bright outside and has been for a while.

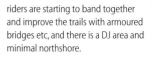

Mereworth Woods

Train station Borough Green & Wrotham
Nearest city London
Sat Nav ME18 5JY

Location Mereworth Woods are around 12 km northeast of Tonbridge. Leave the M25 at Junction 5 and take the A25 until you reach the A228 (which is a right onto Ashton Way). It's about 2 km until you reach Mereworth village. Keep following the road until you are able to take a right here on Beech Road, and go to the end T junction. Mereworth Woods are just opposite this T junction.

Facilities Nearby Mereworth has shops and amenities.

Rough round-up MOD-owned Mereworth Woods contains a collection of trails that local riders have slowly added features to in order to create some short but feature-full DH trails. There are a few jumps, drops and berms, and it's all pretty low-budget, but worth a look if you're in the area. There is a good local scene and the riders are starting to band together and improve the trails with armoured bridges etc, and there is a DJ area and minimal northshore.

Conditions This is all singletrack through forest. Avoid when muddy.

Peaslake

Train station Gomshall
Nearest city London
Sat Nav GU5 9RR

Location Peaslake is a beautiful village on the Surrey/Sussex border and easily found from the M25. Exit at junction 9 and head south through Leatherhead following signs for the A24 Dorking. At Dorking turn right onto the A25 Guildford Road, and carry on for 7km to the village of Abinger Hammer. Turn south on the B2126, then second right into Hoe Lane which leads to Peaslake village. Park at The Hurtwood Inn, on the corner of Walking Bottom and Peaslake Lane.

Facilities Peaslake village has a couple of shops and the Hurtwood Inn pub.

Rough round-up Head up Walking Bottom and turn first left. This parking area gives access to a network of XC routes in some spectacular forest (home to the Germanic battle scenes in the film Gladiator), which summits out with views over the south and north downs. There are a few short but sweet DH tracks to be found up Radnor Road from the village centre. Expect to see plenty of riders who are by-and-large very friendly and only happy to show their trails off.

CHRIS MORAN

Conditions Most routes are singletrack or bridleways and tend to be shared with dog walkers etc.

ⓘ **More info** There's some MTB Orienteering from peaslakemtbo.com which is the best place to find out some local knowledge of the trails.

---

⑨40 Peckham BMX Track
Ⓑ

Train Station South Bermondsey/ Queens Road Peckham
Nearest City London
Sat Nav SE5 0AN

Location These BMX tracks are easy to find when travelling through London. Driving south from Elephant and Castle, drive down the A215 until you reach Albany Road on your left. Take this turning and you'll see a turning off into a car park just past Canal Street.

Facilities Peckham is full of shops and amenities.

Rough round-up Both BMX tracks have benefitted from substantial investment recently and are both top BMX tracks. As with most BMX tracks, it's not worth a long journey but if you're looking to start out on dirt jumps, it's a good place to learn bike control.

Conditions This is a small clearing of land in a densely built-up area of London.

ⓘ **More info** Peckham BMX track has its own website and club membership – peckhambmx.co.uk.

CHRIS MORAN

↘41 PORC (Penshurst Off Road Club) aka Viceroy's Wood

Nearest train station Penshurst/Cowden

Nearest city London

Sat Nav TN11 8DU

Opening times 0900 until dark. Day pass for adults – £5, under 18s – £3, and £3.50 for students. There are annual memberships available at £125 for adults and £75 for under 18s.

Location The Penshurst Off Road Club (PORC) also goes by the name of Viceroy's Wood, and can be found next to the village of Penshurst in Kent. Take junction 5 from the M25 and down the A21 towards Tonbridge. When you reach Tonbridge, take the A26 south and turn off right towards Penhurst

on the B2176 (Penhurst Road). At the village turn left on the B2188 Fordcombe Road, and carry on for 1 km then turn right into Grove Road. Go 1 km down this road and PORC is signposted off to the left.

Facilities A Visitor Centre, café, showers and stunning views of the woodland, PORC has a lot of facilities for the mountain biker. Penshurst itself is an historic English village where you can expect to see thatched roofs and quaint old cottages nestled around the old town hall and church. Its location also lends itself to serve much of London, and yet the contrast from the nation's capital to this sleepy village couldn't

Southeast England — PORC (Penshurst Off Road Club) aka Viceroy's Wood

90

be greater. The riding area manages to cram a lot into a small space. That said, it's still a great place to spend the day honing your skills on the range of short courses and features.

XC Don't travel to PORC purely with the intention of trail riding as you'll be very disappointed. There are some marked out XC trails but most people come here for the DH and 4X. It's suggested that you try out some of the other downhill and freeride tracks as none of them are too steep for an XC bike. The ride around the perimeter is 5.5 km long, and perfect for everyone, including families.

Downhill There are a number of short downhill routes at PORC/Viceroys which will keep you busy for a day; being a small hill it means the runs are short but that has the advantage of the push back to the top being far easier than some venues.

Freeride For all freeriders out there, the 4X track is enough to quench your thirst but there are also some gaps and a quarry area full of DJs.

Not to miss The DJs are top class.

Remember to avoid Not checking out the view from the Shimla centre. Apparently it's the 'Best in Kent'.

Nearest Bike/Hire shop Nearby Tunbridge Wells has a large cycle dealer called Wildside (01892 527069) who stock just about everything you'll need.

Local accommodation
Check ahead if you are interested in camping at PORC (contact is on their website) or there are plenty of places nearby. For example, Manor Court Farm B&B (T01892 740279).

Eating The Spotted Dog (T01892 870253) serves great food using locally sourced products in Penshurst. The new Shimla Centre should be offering plenty of locally-sourced food.

ⓘ **More info** P.O.R.C – T01892 870136, or check out their website at – porc.uk.com. Alternatively, Mud Trail has a page dedicated to the area at mudtrail.co.uk/where-to-ride.php.

> **Lowdown**

☺ **Locals do**
Have quite rounded bike skills due to the riding here.

Try out the 4X track when they can – it's a lot of fun

☹ **Locals don't**
Ride here in the wet – jumps are no fun unless they're dry.

✔ **Pros**
Good on a hardtail or a suspension bike.

✘ **Cons**
Could do with a full bike shop on hand.

⟨↘42⟩ Redlands

Train station Gomshall
Nearest city London
Sat Nav RH5 6QH

Location Just near the village of Wotton in Surrey, just west of Dorking, are the Redlands Trails. Exit the M25 at junction 9, heading south through Leatherhead and for the A24 in the direction of Dorking. When in Dorking, follow the signs for the A25 travelling towards Guildford. After about 2 km you'll arrive at Wotton, take a left here down Sheephouse Lane, and then another left after 400 m into Wolvens Lane. The parking area for Redlands is around 500 m up here on the left.

Facilities Nearby Wescott or Wotton have small shops and a few amenities, but it might be best getting all supplies from Dorking.

Rough round-up This is a huge expanse of mixed-owned land, and a brilliant example of what groups of mountain bikers can achieve when they form a club and treat the land and its owners with due respect. There are tens of purpose-built trails here, criss-crossing the area using either fire-roads, bridleways, or – increasingly as they are built – mountain bike-specific singletrack.

Terrain Gentle, hilly country at its best, covered in large coniferous forest. Some of the land is privately owned, some owned by English Heritage but it's all managed in one way or another. Avoid the budding trees or any closed areas, and only build in conjunction with the Redlands riders club.

XC From easy blue runs to more difficult reds, they're all waymarked and clearly signed as to whether they're bike, walker or horse paths (keeping everyone out of the way of everyone else!).

Downhill This is no place for DH riders as there are only short sections to ride. Nearby Leith Hill has a DH section named 'Deliverance' that is renowned, and has a few drops and rootsy sections, but not worth a long journey.

Freeride There are no specific DJs or a freeride area but there are some great features to ride, with plenty of roots, banks and small jumps to hit for the adventurous riders.

Conditions The XC routes are hard-packed dirt singletrack. The area is very popular with walkers and horse riders, and is also home to several residents in cottages etc, but well known as a mountain biking centre so expect to see plenty of bikes. It's also known, by the locals, as a pretty unrideable place to be when it's been raining so make sure you go on a dry day.

ⓘ **More info** There are loads of great local riders who regularly get together and help maintain the Redlands area through redlandstrails.wordpress.com.

SH43 Shoreham DJs

Train station Shoreham by Sea
Nearest city Brighton and Hove
Sat Nav N/A

Location Shoreham Dirt Jumps are in Shoreham-by-Sea, a town just to the west of Brighton. Driving west on the A27 in the direction of Chichester, exit, taking the A283 heading towards Shoreham and drive in the direction of the sea. Take a right at the roundabout and cross over the estuary inlet where the road turns into the A259 (driving away from Brighton). As soon as you've crossed the water, take a right (remembering that this is an illegal turn – head to the roundabout and double back to do it legally) and you'll find the DJs at the end of this road.

Facilities Shoreham has plenty of shops and facilities and is just on the other side of the bridge.

Rough round-up Originally Shoreham's Adur BMX track but was turned into dirt jumps. Recently they local riders have been in discussions with the council to build new dirt jumps but it's still yet to be decided (at the time of writing). There are still some jumps there but it's not worth rebuilding anything as it may get demolished.

Conditions The ground here dries fairly quickly, but still avoid if it's been raining heavily.

ⓘ **More info** The Brighton local scene has a website at brightonmtb.org.

SH44 Shorne Wood Country Park and DJs

Train station Higham/ Sole Street/Cuxton
Nearest city London
Sat Nav DA12 3HX

Location Just east of Rochester Kent is Shorne Wood Country Park and its dirt jump brother. Exit the M25 at junction 2 onto the A2 heading to Rochester. After 10 km, exit the A2 in the direction of Gravesend east, (the exit after Singlewell). Turn right and head back over the A2, and the road follows the A2 in parallel until a roundabout 1 km along. Here carry straight on to Brewers Road (direction Shorne), after 500 m Shore Country Park is on the left.

Facilities SWCP has a brand new Visitor Centre, toilets, disabled access and waymarked routes. The Visitor Centre has a café with refreshments so no need to trek to the nearest town.

Rough round-up Although this is seen primarily as a walkers and horse-riding destination, and originally used to be banned to mountain bikes completely, the park now officially allows cyclists. It's a great XC area with no strenuous DH or horrendous climbs – and mostly naturally singletrack. Just to the north on Brewers Road are a series of dirt jumps ranging from easy to medium gaps and tables. Please note the area isn't as family friendly as you might imagine.

Conditions Avoid if muddy and can be very choppy with the horse tracks.

ⓘ **More info** You can find all info on the Kent website – kent.gov.uk.

SH45 Sidley Woods

Train station Bexhill-on-Sea
Nearest city Brighton and Hove
Sat Nav TN39 5BY

Location Sidley Woods are in the sleepy, seaside town of Bexhill-on-Sea, on the south coast. Heading into Bexhill on the A269 (Ninfield Road), take a left into Sidley Street, then right onto Preston Road. The trails are in the woods at the end of this road, so park cul-de-sac and head into the woods (next to the Lovett's Wood sign), and the DJs are right there.

CHRIS MORAN

CHRIS MORAN

after the houses on the left (around 300 m), park up and ride into the quarry entrance, which is closed off by a couple of poles and a chain.

Facilities Fontwell has a corner shop for immediate supplies.

Rough round-up The quarry is a relatively remote patch of land where local riders have built plenty of drops, berms, doubles, gaps and table tops, and the surrounding area has plenty of unofficial trails for the adventurous XC rider to explore. This is prime South Downs territory, and the area is criss-crossed with plenty of fire-road, single and double track, and has the Cocking Mountain Bike Route 16-mile all-weather loop. Please note that this is private land (and is used for 4X4 and motocross riding, so ride with caution and obey any requests from the landowner.

Conditions The surrounding area can be prone to muddy sections and the quarry itself is used as a 4x4 training area, so the area is very, very muddy after heavy rain.

jump area than anything else so make sure you respect the jumps and people who use them. It's worth getting in touch with the Source BMX Crew (who run a shop in Hastings) first.

Conditions There is little here to hold off the bad weather, so only take a journey if it's bright outside and has been for a while.

ⓘ **More info** The Source BMX Crew are the people to contact – T01424 460943, sourcebmx.co.uk.

N46 Slindon Quarry
ⓧⓒ ⓓⓘ

Train station Arundel/Barnham
Nearest city Brighton and Hove
Sat Nav BN18 0LT

Facilities Sidley Street has plenty of shops and supplies.

Rough round-up These jumps are infamous in the BMX community and were nearly bulldozed in 2013. They have, luckily, been saved but are now very exclusive. It's more of a private dirt

Location Heading east on the A27, drive for around 10 km from Chichester until you hit the village of Fontwell. Take the A29 (Fairmile Bottom road), in the direction of Pulborough and go down this road for about 1 km. Take the second right into Shellbridge Road (the B2132), then

⌐47⌐ Swinley Forest

⊗ ⊕ ⊛ ⊙ ⊚ ⊕ ⊖ ⊕ ⊙ ⊘

Train station Bagshot/Ascot/
Martins Heron
Nearest city London/Reading
Sat Nav SL5 8AY

Location Between Bagshot and
Bracknell is Swinley Forest, a tract of
Crown Estate, just off the M3 and next
door to the Berkshire Golf Club. Exit
the M3 at junction 3 and head north
past Bagshot on the A322. Around
2.5 km up this road and to the right is
Swinley Forest. Turn off first roundabout
heading up the A332 and the entrance
is 150 m on the right. Follow signs for
'The Look Out', or The Coral Reef Water
World just opposite.

Facilities As you would expect from
a big forest like this, you have a Visitor
Centre (named 'The Look Out'), which
houses a café, ranger office, toilets and
various facilities. The Wellington Trek
Bike Hire have bikes for hire at £25 per
day and £10 for every additional day
after that.

Rough round-up This forest used
to be a haven for riders as there were
many trails to discover and ride. In 2012,
the Crown Estates worked to get rid of
these trails and have since opened a
few more purpose-made runs for riders.
They don't charge for permits anymore
but the real loss is the vast selection of
riding that is now banned.

Terrain The trails are now purpose-
maintained singletrack. The area is
also popular with a range of out-door
users, and although mountain biking
is popular, you can still bump into dog

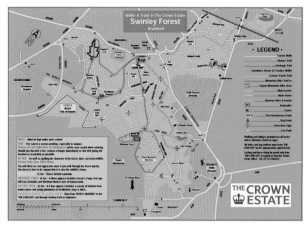

walkers. The forest riding that Swinley
was popular for is now discouraged but
there is plenty to ride and it's well kept,
so there's still plenty of fun to be had.

XC There are 4 trails at Swinley
now – green, blue, red, black – with a
freeride area as well. The green is short
and perfect for families, whereas the
blue and red are for riders looking to
progress their riding. There are many
other trails but these are now off-limits.
The red trail is the longest at 13 km.

Downhill Despite Swinley being
a predominantly XC area, there is a
purpose-built 'Downhill Zone' that will be
good enough for most riders. However, if
you're a seasoned downhiller, you might
get bored quickly.

Dirtjumps Like the Downhill Zone,
there is a dedicated freeride area with
dirt jumps aplenty. It's well worth a visit
but pure dirt jumpers are advised to
head elsewhere.

Conditions The XC routes are hard-
packed, man-made and purpose-
maintained dirt singletrack. The area is
popular with walkers but well known as
a mountain biking centre so expect to
see plenty of bikes.

ⓘ **More info** Bike hire info can be
found on the Wellington Hire website
(wellingtontrek.co.uk/) and there's also
an online map on the Crown Estates
website. There's also a website for the
local riding scene (swinleyriders.co.uk).

⃝48 Sloughbottom Park

Train station Norwich
Nearest city Norwich
Sat Nav NR6 5BB

Location Sloughbottom Park is a competition-standard BMX track in northwest Norwich, East Anglia. Driving from the south on the A11, take a left at Daniels Road (the A140) heading north and follow signs for the Sweet Briar Road Industrial Park, then turn right onto Hellesdon Hall Road, and park up on the right next to the football fields. You'll find the BMX track at the south end of the fields.

Facilities Norwich is full of shops and amenities, and there are facilities at Sloughborough Park.

Rough round-up This is another classic, old BMX track with plenty of whoops, berms, doubles, and tabletops. Perfect practice for those looking to up their game on jumps. Merlins Trails (a local secret spot) have incredible dirt jumps that are not for beginners. Most riders around here cut their teeth on the BMX track first.

Conditions Avoid after rain but this drains well so shouldn't be too long after a shower before it's dry.

ⓘ **More info** Norwich BMX track is home to the Norwich Flyers BMX website (norwichbmx.co.uk).

⃝49 Teddington DJs

Train station Teddington/Strawberry Hill
Nearest city London
Sat Nav TW10 7YJ

Location Teddington DJs are on the other side of the river from Teddington in SW London. From Richmond take the A307 south towards Ham. In Ham town centre, turn right into Ham Common, then carry on straight down Lock road. Turn left onto Broughton Avenue, then right onto Riverside Drive and left into Locksmeade Road and park up. The DJs are just another 100 m along Riverside Drive, then a left into the common land and head to the waterside on the fire-road.

Facilities Lock Road and nearby Ham has corner shops and amenities.

Rough round-up These are small-ish DJs in the corner of a large expanse of common land next to the water. Don't expect too much, but if you're in the area this is a fun playground with some XC riding to be had around the parkland and some decent freeriding practice on the few lines through the DJs. The park also has some drops and is small enough to explore thoroughly in a few hours. But this is practice only – not worth a journey. The local riders head to Esher or Swinley.

Conditions The jumps are fairly well made and the soil packs well. Please fix any bad landings.

Thetford Forest

◎ ◎ ◎ ◎ ◎ ◎ ◎ ◎ ◎ ◎

Train station Brandon
Nearest city Cambridge/Norwich
Sat Nav IP27 0TJ

Location Thetford Forest is just to the north of Thetford town, East Anglia. From the M25, take the A11 towards Norwich and Thetford is around 45 km down the A11. When you reach Thetford, take the B1107 north (Thetford Road) towards Brandon. You'll find the forest around 2 km down this road with public parking signposted off to the right.

Facilities Thetford is home to the High Lodge Forest Centre, which houses a Go Ape rope access playground, Bike Art cycle hire and bike shop (T01842 810090 – they also sell trail maps and give guided rides), a café, and plenty of amenities such as bathrooms, education centres etc.

Rough round-up East Anglia is well known for being flat and Thetford is no exception. The park has made the most of the terrain with fast flowing routes but it falls victim to the weather. When dry and hardpacked the trails actually run very fast and are best suited to hardtails, when it's wet the trails can cut up and run slower.

Terrain There's plenty of singletrack, and four designated routes from family to expert. The two red runs even have an age restriction!

XC A great XC area, the forest regularly hosts a round of the national XC race series and the lack of any big hills or descents means that any loop around this forest can be ridden hard and fast. There are four official waymarked routes from green through blue and to red. There is unfortunately no black run anymore as the Forestry Commission have graded the original black run down to red. The green and blue are really only of any appeal to young children and leisure cyclists. The red routes offer more typical singletrack riding and these can be complimented by the host of unmarked tracks and trails that make up the bulk of the riding for the race courses. Expect swooping singletrack that snakes its way through the forest over whoops and in and out of bombholes.

Downhill and Freeride Forget it!

Conditions The XC routes are hard-packed dirt singletrack. The area is very popular with walkers but well known as a mountain biking centre so expect to see plenty of bikes.

ⓘ **More info** Thetford has its own series of races, the Dusk Till Dawn XC challenges – thetfordmtbracing.com, and the Forestry Commission website loads of great info on the forest and trails – forestry.gov.uk.

Southeast England Thetford Forest

51 Tilgate Forest and St Leonards Forest

🚲 🏕 🅿

Train station Horsham
Nearest city Brighton/London
Sat Nav RH13 6EH (for the Forester's Arms pub)

Location St Leonards Forest and Tilgate are located between Crawley and Horsham, in the North Downs area of Sussex. For St Leonards, park at the Forester's Pub. From the M23 carry on down the A23 (the same motorway really), and take the Handcross exit onto the B2110 heading towards Horsham. After 5 km you'll hit a T junction. Turn right on the A281and turn right into St Leonards Road. The pub is around 50 m along and to the left. To ride in the woods, carry on up St Leonards Road, and take a right into Hammerpond Road. The forest is on your left.

PAUL BLACKBURN

Facilities The pub has everything you should need, or nearby Horsham is a large town with plenty of shops and amenities.

Rough round-up St Leonards is chock-full of bridleways, fantastic singletrack, fire-roads and open land, and with a flint, chalky base it's pretty good year round. There are no waymarkers, and there's no map available, but there are tens of kms worth of riding to be had and the local scene is relatively small so you're unlikely to find traffic. There are also soma escort DH trails that are named after films, along with a pump track. Jumps, drops and berms can all be found on these DH runs and they're all graded as well. You will have to pay to use this location so make sure you have change in your pocket if someone turns up for payment.

Conditions Flint and chalk so is still rideable after some rain though can have unbelievably slippy sections!

ⓘ **More info** Sussex Mountain Biking has a dedicated page on Tilgate (sussexmountainbiking.com), as does MudTrail (mudtrail.co.uk/where-to-ride.php).

52 Track 40

🚲 🏕 🍴

Train station Banstead
Nearest city London
Sat Nav SM7 3RA

Location Track 40 is a small area of dirt jumps and tiny DH trails next to Banstead Downs Golf Course. From central London head south towards Brighton on the A23 through Brixton. Continue through Croyden, and at

Purley take a right onto Foxley Lane (the A2022) heading to Banstead. At the next roundabout, take the right exit – (the B 2218 Sutton Lane) and head up here for 500 m, then turn right into Freedown Lane and park. Banstead Downs are just on the other side of Sutton Lane. Head directly west into the downs, and cross the railway tracks using the bridge. The DH trails are just on the other side of this crossing.

Facilities Banstead has plenty of shops and local amenities.

Rough round-up Banstead Down has some easy XC riding, and on the Track 40 side of the common you'll find a few dirt jumps and some fun riding for those local to the area. Not worth a journey, but for everyone local it's a winner.

Conditions Works well in most conditions, and drains well, but still avoid after heavy rain.

ⓘ **More info** The Muddy Moles are a collection of Surrey Riders who have links to the area – muddymoles.org.uk.

⊙ ⊙ ⊙ ⊙ ⊙

Train station Tring
Nearest city London
Sat Nav HP23 6EE

Location Tring Park is easily found just around 10 km from Hemel Hempstead. If you leave the M25 at exit 20 and head north on the A41 and turn off just before Tring in the direction of Wiggington. Just after the exit, carry along Fox Road for 400 m and then park up. Tring Park is to the right hand side of this road.

Facilities Wiggington is a quant village and a few hundred metres further down the road with some shops and amenities.

Rough round-up There have previously been dirt jumps in this wood, and they sporadically appear and disappear. The DH trails are easy to find, and short but fairly feature-full although a stronger local scene would create better terrain. That said, the XC is fantastic, and part of the Central Chilterns Cycleway, a network of singletrack, bridleways, canal paths and colour-coded paths for families and intermediate riders.

⊙

Train station Brentwood
Nearest city London
Sat Nav CM13 3DP

Location Just south of Brentwood in Essex you'll find Warley dirt jumps. From the M25 exit at junction 29 heading east on the A127 towards Basildon. After 300 m, turn off left on the B186 Great Warley Street towards

Great Warley. Go through the village, take right onto Warley Road for 400 m then turn right onto Warley Gap. Keep on this road for another 400 m and the dirt jumps are just to the right, off the road in and the trees behind the Brentwood Go Karting Centre.

Facilities The nearby Karting centre has supplies and there are plenty of shops in Warley and Brentwood.

Rough round-up This is a pretty cool set up with loads of BMX and mountain bike riders constantly adding to the impressive DJs. There are small gaps to learn, then craters, drops, big gaps, tables, wall ride and a six-pack.

Conditions Solidly built DJs with some carpet on top of solidified dirt. Avoid in the rain as usual.

⊙ ⊙ ⊙ ⊙ ⊙

Train station
Nearest city Watford/Oxford
Sat Nav HP22 5NF

Location Wendover Woods is just south of Aylesbury and is the neighbour of Aston Hill. Driving north from the M25, leave at junction 20 and head north on the A4. Take the B4009 and follow this road until you see the signs for Wendover Woods/Forestry Commission.

Facilities As it's close to Aston Hill, Wendover benefits from a lot of the facilities. That being said, it has its own 'Café in the woods' for riders to stop off and buy refreshments.

Rough round-up It's open 364 days of the year and gates open at 0800.

However, it's probably not worth a long drive unless you're a family that needs a 6-mile bike trail. It's a XC trail that is steep in places but exciting enough to keep the family entertained. Anyone looking for anything more than that should head off to nearby Aston Hill.

Conditions Perfect ride in the summer but probably not advisable in the wet.

More info You can download a leaflet and map from the Forestry Commission website – forestry.gov.uk.

⊙ ⊙ ⊙ ⊙ ⊙

Train station Arundel/Barnham
Nearest city Brighton and Hove
Sat Nav N/A

Location Whiteways is the local name for this area of the South Downs Way, an incredible network of bridleway, singletrack and walker's paths that stretch for over 130 km from Winchester to Eastbourne. It's also known as Houghton Forest. Whiteways Car Park is located just next to the roundabout where the A29 meets the A284 around 6 km north of Arundel. From the A27, head north from Arundel on the A284 (London Road), and park just after the first roundabout on the left.

Facilities This car park is a popular start for XC riders because of Hikers Café, which has hot food and drinks and some toilets to the south side. Arundel has plenty of shops or nearby Houghton (which can be incorporated into some XC loops) has some shops and amenities.

Rough round-up The South Downs Way holds perfect singletrack and bridleway for the rambling XC rider who wants to get out into the country for good riding and spectacular views. You can find challenging routes but you'll have to head into the forest to discover them, or just use the knowledge of local riders. The designated and waymarked trails are likely to be fairly simple – if that's what you're after. The amount of routes here and the distances available is incalculable, but many riders cite the route from here to Devils Dyke in Brighton as being a bit of a classic.

Conditions This is chalky, flinty and sometimes muddy, but generally good year round if it's not been raining too much.

ⓘ **More info** Check out the local Arundel/Brighton scene (brightonmtb.org), while the South Downs Way has its own page at nationaltrail.co.uk.

Ⓢ57 Wild Park

ⓧⓒ ⓕⓡ ⓓⓗ

Train station Moulsecoomb/Falmer
Nearest city Brighton and Hove
Sat Nav BN1 9JQ (for Barcombe Road)

Location Just northeast of Brighton, where the A270 Lewes Road meets the A27, is Wild Park. When traveling on the A23 coming into Brighton from the north, turn onto the A27 heading in the direction of Lewes. Leave at the second exit, and follow the signs back on the A27 going the other way towards the University (you can't exit the A27 in this direction, hence the back-on-yourself detour). This exit is the A270 Lewes Road, head down here for 400 m and Wild Park is on the right. Park just

opposite in Barcombe road (running parallel with the A270 Lewes Road)**.**

Facilities Brighton has plenty of shops and amenities and is just down the road. Nearby Moulsecoomb has corner shops and supplies.

Rough round-up Wild Park is home to the local DH and freeride mountain bike scene. There are some pretty spectacular views of the city and over the University. The trails are short, but feature-full and well loved by the local riders. Not worth a long journey but for those in the area it's a fun day out.

Conditions Like most places on the southeast coast, this is chalky and flinty and can be prone to mud in winter.

ⓘ **More info** The local Brighton scene at brightonmtb.org.

N58 Willen Lake BMX Track

Train station Milton Keynes
Nearest city London
Sat Nav MK15 0YA

Location Willen Lake is in the north suburbs of Milton Keynes, just next to the M1. Exit the M1 at junction 14 and take the A509 signposted to Milton Keynes, then at the first roundabout take the third exit onto Portway, take the third exit at the next roundabout onto Tongwell Street. The BMX track is about 500 m down this road on the right.

Facilities The town of Willen is a few hundred metres further up Tongwell Street and has plenty of shops and amenities.

Rough round-up This is another classic 80s-style BMX track, and great for those wishing to get into dirt jumping but are too intimidated by straight dirt jumps with near-vertical take-offs. The track has a drop in, and some decent berms, doubles, gaps and tabletops.

Conditions The track is a mixture of clay-shale, in open grassland next to a lake.

ⓘ **More info** The Willen Lake track has its own website (mkbmx.com).

N59 Wisley Trails

Train station West Byfleet/Byfleet and New Haw
Nearest city London
Sat Nav GU23 6QD

Location Wisley Trails are just off the M25 near Woking, and just next to the village of Wisley. Exit the M25 at junction 10 and head south on the A3 (Portsmouth Road). You'll find the trails about 200 m on the right, next to Wisley Common. It's not possible to park on the A3 so best thing to do is to take the next right onto Wisley Lane, and park up there and ride through.

Facilities Wisley (200 m up Wisley Lane), has shops and amenities.

Rough round-up Wisley Trails are high-skill level dirt jumps shaped mostly by BMXers with huge gaps, tables and short preparations. Riders need to pay an annual fee to ride there, contact Gareth by email: gbmx666@hotmail.com or go his website for more details (see below). Wisley played host to the 2007 King of Dirt comp.

Conditions Hard-packed soil trails in the forest with some carpet take-offs.

ⓘ **More info** Check out the local scene through digitalbmx.com.

CHRIS MORAN

Woburn Sands

Ⓧ Ⓓ Ⓕ Ⓓ Ⓝ Ⓞ Ⓣ Ⓐ

Train station Aspley Guise/Bow Brickhill

Nearest city Milton Keynes

Sat Nav MK17 8DE (for the Old Stables Guest House)

Opening times The trails are open 24/7, 365 days of the year, although you may have to pay a fee if you see the ranger. At last check, this was £10 for the year. The land belongs to the Duke of Bedford and welcome to all-comers but there are some rules (easy ones – see the website) and respect is asked from visitors.

Location Woburn Sands completes the incredible trio of riding just 40 km north of Greater London (Aston Hill and Chicksands being the other two). Woburn is located right next to the M1, just east of Milton Keynes. Leave the motorway at junction 14 and head toward Wavendon on the A5130. From there follow signs for Woburn Sands on the same road, go through the village and towards the end (passing the garage on your left) go straight over both mini roundabouts. Pass the Fir Tree pub on the left, and head up the hill for about 500 m. Park on the grass verge to the right – the gate is the entrance to the trails.

Facilities No facilities on site, but nearby Woburn has shops and amenities. Ever since the Quarry closed years ago, the Woburn locals have used Old Wavendon Heath at Woburn Sands for walking and horse riding, in the last decade mountain bikers have found the dry, sandy soils perfect for season-round riding. It actually works better throughout winter when the ground is firmer when cold.

TOM CALDWELL

Downhill Woburn is classed as a dirt jumper's paradise so the downhill trails are heavily weighted towards the freeriders. There are a collection of short trails, no more than 30 seconds long. That being said, they're packed full of features.

XC Again, this is Freeride/Dirt Jump terrain really, but there are plenty of XC trails ranging from 3-km laps to 20 km. With a sandy base, the area can get slow in the summer.

Freeride Due to safety concerns, the dirt jump area was recently flattened. The locals are working closely with the group in charge of the forest to bring back the freeride area but it's still in talks (at time of printing). With such a large mountain bike community, it's only a matter of time before all the jumps are rebuilt again. There are plenty of features on the short DH runs to satisfy your hunger.

Easy When the jumps are rebuilt, it's recommended that you start on the beginner jumps. It's the best way to build confidence and master what you're riding before moving onto something much bigger.

Hard This is a virtually unlimited spot for the advanced jumper.

Not to miss The dirt jumps – first class.

Remember to avoid In periods of hot weather. The sand gets mushy.

Nearest Bike/Hire shop Try Phil Corley Cycles in Milton Keynes, philcorleycycles.co.uk.

Local accommodation
The Old Stables Guest House (T01908 281340) is a cheap B&B in Woodleys Farm, Bow Brickhill Road, Woburn Sands.

ⓘ **More info** Woburn Sands has its own website at woburntrails.co.uk and keep updated on their Facebook page as well (facebook.com/groups/WSbikepark).

＞ Lowdown

● Locals do
Ride amazingly well.
Mix things up with the odd DH line.

● Locals don't
Mind the ludicrously cheap annual fee.
Leave litter in the woods.

● Pros
One of UK's top dirt jump facilities.
Friendly atmosphere, rides well in winter.

✖ Cons
Not many immediate facilities.
Short DH.

The Midlands

Hopton Castle's last uphill push before one of the best DH tracks in the UK. [CHRIS MORAN]

The Midlands

CHESHIRE

DERBYSHIRE

Crewe

Wrexham ⊿12 Nantwich

Matlock ⊿3 ⊿5 Mansfield ⊿14 Newark-on-Trent

Newcastle-under-Lyme ⊿9 Ashbourne Ambergate NOTTINGHAMSHIRE

WREXHAM Whitchurch Stoke-on-Trent Nottingham

Sherwood Forest

A47

Oswestry Hodnet Stafford ⊿4 Uttoxeter Derby Castle Donnington A50 Melton Mowbray

SHROPSHIRE Newport Rugeley Ashby-de-la-Zouch ⊿15 LEICESTERSHIRE

Llanymynech Shrewsbury Cannock Tamworth M1 Leicester

Welshpool ⊿7 Telford A49 M54 Wolverhampton Hinckley Market Harborough

Newton Ironbridge The Long Mynd ⊿2 Sutton Coldfield M42 Nuneaton M69

Bridgnorth Dudley Birmingham M6 Coventry NORTHAMPTONSHIRE

Knighton ⊿8 Stourbridge Redditch ⊿16 M42 Rugby M45

Craven Arms ⊿11 Kidderminster M40 Warwick

Ludlow A456 WORCESTERSHIRE Droitwich Spa WARWICKSHIRE Royal Leamington Spa ⊿10 Daventry Northampton

Kington ⊿1 Leominster Worcester Stratford-on-Avon Farnborough A14

Much Cowerne Upton-upon-Severn M5 Evesham Chipping Camden Banbury Brackley BUCKINGHAMSHIRE

Haye-on-Wye A49 Hereford Vale of Evesham Morton-in-Marsh

HEREFORDSHIRE Ledbury M50 Tewkesbury Stow-on-the-Wold Chipping Norton Aylesbury A41

The Black Mountains Ross-on-Wye Gloucester Cheltenham Northleach Great Barrington

Crickhowell Pandy Cinderford Witney Oxford

Abergavenny Monmouth GLOUCESTERSHIRE Stroud Cirencester OXFORDSHIRE Faringdon Abingdon M40 Chiltern Hills Henley-on-Thames

Chepstow Wotton-under-Edge Tetbury Didcot Reading

M48 Malmesbury Chipping Sodbury M5 Swindon A34 Newbury

Bristol Corsham Chippenham Marlborough Hungerford A41

BANES Bath Melksham Devizes Pewsey A346 Basingstoke

Radstock Bradford-on-Avon Trowbridge WILTSHIRE Andover Farnh

Midsomer Norton Frome Westbury HAMPSHIRE

Wells Warminster

The Midlands, the heartland of the UK and home to its second largest city Birmingham, boasts some fantastic terrain. Riders from the outside the counties of Herefordshire, Shropshire, Worcestershire, Warwickshire, Northamptonshire, Cambridgeshire, Suffolk, Norfolk, Staffordshire and Leicestershire may think that this turf isn't as much as a challenge as the mountains of Scotland to the north and Wales to the west, but they would be hard pushed to find better riding.

The Midlands should be thought of as a destination in its own right. After all, the trails here are often empty and the infrastructure is incredible: Hopton Castle is one of the best DH venues in the country, and a place where World Champions are often seen training. And while the area is home to some dense population pockets, there are some surprisingly picturesque areas, even in the middle of urban areas. Cannock Chase, a 26 square mile plot of forest land is just to the north of Birmingham, and nestles nicely between Rugeley and Cannock itself. Many would think of it as an interesting park, perhaps with a trail or two. In fact, it is one of the coolest trail centres in the UK, and has a huge weekend following, drawing in riders from all over the region. Meanwhile, Sherwood Pines has undergone a lot of work since the first edition of this book was printed. The free ride area has doubled in size due to popularity, complete with dirt jumps, berms, rollers and more, alongside plenty of cool XC to ride.

If you live in the south of England and are taking a trip north, or vice versa, then the Midlands will offer some difficult terrain without having to go to the ends of the earth. Champions of the future will find this place overflowing with potential, and of course, some great riding.

Local scene

There must be something in the water in the Midlands, as the area is teeming with mountain bike enthusiasts. They prefer to stay under the radar, however, to keep their trails and parks relatively quiet. Most head to either one of the three dedicated centres at the weekend – Cannock, Sherwood, or Hopton, but there are plenty of standalone sites that are definitely worth travelling to. Marc Beaumont's work at Eastridge has resulted in a brilliant all-round set up, while families will love the scenic Rutland Water Way, especially if it's their first time on a group outing. I've decided to include the very popular Peak District area in the North section, though very clearly there is good riding to the south of this area that is probably covered by Midlands riders. Apologies to local riders in advance if their allegiances are with their fellow Midlanders.

Hubs

The three main areas in this region would be Hopton, with a healthy DH following loyally gracing its trails for over a decade. Sherwood Pines, which has major plans to become one of the UK's best trail centres. Last but not least the fantastically surprising Cannock Chase, which is basically a huge, beautiful forest with some of the best riding facilities in England.

Below: Cannock Chase
Opposite page: Leamington Spa first corner.

❺ Best rides in The Midlands

The Midlands has a lot to offer its local riders,
as well as those who are up for an adventurous trip to the
heart of the UK. Here are five of its best attributes:

❶ Cannock Chase, page 112

The Chase is the number one spot in the Midlands,
featuring the epic Follow the Dog trail, some great
downhill and northshore, a brilliant Visitor Centre and
fantastic bike shop in Swinnerton Cycles.
And we didn't even mention the cake in the café.

❷ Hopton Castle, page 116

If you're a fan of empty downhill tracks, a bucket-load of
features and some stunning scenery, then this is the trail
for you. Our advice: book the uplift!

❸ Rutland Water Cycle Way, page 120

The Guardian have already classed this as one of Britain's
Best Bike Rides, so what more do you need? With a
plethora of cafés on site and a lot of family-friendly
routes, it's a great place for a group trip.

❹ Sherwood Pines, page 121

Sherwood is Cannock's closest rival with over 70 km
of unofficial single track running alongside a few way
marked routes. It's not downhill heaven but there's a bike
park that will keep you entertained for hours.

❺ Eastridge Woods, page 115

Despite there not being much in the woods apart from
parking and the trails themselves, Marc Beaumont's work
has resulted in some incredible riding. A definite for any
downhill enthusiast.

Train station Ludlow
Nearest city Ludlow/Kidderminster
Sat Nav SY8 2HU (for the Downton Estate).

Location Deep in the Shropshire countryside are the Bringewood downhill tracks, around 8 km west from Ludlow. From Ludlow, head to the south side of the river and take Whitcliffe Road signposted towards Wigmore, and after 1.5 km take a left at the hairpin into Lower Wood Road which is signposted 'no through road'. Bringewood is just up this road. When leaving, it's best to follow the Downton Estate one way exit system.

Facilities There isn't a great deal at Bringewood itself, but nearby Downton on the Rock is a beautiful Estate with the award winning Jolly Frog restaurant, and is where the recent Kiera Knightley and James McVoy film *Atonement* was filmed.

Rough round-up You won't find a more full-on downhill territory, all set in some remote, beautiful countryside. It's a fantastically well-built course and has been used for National Champs as well as local races. Some features include hefty road gaps, rock sections and some off-camber drops in a dense forest. Definitely not for beginners. Pearce Cycles in nearby Ludlow run uplifts here and at Hopton Castle, so check their site or shop for dates and availability.

Conditions This is pretty remote countryside, where phone reception is patchy at best. You're only a few kilometres from Ludlow, but it'll take a while to get there, so don't ride on your own.

ⓘ **More info** Pearce Cycles in Ludlow organise plenty of events and uplifts and are the place to head before you go to Bringewood, either online or in person, pearcecycles.co.uk, T01584 879288.

Birmingham BMX

Train station Perry Barr/Hamstead
Nearest city Birmingham
Sat Nav B42 2LB

Location Birmingham BMX is around 4 km to the north of Birmingham town centre, and just on the south side of the M6 (not the toll). From the motorway, exit at junction 7 and head south on the A34 towards Birmingham centre. After 2 km Perry Park is well signed on the left of the road. Park by turning left after the allotments into Church Road and then left again into Perry Park's car parking area.

Facilities The BMX track has a tuck shop on site for refreshments but you can pop into the local town for any other supplies you might need. It's also floodlit so night riding is always an option.

Rough round-up This was originally an old-school BMX track, but after investment from the local council, this track has gone through a lot of change. It's now one of the best BMX tracks in the country and remains popular with the local BMX scene. With a pump track running alongside the BMX track itself, there's a lot for riders to get involved with.

Conditions This is a track built in open fields in the corner of a popular, large park with plenty of copses and woods. The investment has helped with drainage but avoid after heavy rainfall.

ⓘ **More info** Check out the Birmingham BMX Club website for all the info you'll need, birminghambmxclub.com

Brackley DH

Train station Duffield
Nearest city Derby
Sat Nav DE21 5AU

Location Just 10 km north of Derby are the Brackley DH trails. Exit the M1 at junction 26 and drive westwards on the A610 towards Eastwood. From there take the A608 and drive through the village of Heanor, continue driving until you see a sign off to the right heading to Horsley Lodge Golf Club on Woodside Road. Take that, then a left onto Cloves Hill, and follow the road around for 1 km (through Brackley Gate) until it changes name to Moor Lane. The trails are just to the south (left) of this road around 600 m after Brackley Gate.

Facilities Brackley Gate has a shop for supplies.

Rough round-up These are very low-budget downhill trails and are built by local riders. They're short and not especially steep but are packed with features and hold enough for local freeriders and DH riders to keep an interest. Expect plenty of large drops and jumps. The woods also have some unofficial singletrack for XC riders though the forest is quite dense.

Conditions This is a tract of unmanaged forest land which isn't very popular. It isn't waymarked so only go if you're happy and confident about doing some exploration.

ANDY HEADING

⊿4 Cannock Chase

ⓧ ⓢ ⓡ Ⓝ ⓢ ⓞ ⓢ ⓞ ⓣ ⓣ ⓢ ⓕ

Train station Rugeley Trent Valley
Nearest city Wolverhampton
Sat Nav WS15 2UQ

Opening times 365 days a year and all for free. Just turn up and ride. You will, however, have to pay for parking – £1.50 for one hour or £3 for the day.

Location Cannock Chase is an area of outstanding natural beauty located between Cannock and Rugeley, both to the north of the M6 toll road. There are a couple of starting points to the trail but it's best that you head to the Birches Valley Forest Centre. Take junction 11 from the M6 and drive towards Cannock on the A460. At Hednesford, take a left into Station Road (just after Chase Car Sales), then take the first right after 50 m, and go about 3 km along this road until the crossroads – ignore the Visitor Centre on the right. Take a right at the crossroads onto Birches Road, and the Birches Heath Visitor Centre (home to Swinnerton Cycles) is about 1 km down this road on the right.

Facilities Cannock lends its name to the famous chase – 65 square km designated as an Area of Outstanding Natural Beauty that includes an array of important and unusual wildlife and some 600-year-old woodland. As Cannock Chase has many kilometres of woodland riding, it's become somewhat of a hub for the Midlands mountain bike scene. The trail network

JOHN MCFARLANE/FORESTRY COMMISSION

> **Lowdown**

☺ **Locals do**
Run their tyres quite firm to cut into the fresher loamy sections.

Get involved with building the trails as well as riding them.

☹ **Locals don't**
Leave their bikes unattended. While not a crime hotspot, this is an area between plenty of towns and cities.

✔ **Pros**
Great riding within easy reach of plenty of people. Good family riding and novice/intermediate mountain bike area.

Lots of good unmarked singletrack, great for weekend stop-over.

✖ **Cons**
Hills not big enough for downhill purist.

Not enough riding to sustain a week's break.

CHASE TRAILS

consists of a number of official and many unofficial trails to meet demand. You'll be able to find all other facilities on site, such as toilets, bike shop, bike wash, café and more.

Downhill There are two official tracks: one fully machine built and greaded red, the other a more natural, hand built run with roots and features to challenge riders – both are found at the site of Stile Cop. There aren't a lot of long runs or giant hills but there's plenty to ride when you factor in the many unofficial runs.

XC 'Follow The Dog' is Cannock Chase's original mountain bike trail. It's a technical singletrack that's graded red and very popular with the locals. There have been more trails added to increase popularity but the real charm lies within the many kilometres of unmarked, classical singletrack. There are also a number of leisure green graded trails

which follow flat lowland routes for gentler, more family-oriented rides.

Freeride If you're looking for freeriding then you will need to stick to the downhill trails found in the Stile Cop Bike Park. You can session them but only for so long. If freeriding is all you want for the day, you're probably better off elsewhere.

Easy Start out on the beginner jumps, there is so much here that it is definitely a case of building up slowly to make sure you have mastered what you're riding now before moving onto something much bigger.

Hard There are plenty of hard lines to try for the more advanced jumper. The only limitation in a place like this is your imagination!

Not to miss The main reason to visit – the singletrack.

Remember to avoid Travelling a huge distance. It's a great place to ride but if you're looking for DH, you're better off heading into Shropshire.

Nearest bike/hire shop Swinnerton Cycles Forest Centre is the local bike shop and hire, T01889 575 170, bikechase.co.uk, and there are bike maps available from the Birches Valley Forest Visitor Centre.

Eating Unlike the park itself, the Birches Valley Forest Visitor Centre is closed on Christmas Day but is open the other 364 days of the year. It serves hot and cold drinks as well as snacks. Being a reasonably sized town Cannock offers everything from fast food through to world foods and restaurants.

Local accommodation Try the Oak Farm Hotel (T0870 4784319) located close to the M6, or for budget accommodation, you can look into Tackeroo Caravan site (all info on the Forestry Commission website).

ⓘ **More info** Cannock Chase has a riders association which is ran in conjunction with the Forestry Commission – chasetrails.co.uk, and the Forestry Commission page itself, forestry.gov.uk.

JOHN MCFARLANE/FORESTRY COMMISSION

Train station Mansfield/Sutton Parkway
Nearest city Nottingham
Sat Nav NG18 5BP

Location You'll find Cauldwell Woods on the south edge of the town of Mansfield, Nottinghamshire. When driving along the M1, exit at junction 28 and head towards Mansfield on the A38. After around 4 km, take a right onto the A617 heading towards Rainworth/Newark-on-Trent. After about 1 km you'll see Couldwell Woods on your left. Carry on, and exit at the next junction, head north towards Mansfield on the A60 (Nottingham Road), and continue up this road. There will be parking spaces on your left. Head into the woods at any available singletrack entrance.

Facilities Head back up Cauldwell Road for the nearest shops and facilities.

Rough round-up These woods are a popular local site for some XC being criss-crossed with plenty of tracks and hidden trails. Near the middle are some rudimentary dirt jumps that include two lines – both graded somewhere between beginner and intermediate.

This isn't a site worth a journey, but for local riders who want to improve their freeride skills, or to start dirt jumping, this is the place to head.

N6 Deeping BMX

Train station Peterborough
Nearest city Peterborough
Sat Nav PE6 8HT

Location Around 10 km north of Peterborough is the small town of Market Deeping. From the A1(M), carry on north as it changes to the A1 at Peterborough, then turn off at the A1139 (Fletton Parkway) and continue along this road until you reach a roundabout with the A15 being the first exit. Take this exit and drive for about 4 miles until you reach a roundabout with 4 exits, the first being Maxey Road. Take the third exit onto Lincoln Road and drive until you get to a roundabout just after the river, take a right along the river front and then a left at the roundabout onto Godsey Lane. The park is about 600 m up the road, on your left.

Facilities This track is in the heart of Market Deeping, which has plenty of shops and facilities.

Rough round-up This was an old BMX track that a few years ago had a complete make-over into a 4X and BMX venue. Expect a competition-level course with a drop in start and plenty of doubles, gaps and tabletops.

Conditions The purpose-built track has a concrete drop in and is well drained but still to be avoided in the wet.

JONATHAN CHEETHAM

🏠 🔢 🎿 🚆 👤

Train station Shrewsbury

Nearest city Wolverhampton

Sat Nav SY5 0DF

Location Deep in the Shropshire countryside, about 10 km southwest of Shrewsbury is Eastridge Woods. When driving from Shrewsbury, take the A488 towards Minsterley, then take a left into Callow Lane in the direction of Habberley. Carry all the way down this road to the T junction, then take a right, then a right at the fork and take the first turning on the right up the narrow lane towards the entrance to the wood and car park.

Facilities There is parking, but little else at the wood.

Rough round-up As part of The Marches, Eastridge Woods are a spectacularly remote and beautiful part of the world. But it's the two brilliant downhill tracks that brings the riders rather than the scenery. There's enough here to challenge all riders, as well as downhill champ Marc Beaumont (the local pro). Marc also helped build a load of incredible, waymarked trails into the forest, which offers the best XC in the area. However, most riders come here because of the two brilliant DH tracks, with plenty of serious gaps, roots, and switchbacks, and the reason Marc is so good.

Conditions The land is maintained by the Forestry Commission, and you can tell. They're well looked after. The tracks are waymarked and all weather but still best avoided after periods of bad weather.

ⓘ **More info** The Forestry Commission site, forestry.gov.uk, has loads of info on Eastridge Woods. For anyone wanting to help out on a dig day, contact the Eastridge Facebook page, facebook.com/groups/eastridgetrailpartnership, as anything built without permission will be removed.

DAVID BAGNALL/FORESTRY COMMISSION

⌄8 Hopton Castle

Train station Craven Arms

Nearest city Birmingham

Sat Nav N/A (though Shropshire Hills Discovery Centre, where maps of the area are available, is: SY7 9RS.

Opening times Hopton Wood is a working forest so areas can be closed at any time due to forest operations, but it's generally open 365 days of the year.

CHRIS MORAN

CHRIS MORAN

Location Around 10 km west of the town of Craven Arms, on the Shropshire/Mid-Wales border is Hopton – an area of Forestry Commission land to the west of Hopton Castle. From the east, head in on the A49 from either Shrewsbury or Hereford, and turn off at Craven Arms onto the B4368 and follow this road for 6 km, then turn south onto the B4367 heading to Hopton Heath and turn off to the right after 2 km heading towards Hopton Castle. The riding area is difficult to find but around 1 km past the turn off to the Castle. Call in at Pearce Cycles in Ludlow for more detailed directions, or at the Secret Hills

Discovery Centre in Craven Arms for a waterproof trails map (£1).

Facilities There's really not much at Hopton Castle save for Pearce Cycle's Land Rover and bike trailer (only on certain days and when you book in advance). It's best to take supplies from nearby Craven Arms as you'll be quite far from civilisation when riding. You'll find that the trails in Hopton are varied, from gently and smooth family trails to the highly technical, black-diamond-graded downhill courses. The riding is all enclosed in this plantation wood so its conifer trees-a-plenty and as a result the more technical trails are strewn with roots and stumps. The ground bakes hard in the summer but can be quite greasy when wet. All in all, it's a fun place for a rider of any ability.

Downhill The downhills are known for their tight turns and having loads of roots, it's a great place to perfect your

bike handling skills and is regularly used by some of England's best riders as a training ground – that should convince you! The hill is not very steep so it's easy to session the trails here.

XC Hopton offers the perfect mix of XC trails, with short flat rides for novices and kids, and harder red trails for the more experienced XC riders with some tough climbs and switchbacks. The recently opened Pearce XC trail has proved to be very popular with riders as they're thrown onto a trail with technical climbs, rocks roots and more. For more experienced riders, it's worth trying the DH routes as XC bikes can be comfortably ridden there.

Freeride No specific freeride routes/ areas but the DH trails contain various small jumps and interesting sections so those who like to be in the air will find something to ride.

> **Lowdown**

⊕ **Locals do**
Take advantage of Pearce Cycle's uplift days. You can get 10 good descents in a day and improve immeasurably.

⊕ **Locals don't**
Ride without a phone – a slam here is a long way from help.

✔ **Pros**
One of England's best downhill venues.
Uplift (on certain days).

✖ **Cons**
Very rooty, and hence slippy on bad weather days or after periods of rain.

Easy There's a 'warm-up' loop for novice riders and another blue graded run to help build up confidence before hitting a red.

Hard There are three downhill routes that can all be ridden by the competent XC rider, so from the top of the hill take each one in turn and spin back up the access road. The hill may not be massive but three runs and climbs of this will tire anyone.

Not to miss The uplift days.

Remember to avoid Riding on a day when the Forestry Commission are felling. Call ahead first otherwise your day of riding will be ruined (see below for details).

Nearest Bike/Hire shop Pearce Cycles in Ludlow is the place to head for all local knowledge and equipment (see below for details).

Eating The Craven Arms Hotel (T01588 672888) offers a daily carvery for those of you needing a slap-up meal. There are also plenty of other pubs serving traditional home cooked food in the surrounding area.

Local accommodation Take in Stokesay Castle during your stay at the Castle View B&B (T01588 672304). Also offering B&B accommodation is Hopton House (T01547 530885).

ⓘ **More info** Pearce Cycles, pearcecycles.co.uk, T01584 879288, and the Forestry Commission can be found at forestry.gov.uk.

N9 Keele Woods and DJs

XC DH CJ

Train station Stoke on Trent
Nearest city Birmingham
Sat Nav ST5 5BG

Location Two locations here – the small woods to the north of Keele University (known locally as Keele Woods – home to the dirt jumps), and Springpool Wood, south of the Uni, which has the XC riding. From the M6 exit at junction 15 and at the first roundabout turn left on the Clayton Road (A519), carry on up this road for 3 km (straight over both roundabouts), then a left when the road splits into two and head towards Keele University. Carry on up this road for another 3 km, and Keele Woods are just to the north side (the right) of the road just after the University turn off to the left. Park at the Uni. Springpool Wood is directly to the south, where the university land meets the M6.

Facilities Keele University is next door to both these locations and has a host of bars, shops and amenities.

Rough round-up Perfectly suitable jumps for beginners to intermediates but not worthy of a long journey. But for local or Uni riders this is a half

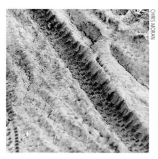

CHRIS MORAN

decent practice area. Springpool Wood is home to some very tame DH trails and some pleasant XC singletrack, but again, not worth a long journey.

Conditions Both woods are beautiful areas of relatively wild land, and popular with some dog walkers and flower hunters, but often rarely used.

N10 Leamington Spa 4X Track and DJs

4X CJ

Train station Leamington Spa
Nearest city Coventry
Sat Nav CV32 7UA

Location Leamington Spa 4X and Dirt Jumps are to the northeast of the city with the same name. From the M40 exit at junction 15 and head in the direction of Warwick on the A429. Drive through Warwick and take the A445 towards Leamington Spa. After crossing the river, take a right onto the B4099 heading on Warwick New Road into Leamington town centre. After 300 m, take a left into Warwick Place, left on Dale Street and then first right into Clarendon Avenue. It will turn into

Leicester Street after 500 m. The 4X track is just to the right in the fields as Leicester Road bends to the left.

Facilities The leisure centre nearby is the closest place to get supplies, although Leamington is full of shops and amenities.

Rough round-up This is part of a council park so is open all year round and is free to ride. It's an old BMX track with a variety of whoops, berms, tables and doubles that will excite all riders. It has held stops on the British 4X series in the recent past so it's a track of high standards – a track with a stoney, hardened surface that's good for most weather. Next door is a fantastic dirt jumping site and with enough trails to satisfy beginners through to pro riders. Definitely worth a visit if you're nearby and fancy improving your jumping and speed skiils.

Conditions This is a well-maintained site, with a surface on the BMX track that's been designed to drain well, and the DJs are well made.

⬆11 Ribbesford DH

ⓧ ⓔ ⓦ

Train station Kidderminster
Nearest city Birmingham
Sat Nav N/A

Location You'll find Ribbesford around 5 km west of Kidderminster. If you leave the M5 at junction 3 and head south towards Kidderminster on the A456. Pass directly through Kidderminster, following directions for Tenbury Wells. As you pass Bewdley on your right, look for the B4194 crossing the road. Don't take that road, but take the second left (Heightington Road). Head up here for 300 m and Ribbesford DH is on the left.

Facilities All the shops and supplies that you'll need, you can find in nearby Bewdley.

Rough round-up The DH trails are divided into three sections – the black, green and red runs, all delightfully named (the red run being called The Rib Tickler). All have plenty of interesting features and plenty of roots, jumps, bomb holes, tabletops, reinforcements and purpose-built gaps. Each varies in difficulty, and although there is plenty to test advanced riders, they might be better advised to head to Hopton or Bringewood if they're in this part of the world. For learners or intermediates, this is a fantastic DH place.

Conditions This is an area of beautiful forest with plenty of exposed roots and a clay soil that packs well and is perfect for sustaining the many jumps down this DH trail.

CHRIS MORAN

119

N12 Tipkinder Park
(Shanaze Reade BMX Track)

Train station Crewe
Nearest city Crewe
Sat Nav CW2 7SE

Location The Shanaze Reade BMX Track is in Tipkinder Park, in the middle of Crewe, Cheshire. From the M6 exit at junction 16, head into Crewe on the A500. At the first roundabout take the A5020, go straight on at the next two roundabouts and then left at the third onto Nantwich Road (the A534) and go past Crewe Railway Station. After 300 m, take a right into Mill Street, and at the end a left onto Oak Street. This turns into Wistason Road which turns into Victoria Avenue. Tipkinder Park is about 500 m up this road on the left.

Facilities Victoria Avenue has shops for immediate supplies.

Rough round-up Originally named as the Cheshire Ghost Riders BMX Track, it was renamed after Crewe's Olympic BMX talent, Shanaze Reade. In January 2009 was completely renovated to improve the shape, drainage and surface. It's floodlit until 2200 on certain days and has CCTV protection and a very organised club regularly racing there.

Conditions This is a well-maintained site, with a surface on the BMX track that's been designed to drain well.

ⓘ **More info** The Cheshire East Council has a web page with info on the track, cheshireeast.gov.uk. Also check out the Cheshire Ghost Riders Club Facebook Page, facebook.com/pages/Cheshire-Ghost-Riders-BMX-Club/148289701864837.

N13 Rutland Water Cycle Way

Train station Oakham
Nearest city Leicester
Sat Nav LE15 8BL

Location Famous for being the largest man-made lake in Europe, and to the east of Oakham, Rutland Water is between Leicester and Peterborough. From the A1(M) heading north to Peterborough and carry on past the city on the A1 in the direction of Stamford. Here turn left onto the A606 and after 6 km take a left at Whitwell into Bull Brig Lane signposted Rutland Water.

Facilities There is official parking at both north and south entrances, two bike shops (one in between Normanton and Edith Weston and one at Whitwell) and plenty of cafés around this cycle route.

Rough round-up *The Guardian* has classed this route as one of 'Britain's Best Bike Rides', being one of the most picturesque waterside routes in the country. Rutland's riding is essentially family/novice XC, offering great views, some lovely singletrack and bridleway (all waymarked), and the chance to go round the entire 3,100 acres of lake in a 40-km loop (families might wish to stop at one of the many rest areas or pubs and head back for a shorter ride). There are several places to park around the lake, and for the more adventurous there are suggested harder XC distances in the vicinity, specifically Leicester to Oakham (see website below).

Conditions This is an all-weather surface, but is still prone to some muddy areas in heavy conditions.

ⓘ **More info** Try Rutland Cycling on rutlandcycling.co.uk (T01780 460705).

⌖14 Sherwood Pines Forest

Train station Mansfield/Mansfield Woodhouse

Nearest city Nottingham

Sat Nav NG21 9JL

Location The Visitor Centre for Sherwood Pines Forest Park is around 6 km to the northeast of Mansfield, Nottinghamshire. Make sure you leave the M1 at junction 28 and follow the A38 into – and through Mansfield. Head left onto the A60 into the town centre, heading out of the town and into Mansfield Woodhouse, turn right at the traffic lights onto the A6075 (Peafield Lane) signposted towards Edwinstowe. Go down here for around 5 km then turn right at double mini island in the direction of Clipstone. At the village, turn left at the T junction onto the B6030 and Sherwood Pines forest is on your right after 700 m.

Facilities The SPFPVC is a newly-built Visitor Centre with Go Ape (high rope adventure park), cycle shop and hire, café, toilets and a forest classroom. It's open from 0800 until dusk, 364 days of the year (closed on Christmas Day). Times may change for the winter so check before going. Parking for cars ranges from £1 for an hour up to £4 for the day.

Rough round-up Sherwood Pines is the perfect set-up for riders of all abilities, with a great set of dirt jumps, a bike park and lots of singletrack for the XC lover. There used to be northshore in the forest but it has since been removed. Well worth a visit.

ISOBEL CAMERON/FORESTRY COMMISSION

Terrain Sherwood Pines Forest has over 45 miles of unofficial singletrack, plus a few purpose-built areas.

XC For families and those looking for gentle terrain, there are four waymarked trails. The Green Route, the Blue Route, a newer Green Route and the Adventure Trail. All have varying degrees of technicalities to challenge younger or less skilled riders and all are purpose built and all-weather surfaced. There are plenty of rest areas and shortcuts. For more hardcore riders, the Kitchener Trail, a 13 km technical loop should hold some challenges, and there's a Skills Loop being planned.

Downhill If you're a serious downhiller, it's not the best place to ride but the Kitchener Trail should hold some fun.

Dirtjumps/Freeride The original dirt jump area was so popular with riders that the Forestry Commission decided to double its size – something that was welcomed by everyone. With plenty of tables, gaps and rhythm sections, there's something here for riders of all abilities.

Conditions The routes have all been built with all-season conditions in mind (with limestone coverings), but still expect to find some mud and boggy conditions in the middle of the forest.

ⓘ **More info** Local bike shop Sherwood Pine Cycles has a wealth of info on the area at sherwoodpinescycles.co.uk, while the Forestry Commission has dedicated a page to Sherwood at forestry.gov.uk.

⬊15 Swithland Woods

Train station Loughborough/Leicester
Nearest city Leicester
Sat Nav LE12 8TN

Location Swithland Woods are part of the ancient Charnwood Forest near Newton Linford, Leicestershire. From the M1, exit junction 22 and head towards Leicester on the A50. After 2 km, take a left into Markfield Lane in the direction of Newton Linford. At Newton, turn left onto Main Street and head north in the direction of Lingdale Golf Club. Continue driving and the road will turn into Sharply Hill and then Warren Hill. When you reach the crossroads, take a right onto Roecliffe Road and Swithland Woods are to the right of this road.

Facilities There is parking, but little else at the Bradgate Road entrance. Cropston has a few shops and a pub.

Rough round-up Plenty of public-access bridleways and unofficial singletrack criss-cross the woods and

makes this a beautiful XC site to ride. None of the riding is particularly hard, but due to the area being relatively wild and un-marked, novices and those without wayfinding skills are advised to head elsewhere. Originally there were dirt jumps here but they were demolished by the National Trust. If there are any new ones in the forest, it'll be kept very quiet, so if you do find them, don't shout about it too loudly!

Conditions This is forest land maintained by The National Forest, and is a popular horse-riding venue. Expect well kept bridleways and fireroads, but the singletrack can be relatively muddy after rain.

ⓘ **More info** There's no specific bike section of the website but The National Forest is nationalforest.org.

Stirchley BMX Track

Train station Bournville
Nearest city Birmingham
Sat Nav B30 2RY

Location Stirchley BMX Track can be found about 8 km south of Telford. Drive west on the M54 (best found when driving north on the M6, at junction 10a) and take the turning off onto the A464 at junction 4. Take a left at the second roundabout onto Queensway (A442), then take a right onto Holmer Farm Road at the next roundabout and take the first right onto Sandino Road. Park where you can and you'll find the BMX track in the copse of trees to the southwest, next to the roundabout.

Facilities None on site but nearby Stirchley has local shops and amenities.

Rough round-up It's a small but technical track, suitable for intermediate and experienced riders. It's occasionally used for coaching but it's generally quiet. Not worth a long drive to visit but worth a trip for local riders looking to enhance their jumping and bike handling skills.

Conditions This isn't a purpose-built track with great drainage so best to avoid during bad weather.

The North

Gisburn Forest. [ISOBEL CAMERON, FORESTRY COMMISSION]

North Sea

Motorway
A Road
B Road
✈ Airports
⛴ Ferries

outh

Morpeth

Newcastle
Gateshead
↘ 6 **Sunderland**

A19

Easington

↘ 15

Hartlepool

ockton-
n-Tees
Middlesbrough ↘ 14

A66

lington

A19 Whitby

smotherley *North York Moors*
↘ 12

↘ 33 ↘ 1 ↘ 9

Thirsk Helmsley Pickering **Scarborough**

7

ipon A19 Thornton- Filey
le-Dale

Helmsley

A64

1(M) Kirkham
sborough ↘ 16 ↘ 32 Bridlington

YORK A165

ewood **EAST RIDING**
OF YORKSHIRE

↘ 44 **York**

eds ↘ 39 ↘ 24 Beverley

Selby

A164 **Kingston**
upon Hull

field

A1 Barton-upon-Humber

M62 M18

↘ 30 **NORTH LINCOLNSHIRE**

Scunthorpe **Grimsby**

Doncaster

A180 Nettleton

↓ 22 Waddingham

M18 Louth

Gainsborough Market
Rasen

field A46 A16

sterfield Lincoln Ashby
by Partney

↘ 4 **Lincoln** Horncastle

YSHIRE A1 **LINCOLNSHIRE**

M1 Mansfield Skegness

gate **NOTTINGHAMSHIRE**

A46 Newark-on-Trent A16 Wells-next-
the-Sea Cromer

by **Nottingham** A1 A17 Sleaford Boston

Castle Donnington Erpingham
Donnington Grantham Sandringham Fakenham Happisburgh

n upon Trent Melton Spalding Holbeach **NORFOLK**
Mowbray **King's Lynn** A148

EICESTERSHIRE A47 Swaffham **Great**
Leicester Empingham Stamford **Norwich** A140 **Yarmouth**

The North is a multi-faceted, multi-geographical area. How to combine an area that includes the between-city riding spots of Manchester, Leeds, Sheffield, Bradford and Halifax, whilst also covering the absolute beauty of five of the UK's best national parks: The Lake District, Peak District, Yorkshire Dales, Yorkshire Moors and Northumberland and Kielder Forests? It's a big ask, but we've collated the counties of Northumberland, Tyne and Wear, Durham, Cumbria, North Yorkshire, East Riding of Yorkshire, West Yorkshire, Lancashire, Merseyside, Greater Manchester, South Yorkshire and Cheshire to fit all the trail centres and spots in.

An area so big is naturally very diverse. We would imagine that many of the places mentioned in this chapter are for local riders only. Visitors to the region are probably drawn by the incredible riding to be found in the Lake District. But there is so much more to the North than the Lakes. Northumberland has to rate as one of the most unspoilt counties in the whole of the UK. To ride around Kielder, where one can pop over the border into Scotland, is one of the coolest routes in the whole of the British Isles. The forests of the northeast are absolute world-class centres, with Hamsterley and Chopwell being on any serious UK riders' 'must see' lists. And if you fancy some old-school, self uplift DH skills, then the moors of Yorkshire and the Peak District are your number one places to visit.

Local scene

The northeast has the major freeride and downhill presence in the area. In fact, riders around Newcastle, Sunderland, Durham and Middlesborough are spoilt for choice, with Kielder and Chopwell right on their doorstep. Leeds is littered with cool little venues and, if you're into dirt jumping, a visit to Stockport just outside Manchester is hugely rewarding. The North boasts some of the coolest, best-organised and most welcoming clubs in the country and a directory of their websites and contact details is listed at the end of this book.

Hubs

As one would expect, the national parks of the North hold the majority of the XC riding, but there are incredible, stand-alone spots literally everywhere. Riding hubs would include the diverse terrain to be found around Leeds, Bradford and Halifax, while the Lancashire areas around Blackburn, Clitheroe, Burnley and Rawtenstall are definitely on the up (check out Adrenaline Gateway above Rossendale – the North's own 7 Stanes-esque, purpose-built area). Meanwhile there's the ever-present Dalby Forest, featuring one of the UK's best bike parks, and of course, the brilliant spots in the Lake District, including the Whinlatter trail and the and the ever-popular TNF Grizedale centre whichwould stand out even if they were in the Alps. .

Below left: Dalby Forest's incredible bike park.
Below right: A Keilder Forest rock garden.
Opposite page: Hamsterley Forest's 4X in full flow.

TOM BARTHOLOMEW/FORESTRY COMMISSION

❺ Best rides in The North

Hit the North and you're not going home disappointed. Here are five of the best spots:

❶ TNF Grizedale, page 162

Already one of the most popular sites in the UK, Grizedale is continuing to pull people in from all over the country. Its stunning setting near a beautiful village, with some incredible XC routes make this a place to try.

❷ Roman Lakes, page 154

If you're looking for family riding then the Roman Lakes is the perfect place to go. The routes take in canal paths and gentle forest rides, all amongst a lakeside setting – an incredible setting for a family ride.

❸ Dalby Forest, page 136

It might take some traveling to get to but it's worth it. The riding at Dalby caters for every style of rider, with trails bering worked on continuously.

❺ Ladybower Reservoir, page 150

The visitor centre has a café and a museum so you can learn all about the Dambusters as they practiced on the Ladybower. And it's the gateway to some of the Peak District's incredible XC routes. Good riding and educational!

❺ Hamsterley, page 146

You'll find plenty of family-friendly XC routes, tougher XC rides for the experienced rider, and some great freeride facilities – it has the best of every type of riding. Something only boosted by cafés, a visitor centre, bike hire and more to make it exemplary.

⊻1 Carlton Bank DH and XC

JOHN STOREY/NEFFERIDERS.CO.UK

Train station Northallerton/Thirsk
Nearest city Middlesbrough
Sat Nav TS9 7LQ

Location Situated on the western edge of the North Yorkshire Moors, around 20 km to the south of Middlesbrough is Carlton Bank. Leave the A1 at junction 49 and take the A168 to Thirsk, then the A19 in the direction of Ingleby Arncliffe, then take a right onto the A172 (east). Turn off at Carlton and follow the road through the village. Head up the road to the plateau. There is a car park at the Lord Stones Café, which is just next to the trails.

Facilities The Lord Stones Café (T01642 778482) is one of the best cafés in the UK, with home-cooked meals and a license to serve pints. It is cheap, and very bike-friendly with toilets and washing facilities and is very popular with outdoor users.

Rough round-up The surrounding area of Carlton Bank Downhill has some impressive singletrack XC riding, whereas the downhill trails themselves have been a competition venue over the years. You will be aware that it's also very popular with a variety of outdoor users – hang gliders, walkers and horseriders. But there is enough room for all and the surrounds are incredibly picturesque.

Terrain As it's open moorland, bad weather can make it rather uninviting, more so when it's windy. The area is also prone to harsh mud, and several races have had to be cancelled, but hit it on a good day and it's as good as riding gets.

XC There are an untold number of unofficial and un-waymarked routes criss-cross the moors from the Lord Stones Café starting point. The area is famous for its downhill course that starts at the top of the trig point above the café.

Downhill The course starts with a fairly flat, pedally top section with a decent-sized jump, then a ridgeline run which turns into a technical, rocky descent later on. There are plenty of drops, and jumps down the course, and good riders should be able to get down in under 2 minutes (it's around 1300 m long). The track splits into two trails halfway down so it's as if there are two separate trails to try. There's always scope to explore the trails as the landowner seems keen to keep mountain bikers in the area.

Dirt Jumps/Freeride Despite there being no specific dirt jumps, freeriding or northshore, the DH tracks have seen a lot of work, and house some pretty sizeable jumps. If you like being in the air, you'll find something to ride here.

Conditions This is a popular outdoor area, so expect to see lots of other outdoor types. Can be boggy, so avoid after rain, and expect to be see some incredible views over the moors.

ⓘ **More info** You'll find all the info you need on the Lord Stones area from their website, lordstones.com.

N2 Broomley Trails DJs

Ⓓ

Train station Stocksfield
Nearest city Newcastle-upon-Tyne
Sat Nav N/A

Location Located near the town of Stocksfield, itself around 15 km to the west of Newcastle-upon-Tyne, are the Broomley trails. From Newcastle, take the A695 from the A1 ringroad, heading in the direction of Hexham. After passing through Stocksfield, carry on for another 1 km – passing the turn-off for the B6309 on your left, and take the next left after that signposted towards Broomley. The dirt jumps are on the left, around 250 m after you pass under the train tracks.

Facilities There are no facilities at the dirt jumps, though Stocksfield has a few shops for supplies and is around 1 km away.

Rough round-up This is a low-budget dirt jump spot built in some woods and features a few lines with a decent selection of jumps from some small, beginner lines to a couple of good-sized gaps and rhythm sections. Not worth a long journey, but for those nearby who want to practice their handling skills, or start dirt jumping, this is a great spot.

Conditions The DJs are well built, but this is a remote spot and is prone to serious mud after rain. Please don't ride the jumps when they're wet and try to repair any damage.

N3 Calverly Woods

ⓍⒸ Ⓓ

Train station Baildon/Horsforth or New Pudsey
Nearest city Bradford/Leeds
Sat Nav BD17

Location Around 6 km northeast of Bradford, and 10 km northwest of Leeds, you'll find Caverly Wood. From the M62, take the M606 towards Bradford, then exit at the end of the motorway onto the A6177 ring road around Bradford heading anti-clockwise towards Laisterdyke. Turn right off the ring road onto the A658 in the direction of Yeadon, and after 4 km take a right off this road into Parkin Lane (just after you cross a river). Head down this road, and re-cross the same river into Calverly Cutting. The woods are at the end of this lane.

Facilities Apperley, back over the bridge, has shops and pubs for supplies.

Rough round-up This is a completely natural wooded area with purpose-built trails. However, there are a couple of DH trails descending through the woods and there's some half decent XC to be had. It's a fairly popular spot for local Leeds and Bradford riders.

Conditions This is ancient woodland. Cycling is permitted but please don't build or add to the trails.

ⓘ **More info** For all Leeds mountain biking info, MTB Leeds is the place to head, mtbleeds.co.uk

N4 Chesterfield BMX/4X Track

Ⓧ Ⓓ

Train station Chesterfield
Nearest city Sheffield
Sat Nav S43 1DQ

Location You'll find Chesterfield BMX next door to Ringwood Hall, between the towns of Hollingwood and Brimington, around 2.5 km northeast of Chesterfield. It's a very easy drive and an easy track to find. Exit the M1 at junction 30 and head towards Chesterfield on the A619 Chesterfield Road. After 4 km Ringwood Hall is signposted on your left. The BMX track is just before the Hall turn off.

Facilities Hollingwood is a small village but has plenty of shops and amenities.

Rough round-up This is an old BMX track that has had a revamp in recent years and is perfect for those looking to get some experience before heading out to more serious DJs or to take their jumping skills to the downhill trails. It's also wide enough to have some 4X races on, and welcomes all riders. There's a drop in, lots of jumps (though rollable), and three brilliant berms including one wall ride. The track has been recently upgraded to National Standard.

Conditions This is a well-maintained track with concrete, and chalk surface. Drains well and is in a lovely park.

ⓘ **More info** There's a Facebook page for the track, just search for 'Chesterfield BMX Track'.

⬛5 Chevin Forest Park

🔵 🟡

Train station Menston
Nearest city Leeds/Bradford
Sat Nav LS21 3JL

CHRIS MORAN

Location Otley is host to Chevin Forest Park, with the park itself sitting to the south of the Village. It's also 12 km northeast of Bradford and 15 km northwest of Leeds. From Leeds, head towards Skipton on the A660. After 15 km Otley is on the right. Exit here left onto East Chevin Road, following signs for Chevin Forest Park through Birdcage Walk and Johnny Lane. The car park is at the end of this road.

Facilities There's nothing at the Park (save for The White House, which is for pre-booked groups only), though Otley is full of shops and amenities.

Rough round-up Chevin Forest Park has plenty of gentle XC and downhill trails, suitable for all riders from families and beginners through to good intermediates. There are no official waymarked trails (though Leeds Council has been making noises about putting some official runs in since the success of Temple Newsam). Most

are easy to find though, and there are usually plenty of riders around the park to ask.

Conditions This is a popular site for all fans of woodland and well-kept gardens. Please ride with care and be respectful of the other (often elderly) park visitors.

ⓘ **More info** Chevin Park Forest has its own website (chevinforest.co.uk), though no specific details of the trails are mentioned.

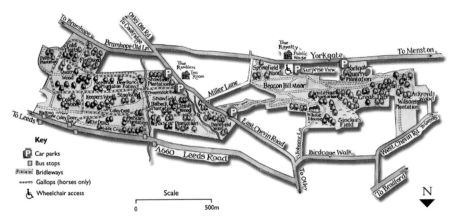

Key
🅿 Car parks
🚏 Bus stops
▒▒▒ Bridleways
⚬⚬⚬ Gallops (horses only)
♿ Wheelchair access

Scale
0   500m

N

Train station Chester-le-Street
Nearest city Sunderland
Sat Nav Various, see below

Location A very easy place to find, Chester-le-Street is around 10 km west of Sunderland, just off the A1(M). Exit the motorway at junction 63 and take the A167 into the town.

Facilities Chester-le-Street is a large town with plenty of shops and amenities. The riding spots are never more than a few minutes from supplies, although those heading to Old Mine Pits should take some food and drink with them.

Overview The western edge of Chester-le-Street is fringed with some cool downhill tracks, and good dirt jumps to the south of town. For those in either Newcastle or Sunderland,

or in the northeast in general, it's worth a look in, though other longer-journeymakers might wish to bypass and head straight to the bigger trail areas, such as Hamsterly, Chopwell or Kielder. The spots are: **Doctors Downhill** off Waldridge Lane (Sat Nav DH2 3RY), **New Road downhill and dirt jumps** off Warkworth Drive (DH2 3TW), **Fox Wood dirt jumps** (200 m east of where the A167 meets the trainline to the south of town), and the best of the bunch – **Old Mine Pits**, a dirt jumping, freeride and downhill spot to the west of Waldridge and just to the north of Fleece Terrace. From Waldridge, head towards Edmondsley and turn to the right halfway down.

Terrain The terrains vary greatly with this handful of trails, with the Old Mine being a mixture of forest land and open quarry freeriding, while the other DH spots are short, forested runs and

the dirt jumps are located in a copse of trees next to the main road.

XC This isn't a location for the XC riders amongst you, it's a spot for a downhill bike or those of you who like air-time. However, there is plenty to ride around the Old Mine Pits.

Downhill Old Mine Pits is the place to head, though Doctors has some short, technical riding.

Dirt Jumps/Freeride The local riders here have worked hard to make sure that at each spot there are plenty of obstacles to mess around on.

Conditions You'll find that the XC routes are hard-packed, dirt singletrack. The area is popular with walkers but well known as a mountain biking centre so expect to see plenty of bikes.

↘7 Chopwell

⊗ ⊙ ⊙ ⊙ ⊙ ⊙ ⊙

Train station Blaydon/Wylam
Nearest city Newcastle-Upon-Tyne
Sat Nav NE39 1LT

Location Just 10 km southwest from the centre of Newcastle Upon Tyne is Chopwell Woodland Park. From the A1(M) exit at junction 65 and take the A1 Newcastle ring road west towards Whickham. Drive for around 8 km and take the A694 south towards Rowlands Gill, then take a right onto the B6315. Carry on up this road for 3 km to High Spen, where the entrance to the park is signposted off to the left, just before Garesfield Golf Club.

Facilities Chopwell Wood has a car park and toilets, but there are no refreshments or supplies to be found. Take supplies with you. The nearest shops are in High Spen.

Rough round-up Chopwell Wood is a 360 hectare Forestry Commission (FC) site which, according to the FC, has only one official route. There are other trails to be found at Chopwell, but they might be slightly hidden. There are family trails and blue-graded trails for moderate difficulty to build your confidence before taking on the Powerline trail (red-graded run).

Terrain These are short but fun and intensive trails that will interest and challenge cross country and novice freeriders with their technical and fast singletrack.

XC The Powerline Trail is a 3.5 km red-graded loop that was the main

attraction for years (the site has had building work since 2001), taking in the river Derwent, the overhead powerlines (hence the name), and packs a technical punch with plenty of built features to ride. There are a few easier runs for riders who aren't as

comfortable on red runs, along with plenty of unmarked runs throughout the forest, ready to be explored.

Downhill There is no specific DH trail here, but the Powerline trail has plenty of short descents that are good for DH practice.

Dirt Jumps/Freeride There are no specific areas for freeriders or dirt jumpers, but the shortness of the other trails means they are packed full of features such as northshore bridges, drops, jumps and berms. Those who like to get in the air will definitely find something to ride.

Conditions This is forest land and open to all, so please be aware of other users and be respectful of the amount of work that has gone into the trails.

ⓘ **More info** The Forestry Commission site has a page on Chopwell, forestry.gov.uk.

↘8 Delamere Forest

Train station Delamere/Cuddington
Nearest city Manchester
Sat Nav CW8 2JD

Location The Delamere Forest Park is a tract of Forestry Commission land 12 km to the northeast of Chester and 18 km southwest from Manchester. Take the B5125 north out of Delamere – itself on the A54. The forest is well marked with plenty of parking along the quiet roads and many access points.

Facilities Linmere Visitor Centre was built a few years back and is the central hub for riders. It has a bike-wash area, which can be accessed by the Delamere railway station (although most mountain bikers arrive by car), and the excellent Delamere Forest Café (delamerecafe.com), which serves food and has WiFi. The closest bike shop is Tracs, situated at the Visitor Centre itself (delamerebikes.co.uk), they also have maps, guide days, pricing and advice on their website, as well as in store. Slightly further afield is The Edge Cycle Works in Chester (theedgecycleworks.com).

Rough round-up It's the largest woodland area in Cheshire, with some great XC trails, a brilliant dirt jump area and some short but interesting downhill. There's a designated 'Skills Area' with an 4X course, the dirt jumps, and some DH which includes some chutes and road gaps.

Terrain There's plenty (and we mean plenty!) of unofficial singletrack, but the majority of the routes here are fire-road.

XC There are a couple of easy XC trails that are suitable for families, named Hunger Hill trail and Whitemoor trail, which both start at the Visitor Centre and shouldn't take you longer than an hour. There's also 12 km loop around the forest which takes in the Skills Area and includes plenty of interesting sections such as drops and well-trodden singletrack.

Downhill The skills area holds some short sections of DH, and there is a longer course named Old Pale nearer to the Visitor Centre, but it's by no means a haven.

Dirtjumps There used to be a plethora of dirt jumps for all abilities but these have fallen beyond the wayside in recent years. Plenty have been demolished by the Forestry Commission but a lot have just not been repaired and so have been forgotten. You might find small jumps in the forest but the likelihood is that they will not be properly maintained.

Conditions The XC routes are hard-packed dirt singletrack. The area is popular with walkers but well known as a mountain biking centre so expect to see plenty of bikes.

ⓘ **More info** Linmere Visitor Centre has its own page on the Forestry website at forestry.gov.uk.

CHRIS MORAN

The North Delamere Forest

135

⬊9 Dalby Forest

XC DH FR AM XL ... ...
... ...

Train station Malton

Nearest city York

Sat Nav YO1 2JN or the Visitor Centre on YO18 7LT

Opening times While the trails are open 24/7, the Visitor Centre is open from 0930 until 1630 each day, although it's best to check with the Forestry Commission website as they often close the XC route for maintenance during bad weather. Car parking is £7 for the day in the summer months, £4 in the winter. Entry to the forest by bike is completely free.

Location Dalby Forest is one of many Forestry Commission sites in the North Yorkshire Moors near Pickering, around 15 km to the west of Scarborough. From the M1 exit at junction 49 and take the A168 in the direction of Thirsk, then turn onto the A170 in the direction of Scarborough. After Pickering, and in the small village of Thornton-le-Dale, take a left at the village square and take the road going north, following signs for the Dalby Forest Visitor Centre.

Facilities/Overview Dalby Forest is considered to be one of the northeast's best mountain biking spots and rightfully so. With everything from family riding, DH trails, plus bike hire and onsite accommodation, you can't really go wrong with a trip here. Being another Singletraction site (like Stainburn and Guisborough Forest), the work here is first class with solid dirt jumps, sturdy northshore, purpose-built XC trails and some good downhill. It is popular with riders from as far as Leeds and Manchester, and has a host

of facilities in the Visitor Centre. There are further café and bike hire facilities at nearby Dalby Courtyard as well as the Tree Tops Restaurant at the Dalby Forest Visitor Centre and shops, maps toilets and bike wash available on site.

XC There are some fantastic XC routes at Dalby – two green grade family trails (Ellerburn Family Cycle Route – a 4 km easy loop from the Visitor Centre, and the Green Cycle route, which is a 19-km loop). There's the blue trail, a 13 km upgrade for those who fancy a gentle, but challenging loop through the forest, the Dalby Forest red trail is 34 km of feature-full riding with plenty of climbing and technical riding, while the Black Trail is a 6.4 km waymarked loop with plenty of off-camber riding and northshore style additions to make the trail as interesting as possible. You'll find that a lot of the loops have been reinforced to make them all-weather trails, and all feature brilliant, flowing singletrack, jumps, rock sections, and enough differences through the seasons to keep even the most technical rider on their toes. There's also plenty of unmarked routes throughout the forest for the more adventurous of you to try out.

Downhill The Downhill trails at Dalby have been getting a bad reputation

in the mountain bike community for being too short. That said, all the DH trails are an on-going project and have plenty of features and obstacles to test yourself. It might not hold the longest DH in the world, but has been carefully planned for maximum entertainment.

Freeride The Pace Bike Park at Dixon's Hollow is a park built in a disused quarry, holding a brilliant, competition-standard 4X track, some great dirt jumps (that will suit beginner to intermediate), loads of northshore and testing riding, and some freeride obstacles to mess around on. This is one of the major attractions to the forest, and includes a corkscrew, some skinny logs and inventive obstacles, though can be slippy in the wrong conditions.

Easy There are some good lines through the Bike Park that learners will love.

Hard You wouldn't class the black run as the hardest in the country but it's definitely challenging.

Not to miss The Bike Park brings 'em in from miles around.

Remember to avoid Turning up when one of the waymarked runs is closed. Check online first.

Nearest Bike/Hire shop
Dalby Bike Barn can be found on site, and their website has a whole host of information (dalbybikebarn.co.uk).

Local accommodation
Thornton Le Dale is host to Warrington Guest House (T01751 475028) for some luxury living in the forest, or why not hire one of the wooden cabins set in stunning locations in nearby Cropton, call Forest Holidays on (T01751 417510).

Eating The Tree Tops Restaurant or the Purple Café are the places to head, otherwise try the Brandysnap Bistro (T01751 474732) restaurant in Thornton Le Dale, one of the prettiest villages in Yorkshire.

ⓘ **More info** Dalby Forest has several pages on the Forestry Commission site, forestry.gov.uk.

> **Lowdown**

😊 **Locals do**
Ride to a super-high standard.

Ride all day and ride whatever is on offer.

😞 **Locals don't**
Really come from here! Lots of the riders here have travelled long distances.

Complain about the parking charge – the forest is worth it.

✅ **Pros**
One of the UK's top mountain bike facilities.

Great chilled, friendly atmosphere.

❌ **Cons**
No uplift for the DH trails despite being short runs.

The trails are very spread out.

TONY BARTHOLOMEW/FORESTRY COMMISSION

⭷10 Devils Cascade DJs

Train station Poynton
Nearest city Stockport/Manchester
Sat Nav SK12 1HE

Location The Devils Cascade dirt jumps are around 300 m to the north of Poynton Railway Station, itself around 3 km to the south of Stockport near Manchester. Leave the M56 at junction 6 and take the A538 (Wilmslow Road) past Manchester Airport – heading towards Wilmslow. Take a right onto the A34 Handforth Bypass, then after 300 m left onto Prestbury Road. After another 300 m take a left onto the A5102 Adlington Road. After 5 km take a right onto the A5149. Poynton is 1 km up this road and the railway station is clearly signed on the left. The next road on the left is Hazelbadge Road, and at the top of this road is a field with the dirt jumps. Please close the gate as there are livestock.

Facilities Poynton has plenty of shops and amenities on hand.

Rough round-up Poynton is a very popular area for dirt jumping, and there are lots of BMXers around who have built numerous sites in the area, some secret, some not so. Ask around and you're likely to find more spots, but Devils Cascade is a well-known spot and a perfect place to start. The jumps themselves consist of two sets of dirt jumps, one for learning, one fairly large, with some more tabletops and random jumps scattered around in the surrounding fields.

Conditions This open grassland belongs to the farm next door. Please respect the farmer's wishes and leave the site as you found it for other riders to carry on enjoying.

ⓘ **More info** Poynton has a fantastic and varied mountain bike scene.

Elland Park Wood

◎ DH

Train station Halifax/Sowerby
Nearest city Bradford/Leeds
Sat Nav HX5 9HZ

ANTONY DE HEVENINGHAM

Location You'll find Elland Park
Wood to the north of the town of
Elland, itself halfway between Halifax
and Huddersfield. Leave the M62
at junction 24 and take the A629 in
the direction of Halifax. Exit this dual
carriageway signed for Elland and
take the Elland Riorges Link. At the
first roundabout take a right onto the
B6114, then after 500 m take a right
over the bridge, then a right onto Park
Road (A6025). After another 500 m the
entrance to Elland Park Crematorium
is on your left. Go through here and
access the park to the rear! The DH
trails are to the east end of the park in
the wooded area.

Facilities Park Road, which rings the
park, has plenty of shops and facilities,
plus there are some good pubs such
as the Collier's Arms on the canal
just opposite the entrance to the
crematorium.

Rough round-up None of the trails
here are waymarked, so you'll have to
use your natural navigational instincts
or chat to some of the local riders to
find where some of the trails start.
That said, this is a great spot for those
just getting into the sport. There are
a few gentle downhill trails, as well as
plenty of XC and freeriding to be had
in both the wooded and open areas of
the park. The crematorium puts many
off riding here but no-one seems to
mind, though there is also access
further down the canal should you
prefer. Again, talk to local riders to get

the lowdown. There should be plenty
around.

Conditions This is a large expanse of
park which is popular with walkers and
dog owners but due to the nature of
its size you're unlikely to meet many
people if you head off following the
singletracks into the woods.

Great Ayton Quarry DJs

◎ FR DJ

Train station Great Ayton
Nearest city Middlesbrough
Sat Nav TS9 6EY (to Roseberry Crescent)

Location Just on the northwestern
edge of the North Yorkshire Moors
and around 10 km southeast of
Middlesbrough is Great Ayton. The
quarry (actually called Roseberry
Quarry, but known locally as Ayton
Quarry), is to the northeast of the
town. Heading north on the A1, exit
at junction 49 heading to Thirsk

on the A168, then north towards
Middlesbrough on the A19 with the
North Yorkshire Moors on your right.
At Ingleby Arncliffe, take the A172 to
Stokesly, then the A173 to Great Ayton.
Head through town and take the next
right after Roseberry Crescent (the last
of the houses in Ayton). Park up where
you can and cross the railway line. You
should find the quarry at the end of
the lane, just behind some trees.

Facilities There's nothing up at the
quarry, but there are plenty of shops
and amenities in nearby Great Ayton.

Rough round-up Roseberry Quarry
has two fantastic attributes: the first
is that it has brilliant access to the
amazing XC riding that the North
Yorkshire Moors has to offer. But most
people come to ride here for the
brilliant dirt jumps and freeride area
that the quarry houses. It's been built
mostly by the local mountain biking
scene, and is perfect for everyone from
beginners through to good riders
looking for some practice. There are
tens of lines scattered around the
quarry, with plenty of drops, gaps,
doubles, rhythm sections, step-ups
and more. Well worth a visit for those
nearby as it's a large site with a lot of
variety.

Conditions This is a well-maintained
site, with lots of jumps that are
always being added to. The ground
is apparently fine-ground dolomite
which is superb for dirt jump building
and drains very well. Park at the main
road or Roseberry Crescent if the
access road is busy (lots of people use
this road to get to the Moors).

↘13 Gisburn Forest

ⓧⓒ ⓓⓗ ⓕⓡ ⓝⓝ ⓞ

Train station Long Preston
Nearest city Bradford/Leeds
Sat Nav BD23 4SQ (for the centre of Tosside)

Location Gisburn Forest is located just southwest of the Yorkshire Dales, around 15 km north of Clitheroe and 4 km to the west of the village of Long Preston. Take junction 13 on the M65 and head north on the A682, in the direction of Gisburn. At Long Preston, turn off to the left on the B6478 heading towards Slaidburn. When you reach the village of Tosside, take a right onto Bailey Lane and you'll find the forest at the top of the hill overlooking Stocks Reservoir.

Facilities There are two car parks and the Forest Den Café. Aside from that, there isn't too much more on offer in Gisburn Forest. The café is open only on weekends from 1000 until 1600, so it's better heading into nearby Tosside for local shops and pubs – The Dog & Partridge Pub is very bike friendly and has a power washer on hand! There is cycle hire available from Cycle Bowland (see website below).

Rough round-up Gisburn Forest is inside the beautiful Forest of Bowland and has plenty of downhill and XC riding in the surrounding woods and hills. The Forest has benefitted from investment into the 'Adrenaline Gateway Project' which has turned the Lancashire Pennines into an outdoor activity area. Currently there are two waymarked XC routes and plenty of unofficial downhill and XC singletrack all over the area.

Terrain There's plenty of singletrack, but the majority of the routes here are fire-road.

XC There are two main routes for the XC lover: Bottoms Beck (blue) and The 8 (red). The blue is more suited for novices and younger riders, whereas the red is for the more experienced – a run that takes in plenty of features and a volunteer-built trail!

Downhill There's one obvious downhill trail at Gisburn and it's the black route at the top of the hill. It's a small section that leads off of the red route but is still nail-bitingly good. There are also plenty of hidden

downhill trails throughout the forest, despite being short, they are enough for the large local mountain biking scene.

Dirt Jumps/Freeride Although there is nothing specific here for freeriders, there's a disused quarry that sees a lot of drop and dirt jump action, but plenty of jumps and features on the XC and DH trails should keep most satisfied.

Conditions This is Forestry Commission land that is still in full working order. Expect well worn tracks and mostly fire-road to ride on, though there is plenty of hidden singletrack to explore. Most of it is in a natural state, so parts become largely unridable after heavy rain. There is man-made tracks, natural tracks, woodland and a quarry.

ⓘ **More info** Visit adrenaline-gateway.co.uk to get more on the whole Adrenaline Gateway area and try Cycle Bowland in Settle on cyclebowland.com for bike hire, maps and more info. The Gisburn Forest Bike trails also have a Facebook page that will allow you to help out with dig days (facebook.com/gisburnforestbiketrails).

⛰14 Guisborough Forest

ⓚ ⓖⓗ ⓖ ⓞ ⓐ ⓔ

Train station Gypsey Lane or Nunthorpe
Nearest city Middlesbrough
Sat Nav TS14 8HD

Location Around 7 km to the east of Middlesbrough, on the northwestern tip of the North Yorkshire Moors, is Guisborough Forest – a small tract of Foresty Commission land. From the A1(M), exit at junction 57 onto the A66(M), which turns into the A66 in the direction of Middlesbrough. Follow this road almost to Middlesbrough town centre, but take a right onto the A19 heading south towards Thirsk. After 2 km take a left on the A174 towards Nunthorpe, then a right off the A174 onto the A172. Carry on this road for 2 km, then take the A1043, and then the A171 towards Guisborough. Just before you hit town, take a right onto the A173 and the Guisborough Forest and Walkway Visitor Centre is sign posted off this road after around 250 m on your left.

Facilities The Visitor Centre has toilets, but for shops and supplies you'll have to go to Guisborough, another 2 km along the A171.

Rough round-up Guisborough Forest is another Singletraction site with two main XC routes: the Blue Route and Red Route (originally a black route but was downgraded by the Forestry Commission due to the state of the trail). The Blue is around 6 km in length, is waymarked and is suitable for learners and families who can already ride, while the Red Route is a 12 km harder course for intermediate/advanced riders. There is also a fair amount of unofficial singetrack, shale

riding and some fantastic, technical descents dotted around the area and it's fairly popular with the local riding scene. This area might not be worth a very long journey but for those nearby or in the northeast, it's high on the list of places to visit.

Conditions Anything Singletraction do is worth a visit. A high level of care and attention to detail plus they work closely with the Forestry Commission. This is forest land with open areas, all waymarked and any problem areas have had work done for drainage and support. But still avoid after bad weather.

ⓘ **More info** The Forestry Commission has a Guisborough Forest page forestry.gov.uk. This is also another Singletraction-built area so join in at singletraction.org.uk. Check the Singletraction site for dig days that you can join in with. They discourage from digging when it's not affiliated with them as your work may be demolished.

JOHN SOTREY/MFREERIDERS.CO.UK

⛰15 Hartlepool 4X

ⓚ ⓑ ⓖ

Train station Hartlepool
Nearest city Middlesbrough
Sat Nav TS25 4LL

Location From the A1(M), exit at junction 60 and take the A689 towards Hartlepool. Pass the Greatham turn off and go through two sets of traffic lights and at the third set take a left on to Owton Manor Lane, then take a right onto Catcote Road through town. Keep following signs for Summerhill, turning left off Catcote towards the Summerhill Visitors Centre. The BMX track is next door and part of the centre's amenities.

Facilities Summerhill Visitor Centre is a council ran initiative with lots of facilities including car parking, toilets, changing rooms, lockers and drinks machines. There is also a rope course, a climbing centre and fitness loop.

Rough round-up The BMX track went under a huge, and much needed, facelift in 2012. Straights have been turned into four with new tarmac berms instead of dirt ones. The jumps are a bit bigger, as well as the tabletops and gaps. Well worth a visit if you're nearby or a fan of 4X riding.

Conditions This is a purpose-built site which drains well and has been designed to work in all weathers.

ⓘ **More info**
Hartlepool BMX has a club website at northeastbmx.co.uk.

The North Hartlepool 4X

N16 Hookstone Woods DJs

Train station Hornbeam Park
Nearest city Harrowgate/Leeds
Sat Nav HG2 8PN

Location You'll find Hookstone Woods to the east of Harrogate, Yorkshire. Exit the A1(M) at junction 47 and head towards Knaresborough/Harrogate on the A59. After 2.5 km take the A658 south towards Follifoot then a right onto the A661 heading towards Harrogate town centre. After 2 km take a left into Hookstone Drive, then another left into Hookstone Wood Road. Near the end of the road, turn right into Hookstone Woods and the dirt jumps are 200 m to the west of this point.

Facilities Hookstone Woods is an area of outstanding natural beauty – part of the ancient Knaresborough Forest – and very popular with the inhabitants of Harrogate. As this is a natural area, there are no on site facilities.

Rough round-up Hookstone dirt jumps are the fruits of the local riders hard work and although small, are well kept and a good place for beginners and intermediate riders to get into freestyle and freeriding. Not worth a huge journey, as there are only a few jumps on offer, but for those in the area, they are well worth a visit.

Conditions This is public forest though you probably won't see many people at the jumps themselves. Avoid after rain as the area is prone to serious mud and please don't ride the jumps when they're soft.

N17 Hulme Park DJs

Train station Deansgate
Nearest city Manchester
Sat Nav M15 6HE

Location Hulme Park is just to the south of Manchester City Centre and incredibly easy to find. coming off the M62, follow the signs into Manchester City Centre, which will lead you to exiting at junction 3 of the M602. Continue as it turns into the A57 and again as it turns right. At the roundabout, take the Chorlton Road exit and head down here for 200 m before turning left into Jackson Cresent, then right into Birchvale Close. The dirt jumps are at the end in Hulme Park.

Facilities Hulme Park is a redevelopment area with plenty of shops and amenities.

Overview This is a dirt-jump specific site built in conjunction with Manchester Council and the BMX group M15 after the demolition of a BMX site nearby. It's a 600 m square area and houses plenty of lines from beginner to expert. Many shy away from coming here with expensive bikes as this is a notorious inner city park, but incidents have been rare and there is a thriving riding scene, though many BMXs.

Conditions This is an inner-city, purpose built BMX and dirt jump venue with good drainage.

ⓘ **More info** Manchester City Council has a website with a Hulme Park page (manchester.gov.uk).

N18 Hurstwood Trails

Train station Hebden Bridge/Mytholmroyd
Nearest city Bradford
Sat Nav HX7 7AZ

Location Hurstwood trails can be found in the moors between Burnley, Halifax and Bradford. From the M65 exit at Burnley and take the A646 towards Hebden Bridge/Halifax. At Hebden Bridge, turn north towards Heptonstall on the Heptonstall Road, then Smithwell Lane, Slack Road and Widdop Road (all the same road which changes name), all of which are signed towards Nelson. After 5 km, park at Widdop Reservoir and cross the dam to the start of the trails.

Facilities There's nothing up at the trails, but Hebdon Bridge is a beautiful town with plenty of quirky cafés and is full of shops and amenities.

Rough round-up This is a brilliant, natural area full of XC trails with some interesting downhill sections, plenty of jumps and drops, all set in some spectacular countryside with beautiful views across the numerous lakes and Widdup and Gorple Reservoirs. The short blue trail at Hurstwood is good for the family but not worth a long journey. The surrounding area will have some nice hidden treasures.

Conditions This is open-land singletrack and shared-bridelways for miles around, with stone walls, reservoirs and small copses over the rolling hills. A lovely XC day out for those nearby.

Opposite page: Hurstwood Trails.

Train station Ilkley or Ben Rhydding
Nearest city Bradford
Sat Nav LS29 8RX (for Escape Mountain Biking in Ilkley)

Location Ilkey is a small village on the road that leads between Leeds and Skipton, around 12 km north of Bradford. From Leeds take the A660 out of the city centre towards Skipton. Pass through Otley and Burley in Wharfdale and, after 15 km, you'll come to Ilkley. The trails are on the moor directly overlooking the town to the south.

Facilities Ilkley is a picturesque village with plenty of facilities and amenities and is a gateway to the moors which are popular with all sorts of outdoor types.

Rough round-up Ilkley Moor is an enormous expanse of the Yorkshire Dales which is criss-crossed with fire-road, bridleway and fantastic singletrack. There is everything here from incredibly XC riding to the most technical and steep downhill. None of the routes are waymarked but it's a fantastic playground for riders. It's also popular with walkers and other fell users, but everyone from families to good riders should be able to find a decent line or two.

Conditions This is open moorland with plenty of shale and gravel singletrack owing to the large amounts of limestone to be found in the area.

ⓘ **More info** The Leeds MTB club has info on Ilkley, mtbleeds.co.uk.

The North Ilkley Moor

Local riders
John Storey

Bike Intense Socom & Giante Trance x3
Local spot Guisborough
Club member Manager of Team NEFR
Age 32
Type of rider Downhill Racer

Where's the one place you'd recommend above all, for those coming to the north?

JS It's got to be Hamsterley Forest – purpose built facility with many different types of tracks for all abilities. There are long or short XC routes, a beginner's skills loop and the expert-level DH Courses and 4X.

Where has the best XC?

JS That would have to be Hamsterley. You can combine different routes together to create your own way. The black route is my favourite and is the most technically challenging trail, with steep technical climbs, smooth flowing singletrack and some superb rooty, rocky descents. It's got some great natural riding that will challenge even the best cross-country bikers.

Where is the best Downhill?

JS Again that'd be Hamsterley Forest with its purpose-built DH facility, featuring numerous tracks with loads of variety. The fast flat out top sections are full of big jumps and sweet berms. Depending on which bottom section you ride the course gets very steep, rocky, rooty and technical and also includes a number of drops and jumps. It's notorious for its rock gardens on the lower sections of the course.

The best dirt jumps?

JS Great Ayton quarry is by far the best Dirt Jump spot in the north, famous for its huge 6 pack. People come from all over the country to ride these jumps. The jumps have been continually modified by generations of local riders and it's bmx and 26-inch wheel friendly! They even shot a section of Earthed DVD series at these Dirt Jumps.

If you were to take a family out – say a cousin who's visiting with his kids – where would you head?

JS The best place for a family ride would have to be Dalby Forest. There are many different family rides to choose from, varying in length and skill level. The facilities at Dalby are also excellent, with loads of parking, toilet and changing facilities, café's and good cycle route signs. The whole forest is very clean and tidy and there's a lovely, friendly atmosphere about the place.

What secret stashes do you know about?

JS Ha ha!! I must admit I do know of quite a few! Guisborough woods, my local training ground is littered with secret trails all over the forest. Steep shale descents and technical short DH tracks are scattered throughout the forest, but you really do need local knowledge to find them. I also know of one or two other secret spots around the Hamsterley area and also at Innerleithen and Glentress in Scotland!

If you were a huge fan of cake and wanted to find the best trail with a foodie pit stop, where would it be?

JS The best foodie pit stop would have to be Castleton Tea rooms. It's a small café in the North Yorkshire village of Castleton. It's lovely little spot and is very popular amongst the XC community. The XC riding around the area is superb! Close to hand you have the North Yorkshire Moors and Guisborough Forest. But to be Honest I much prefer a bag of crisps and a pint after a ride!!!

Where – if anywhere – outside of your area do you often visit with your bike?

JS Innerleithen in Scotland!! It's a great DH venue that regularly holds races for the SDA and NPS series. There are so many different DH trails up there I would be here all day trying to list them. It's one of my all time favourite tracks to ride. Fast, flat out, steep and technical… you name it, it's got it!!

Which websites have the best info on your local area?

JS The best websites for local riding information would have to be my own team website, Team NEFR (nefreeriders. co.uk) and Trailblasters (trailblasters.co.uk). Team NEFR Website is geared more towards the DH and Freeride aspect of the sport with regular information and updates on local DH race series as well as national races, product reviews and race reports. The site also has a number of videos featuring races from around the country as well as the local area. It has a very popular forum where riders log on to organize rides and meet up with each other and find out about the local mountain bike community. Trailblasters on the other hand is geared toward the more general aspect of riding and XC across Guisborough and the North Yorkshire moors. The site has lots of videos made by local riders, which give an insight into the trails,

technical descents and superb singletrack that are on offer in Guisborough woods and surrounding North Yorkshire moors. Between the two websites I think we pretty much have the north of England covered for local information.

Which is the best shop to head to if you're in the North?

JS The best bike shop to head to would have to be Peddlers in Redcar. Peddlers have a great selection of bikes and equipment ranging from kids bikes and BMX, right through to full on DH Bikes. Greg Winspeare the owner actually rides for Team NEFR and my thanks have to go to Greg for all his help and support for Team NEFR.

ꚩ20 Hamsterley Forest

ꚉ ꚋ Ꚍ ꚍ Ꚏ ꚏ Ꚑ ꚑ Ꚓ ꚓ Ꚕ
ꚕ Ꚗ ꚗ Ꚙ ꚙ

Train station Bishop Aukland
Nearest city Newcastle-upon-Tyne
Sat Nav DL13 3NL

Opening times You can ride the XC trails at any time, although the 4X and downhill trails are a little different. You may have to pay a membership fee or buy a day pass to cover insurance costs. It's best to call ahead.

Location Hamsterley Forest is 5 km west of Bishop Auckland, 10 km south west from Durham, 25 km southwest of Newcastle Upon Tyne and 20 km northwest of Middlebrough. To get there, exit the A1(M) at junction 60 and head along the A689 in the direction of Bishop Auckland. Take a left onto the A688 and then a right onto the A68 at West Auckland. The The Hamsterley Forest Visitor Centre is signed from here, but just in case – go up this road for 5 km then take a left onto Saunders Avenue signposted for Hamsterly. Just after Hamsterly take a right into Bedburn Road signed to Bedburn, then straight through the village, cross the

stream, and then left onto Redford Lane. Follow this road for 3 km and the Forest Lodge is at the end. There's a £3 fee to enter and park (£5 on Bank Holidays).

Facilities/Overview This one of the north's best mountain bike centres. It's a very simple but effective set up with all the gravity trails (DH, 4X, duel and dirt jumps) located together on one side of the hill, and the XC trails running out into the forest where blue, red and black runs await all riders. The easier trails are surfaced and skimmed for smooth riding, while the red and black trails contain more natural terrain, which is made up of plenty of roots and can be quite slick when wet. The site is incredibly popular, and constantly evolving, so expect each visit to have new, ever-more-interesting terrain to ride.

XC There are plenty of trails here for every ability of rider. The blue routes are aimed more towards families and novice riders, and the red and black routes for those more experienced. The

Trail Quest Course is a map reading area (on bikes) with the emphasis on finding checkpoints – a great ride for the family, and educational for younger riders.

Downhill Hamsterley is one of the only venues offering official downhill trails in the north of England. There is one main run with plenty of split sections offering different styles from rock gardens, to technical singletrack, wide open berms and jumps. There is usually a good scene on weekends and holidays with plenty of local riders sessioning the track.

Freeride With a 4X track, dirt jumps and a purpose made skills area, there's so much on offer for the freerider. The 4X trail is of a national standard having hosted several rounds of the NPS 4X series and some say is second only to Fort William's impressive set up. The 'Loop Mountain Bike Skills Area' holds a lot of wood and stone northshore and plenty of testing obstacles.

FORESTRY COMMISSION

Easy The Trail Quest is a non-technical ride to get groups out into the forest, but if you are looking for some real riding, it's not until the red route that you will find singletrack. Brush up your skills on 'the loop' a one mile skills training loop with plenty of features to learn the basics.

> **Lowdown**

🙂 **Locals do**
Get involved with the trail building in the forest too.

☹ **Locals don't**
Disrespect the forest.

✅ **Pros**
Hamsterley can offer something for most riders.

A good club and scene at the trails.

❌ **Cons**
Hills rather than mountains.

Can be quite muddy on the unsurfaced trails in winter.

Hard XC riders should head out on the black trail with steep technical lines, singletrack and some rooty descents – it's perfect for the experienced rider. For the freeriders and downhillers, there are plenty of challenges on the hill be it cleaning the rock garden or root sections on the downhill or putting together the rhythm sections on the 4X.

Not to miss Coming here at least once in your riding career!

Remember to avoid The old NPS Downhill track which is quite flat. It does make a great XC route though.

Nearest Bike/Hire shop Hamsterley has its own small bike shop called Wood N Wheels (T0333 8008 222). They offer cycle hire and are more than capable of repairing any problems you might have.

Local accommodation You can find plenty of places to stay in the surrounding area from camping to hotels. For a B&B, try the Dale End (T01388 488091), otherwise check thisisdurham.com for more options.

Eating The Hamsterley Forest Café (found inside the Visitor Centre) has just been refurbished to offer better facilities for all visitors. There are also local pubs in Hamsterley that offer meals to hungry bikers with the closest being the Cross Keys (T01388 488457).

ⓘ **More info** hamsterley-trailblazers. co.uk has a wealth of info on the trails, trail maps (and stats) and is the place to head to gain membership to the area. The Forestry Commission website (forestry.gov.uk) also has a page on the Visitor Centre.

ꡌ21 Kielder Water & Forest Park

ⓒ ⓓⓗ ⓕⓡ ⓝ ⓐⓢ ⓞ ⓜ ⓖ ⓐ ⓔ ⓕ

Train station Gretna Green

Nearest city Carlisle

Sat Nav NE48 1HX

Opening times The trails are open all year round, day and night. The only closures will be due to forest operations. The status of the trails are posted on the websites: visitkielder.com and forestry.gov.uk. All trails are free, though there is a £4 parking fee at the castle car park.

Location The vast expanse that is Kielder Water and Forest Park is on the western edge of the Northumberland National Park. Exit the M6 at junction 44, just north of Carlisle, and head towards Longtown on the A7. Pass through the Scotland/England border, and then take a right onto the B6357 towards Canobie, go through the village, and keep on the B6357 for around 20 km until you hit Saughtree where Kielder Water and Forest Park and Kielder Castle Forest Park Visitor Centre are clearly signed to the right. Follow this road and park at the Visitor Centre at the end of the road, around 10 km down the road.

Facilities/Overview The Kielder Castle Forest Park Visitor Centre is an old Georgian abode, the former hunting lodge of the Duke of Northumberland and has since been transformed into a Visitor Centre with bike shop, a café, parking, toilets, a maze (plus there's lots of info on the castle and the walking and riding trails in the area). Kielder Water is the largest man-made lake in northern Europe, and can be popular with other users, but it's a big enough area to have your own space. You'll be spoilt for choice with numerous trails and a skills loop available.

XC The Castle Wood Skills Loop has been designed to check your level of riding so you can choose which of the routes suits your riding; the Lakeside Way trail is a blue-graded route that takes in 42 km of beautiful countryside; The Borderline Trail is 11 km of green-graded (depending on who you ask), easy riding down an old railway line along the Scottish border; Osprey trail is a 19 km trail that takes in some beautiful sweeping singletrack; Bloody Bush trail is a 32-km ride taking in the Scottish border; Deadwater trails is a 15-km red-graded loop taking in the lake; The Cross Border trail is a 48-km red-graded loop into Scotland and back; the Up and Over trails is a black-graded trail over Deadwater Fell and was designed by world-cup competitor Gary Forrest. All are waymarked and are packed with features suitable for their gradings.

Downhill Despite having no specific downhill trails, the Up and Over black run can be looped for some good runs. A lot of the other trails will have more technical descents to quench your downhill thirst.

Freeride A new trails park has been built with dirt jumps, northshore and a rock garden. You won't be allowed near it without body armour, so turn up prepared.

Terrain At 650 square-km Kielder Water and Forest Park is England's largest forest, and also includes the country's largest blanket bog, which gives you an idea of the going underfoot. All the trails in the forest have had to be constructed from imported aggregate so that riders don't sink into the soft ground.

Easy The Skills Loop is the tool for your fun in this forest. It has been designed to work out your level of riding, with green, blue, red and black graded obstacles to try out, but the Lakeside Way is the easiest route in the forest.

Hard The Up and Over trail peaks out at 1900 ft. A good bit of downhill but a gruelling ride up.

Not to miss A slice of cake in the Castle Café after a good day's riding.

Remember to avoid Taking on a huge route without trying one of the smaller loops first.

Nearest Bike/Hire shop The Bike Place in Kielder (T01434 250457), or try The Bike Place in Newcastle (T01434 220210) who also do bike hire.

Local accommodation
Twenty Seven B&B (T01434 250462, staykielder.co.uk) is the only hotel in Kielder Water and Forest Park so it's best to book ahead. If you wish to look at a variety of local accommodation, check out visitkielder.com.

Eating The Kielder Castle Café is on site and serves hot and cold drinks, as well as meals. If you're wanting a meal more fitting of a mountain biker, there are plenty of pubs offering exactly that. Try The Anglers Arms (T01434 250 072) in Kielder Village. Other Visitor Centres in the Park include Tower Knowe Visitor Centre and Leaplish Waterside Park which both provide food.

ⓘ **More info** Kielder Water and Forest Park (T01434 250 209, visitkielder. com). The Forestry Commission website (forestry.gov.uk) also has a page, Visit North East England (visitnortheastengland.com) has a page on Kielder Water and Forest Park with a breakdown of most of the trails. The organised Kielder Trail Reavers are the people behind most of the trails and can be found at kieldertrailreavers.org.uk.

> **Lowdown**

☻ **Locals do**
Loop back up the forest road to ride the final descent of the Deadwater again.

☻ **Locals don't**
Leave the marked trails as the ground is very soft and can be easily damaged by bikes.

✔ **Pros**
Huge forest with plenty of trails, perfect for all levels.

✖ **Cons**
Unofficial, unmarked XC trails can be boggy.

Train station Glossop
Nearest city Manchester/Sheffield
Sat Nav S33 0AQ (for the Visitor Centre)

PAUL BLACKBURN

Location Ladybower Reservoir is right next to the Snake Pass (A57), which connects Manchester to Sheffield, and it couldn't be easier to find. From either city, follow the A57 and roughly mid-way between the two is a well-signed turn off for Ladybower. Follow the signs for Derwent Visitor Centre Car Park exit for the most facilities.

Facilities Upper Derwent Visitor Centre has a café, museum (for the Dambusters who practiced on Ladybower), parking (you will have to pay and display), bike wash and toilets. Park earlier than the Centre and it's free. The Centre also houses a bike shop with half-day rentals for £13 and full day for £16.

Rough round-up Ladybower is your gateway to some of the Peak District's best XC routes. The sheer amount of riding available is staggering, with the whole of the Peaks – theoretically – at your disposal. If you didn't want to wander too far, there are short loops so you can stay relatively close to the Visitor Centre, or there are plenty of long-haul rides to be had. Highly recommended for those who like their riding very rambling-esque.

Terrain As you could imagine, the Peak District is mostly open moorland but there are plenty of woodland areas and secret copses hidden in the valleys. These are normally seen as short, sharp routes, but the truth is that there is every type of XC riding to be had here.

XC There are so many routes on offer that it's hard to know where to begin. The classic Ladybower route is for those of you wanting to cautiously test limits: leave the Visitor Centre and loop around Derwent Dam and Ladybower, up over Cutthroat Bridge and a climb up the moorland before a long descent back to your starting point – 11 km with gentle climbs. There are many extra trails you could add to this route – just google it and you'll find plenty of added extras. There are plenty of specific Peak District XC guides (perhaps the best

being Dark Peak Mountain Biking: True Grit Trails, and White Peak Mountain Biking: The Pure Trails, which cover the north and south Peak District XC routes respectively), and serious local riders would be well advised to invest in one. Others can simply route find and ask other riders on the climbs – there's plenty to search out for yourself.

Downhill You won't find any purpose-built DH trails but there are plenty of technical descents on the XC routes that are satisfying for downhill riders.

Dirt jumps/Freeride Again, there isn't anything purpose-built here but those of you on full-rig freeride bikes will undoubtedly find things to ride.

ⓘ **More info**
peakdistrict.gov.uk has plenty of advice and information for mountain bikers while the guide books mentioned can be bought online. The best source for local riders to discover more routes and meet each other is mountainbikerides.co.uk.

↘23 Lee Mill Quarry (aka The Adrenaline Gateway)

Train station Rochdale

Nearest city Manchester

Sat Nav OL12 8XG (from the south, heading from Rochdale). OL13 0BB (heading from the north and parking at Future's Park)

Location Lee Mill Quarry is a disused quarry that lies around 10 km north of Rochdale on the A671. When travelling north from Rochdale, take the A671 (Whitworth Road), which turns into Market Street, until the road forks. You will need to take the left turn onto the A6066 heading towards Bacup, then join the A681 (Newchurch Road) and take a left onto Farholme Lane. This road will change to Acre Mill Road and Cutler Lane; park where you can in Cutler Lane and ride to the end of the lane itself. The quarry will be to your right.

Facilities There's nothing up at the quarry itself, but Whitworth is a small village with shops and some amenities, as is Stackstead. The quarry is part of the Adrenaline Gateway project and has recently been linked by singletrack allowing XC riders another route.

Rough round-up This is an old quarry which has been appropriated by the local riding scene for some years. There are plenty of lovely XC trails heading off into the nearby moors, and there are lots of drops, berms and jumps scattered around, some threaded together to make some half-decent downhill trails. Lee Quarry has over 10 km of red and black graded mountain bike trails, alongside Cragg Quarry that has 6.5 km of trails.

Both quarries are linked by 2 km of singletrack, intended for all users, so keep an eye out for walkers.

Terrain There's plenty of unofficial singletrack, but it's mostly rocky riding around here.

XC There are currently two main XC loops – a 4.5-km red route (2 km uphill, 2 km downhill – some gruelling climbs and decent descents), and a 1-km severe black loop which is for experts only (and body armour is advised); there is also a skills area with drops, jumps and tests of balance on the natural rock etc.

Downhill You'll find some short sections of DH around the quarry, but the red route is where you'll have the most fun. It has a decent couple of sections that are testing for most DH riders.

Dirt jumps/Freeride The natural terrain should be enough for freeriders as it has a lot of technical riding (drops mostly) but there's a purpose-built trails bike area and two pump tracks. There's certainly enough here to keep even the most experienced of freeriders busy.

Conditions This is a stone quarry with fields and moorland in the surrounding area. The surface is naturally very rocky, though the red route is fine. The black run requires body armour as a fall could cause damage.

ⓘ **More info** rossendale.gov.uk has info on both quarries and the work being done. Also visit pmba.org.uk for a map of the cycle routes in the area.

N24 Little Switzerland

XC DH ⬤ ⬤ ⬤ ⬤ ⬤

Train station Ferriby
Nearest city Hull
Sat Nav HU13 0LN

Location Little Switzerland is the name given to an area of the Humber Bridge Country Park, which is next door to the mighty Humber Bridge in Hull. From the M62 exit at the end of the motorway, then continue onto the A63 in the direction of Hull. Head towards the town centre and the A63 will take you right to the bridge where the entrance to the Humber Bridge Country Park is clearly signed.

Facilities There are plenty of places to stop and get a bite to eat in the Country Park, including the fantastic Mrs B's Woodland Café.

Rough round-up Little Switzerland is the name given to the chalky edged cliffs in the Humber Bridge Country Park, which house a couple of interesting trails for local riders. Not worth a huge journey, but the old quarry has some jumps, there are some short but interesting DH trails (though more XC oriented), and there is access to a whole host of XC routes by way of the Yorkshire Wolds Way which passes directly through the park and underneath the bridge. Always a good backdrop to a quick ride.

Conditions This is chalk surface, so very slippery when wet – avoid after recent rain and through the winter months.

ⓘ **More info** The Yorkshire Wolds Way has a page on the site nationaltrail.co.uk.

N25 Longridge Fell

XC DH

Train station Preston/Pleasington/Blackburn
Nearest city Preston
Sat Nav PR3 2TY (for Longridge Golf Course)

Location You'll find Longridge Fell to be a popular outdoor venue around 6 km northeast of Preston and 10 km to the northwest of Blackburn. From the M6 exit at junction 31a and head in the opposite direction to Preston, following signs instead to Longridge on the B6243. In Longridge, go all the way through the village to the T-junction, then take a right onto Kestor Lane, then a left onto Higher Road, then follow this road into Forty Acre Lane and continue to the top of the hill, passing the golf course on your left. The start of the trails is around 5 km from Longridge.

Facilities There isn't much up at the fell, but Longridge has plenty of shops and amenities.

Rough round-up This is the local hub for Preston and Blackburn, and is an open spot with a few downhill trails with some jumps, drops and berms. There's also plenty of unofficial singletrack and bridleway to explore, and is suitable for complete beginners through to half decent riders who want to get some practice in. Not worth a huge journey but great for those in the area. This is predominantly natural terrain, with rocks, roots and drops although the local riders have reinforced one or two areas.

Conditions As this is open moorland with some tree'd copses along the way, it's best to avoid in high winds and it can become a real bog in the winter months.

N26 Manchester Road DJs

DH

Train station Accrington
Nearest city Blackburn
Sat Nav BB5 2PQ (100 m to the southeast of the DJs)

Location Just to the south of Accrington, a town between Blackburn and Burnley, are the Manchester Road dirt jumps. From the M65 exit at junction 7 and take the A6185 Dunkenhalgh Way towards Accrington. Carry on towards the town centre (the road changes to Hyndburn Road), then the A680, and head south on Abbey Street (the A680 main road through town) until that road changes name to Manchester Road. After 1 km from the centre of Accrington, there's a break in houses on either side of the road, with woods on your left, and a park on your right. The dirt jumps are in the woods to the left.

Facilities You'll find all the shops and amenities in Accrington.

Rough round-up These are some dirt jumps built by local BMXers and mountain bike crew. Worth a look if you live or ride nearby but not worth a long journey as it's a relatively small area though packed with plenty of decent-sized jumps.

Conditions This is a soil clearing in some public woods. Avoid after rainfall.

N27 Meltham Skills Trails

XC FR

Train station Brockholes/Slaithwaite
Nearest city Huddersfield
Sat Nav HD9 4HL

Location Meltham Skills Trails are just to the east of the town of Meltham, which itself is on the north east edge of the Peak District and around 6 km south west of Huddersfield. Leave Huddersfield on the A616 south to Armitage Bridge, then take a right onto the B6108 (Meltham Road) towards Meltham. Just before entering the town, turn left onto Meltham Mills Road, then left again onto Knowle Lane. Drive another 250 m and the trails are just to the south of the road, in the woods that lead to Meltham Mills reservoir.

Facilities This is an area of forest land next to the town of Meltham. There are no facilities in the woods, but Meltham has plenty of shops and amenities.

Rough round-up The woods here hold many hidden freeride obstacles, drops and jumps, though this isn't a classic dirt jump run with flowing lines. It's not worth a long journey but it's perfect for locals. It's definitely worth combining with some of the other Peak District rides as there's also plenty of unofficial XC riding to be had in the woods around Meltham Mills Reservoir.

Conditions This is forest land on the edge of the Peaks, and is prone to being boggy throughout the winter. It's a popular spot for fell runners and walkers.

N28 Midgley Woods

DH FR

Train station Mytholmroyd
Nearest city Bradford
Sat Nav HX7 5LR

Location Around 5 km to the west of Halifax centre, and to the north east of Mytholmroyd, are Midgley Woods. Exit the M62 at junction 24 and take the A629 north in the direction of Halifax. After 4 km turn left into the A646 (Dryclough Lane), and follow this road for 6 km in the direction of Mytholmroyd. At the town of Mytholmroyd, take a right into Midgley Road, and after 1.5 km Midgley Woods are on the right.

Facilities There's nothing up at the woods but Mytholmroyd has plenty of shops and facilities.

Rough round-up Midgley Woods are a low-budget freeride and downhill spot, with local riders practicing their jump skills on some tabletops, gaps, drops and berms that have been shaped here. Definitely not worth a long journey but for those in Halifax or nearby that want to get some mild dirt jumping on the go, it might be worth a look in. There are more trails planned, though this is an unofficial spot and you'll have to meet with the local riders to get involved in any potential building work.

Conditions This is sparsely wooded land with soil jumps with little work gone into the trails but plenty of natural drops and drop ins to get speed.

N29 Park Bridge 4X

DH 4X

Train station Hollinwood/Ashton-under-Lyne
Nearest city Oldham
Sat Nav N/A

Location Otherwise known as Bankfield Cloud, Park Bridge is around 2 km south of Oldham, just next to the village of Bardsley. Exit the M60 at junction 22 and take the A6104 (Hollins Road) eastwards. Drive to the T-junction, take a right onto the A627 Ashton Road south towards Bardsley, and after 1 km take a left onto Park Bridge Road. Park after 1 km on the left and follow the red topped posts from the wooden bridge on Park Bridge Road. Head to the top of the hill for the start of the 4X.

Facilities This is a disused hill with no facilities on site, but nearby Bardsley has plenty of facilities and amenities.

Rough round-up This is a fantastic set up with a gravity assisted downhill 4X track that was cut into the forested hill by the local mountain bike scene. The track is steep, wide, and has doubles, drops and a large final step-up jump. Everything is rollable but good intermediate riders will undoubtedly get the best from the track. Definitely worth a journey for local riders.

Conditions This is a clay-based track which doesn't drain particularly well so avoid after heavy rain.

⬂30 Ramsden Lane DH

Train station Brockholes
Nearest city Huddersfield
Sat Nav N/A

Location You'll find Ramdsen Lane around 2 km south west of Holmfirth, itself 6 km south of Huddersfield, and just on the edge of the Peak District. When travelling from Huddersfield, head south on the A616 towards Honley, then the A6024 to Homfirth, then carry on towards Holmbridge. Just after Holmbridge village, turn off onto Dobb Topp Road following signs for Brownhill Reservoir on Brownhill Lane. Carry on for 1 km with the reservoir on your right, then turn left into Ramsden Lane, and after 600 m the DH trail is on the left at the top of the hill.

Facilities The reservoir doesn't have a Visitor Centre like many of the other lakes in the Peak District, but nearby Holmbridge has plenty of shops and facilities.

Rough round-up This is a low-budget downhill track that starts at the top of the hill and finishes at the house near the bottom. It's extremely rocky with plenty of shale, and can also be popular with walkers. Local riders flock here as it has the ability of uplift, providing you have a car!

Conditions Very rocky in sections – especially the middle – but essentially this is open field land with beautiful views over Brownhill and Ramsden Reservoir.

⬂31 Rawcliffe Pump Track

Train station Poppleton
Nearest city Bradford
Sat Nav YO30 5XZ

Location The Rawcliffe Pump Track can be found around 25 miles north east of Bradford. Driving north on the A1(M), exit at junction 44 and drive towards York on the A64. Take a left turning onto the A1237, drive for around 12 km and cross over the river. When you reach the roundabout just past the river, take the fourth exit and head towards the roundabout. Find a place to park and the pump track is just to the south in a small copse.

Facilities There are no facilities at the pump track itself but the park is near town, and riders will be able to find shops and amenities there.

Rough round-up These are two purpose-built pump tracks – one for beginners and one for experienced riders. It's a great addition for local riders, especially if you're looking to progress your bike handling skills. Not worth a long journey. That said, expect them to be busy.

Conditions Although they're purpose made, bad weather still can cause the pump track to get a little muddy.

⬂32 Roman Lakes Leisure Park

Train station Marple Central or Rose Hill
Nearest city Stockport/Manchester
Sat Nav SK6 7HB

Location Exit the M60 at junction 27 (signed for Stockport) and follow the A626 signposted Marple. When in Marple, go straight on at the first set of traffic lights – where the A626 goes left – and up the hill through the middle of Marple on the B6101. At the top of the hill, cross the canal and the road turns sharp right, but bear left on Oldknow Road and then cross Arkwright Road onto Faywood Drive. This becomes Lakes Road which leads to Roman Lakes Leisure Park.

Facilities The are plenty of facilities at the park, including a café, free car parking, toilets, picnic area and a boules area! As this is primarily a walking and nature reserve, there are plenty of other forest users, including bird watchers and horse riders. However, it is also a specific mountain bike centre and families are very welcome.

Rough round-up You will be spoilt for choice as there are 12 waymarked trails from 8-40 km loops surrounding the park with family routes that follow bridleways and canal paths, and more serious XC routes can be found by riding over Mellor Moor, New Mills and Hayfield. There is a route maps and brochure called Mountain Bike Rides Around Roman Lakes which costs £1 from the café and is written by Pete Fuller. The book has detailed descriptions of the trails, as well as maps and pictures of strategic sections

Rough round-up As this area has decreased in popularity, the Forestry Commission has decided not to maintain in the route any more. The route itself still remains but any purpose-built features or obstacles have been removed, and the trail has gone into disrepair. There are signs up to notify riders of the change and if any locals wish to be involved in the upkeep – if you are, make yourself known to the ranger or the Forestry Commission.

Conditions This is a Forestry Commission site in an area of outstanding natural beauty. The trails are mostly natural, so avoid after heavy rainfall as it becomes almost unrideable.

ⓘ **More info** Keep up to date on the Silton Forest Downhill Track Facebook page, facebook.com/siltondownhill.

on the routes, and is indispensable for all riders. For those looking for a more serious XC challenge, Roman Lakes offers a 100-km loop start and finish around the Peak District, see the website romanlakes.co.uk/mountain_biking.htm for more info. The park opens at 0800 and closes at dusk. They also challenge you to the Roman Lakes 100 km Challenge, but that's only for the hardened XC riders!

Conditions This is a selection of singletrack, bridleway, canal path and fireroad (possibly some tarmac). Mostly waymarked but some longer routes need navigation.

ⓘ **More info** Check out romanlakes.co.uk as the park often hosts demo days and is a popular bike-testing venue.

Silton Forest DH
XC DH ⊕

Train station Northallerton
Nearest city Middlesbrough
Sat Nav YO7 2JZ (to the Gold Cup Inn)

Location You'll find Silton Forest on the eastern edge of the North Yorkshire Moors, almost halfway between Harrogate and Middlesbrough. Exit the A1(M) at junction 49 and head north towards Thirsk on the A168, then continue onto the A19 towards Middlesbrough. Roughly 5 km north of Thirsk, take a right onto Leake Lane in the village of Leake, heading in the direction of Nether Silton. Carry on up this lane for 2 km, then turn right onto West Lane, then a left after the village of Nether Silton into Kirk Ings Lane, then a right into Skirt Bank/Moor Lane and head to the top where the forest car park awaits. From the car park, ride up the fire road to the crossroads, then go left.

Facilities There's nothing up at the forest but the Gold Cup Inn is a great after ride spot!

SMITHOS

XC DH ◯

Train station Maryport/Workington
Nearest city Newcastle-upon-Tyne
Sat Nav CA13 9HA

Location Cockermouth and Setmurthy are two towns (Cockermouth the bigger of the two), on the northwest edge of the Lake District, Cumbria. Leave the M6 at junction 40 (next to Penrith) and head westwards on the A66 to Kewick and then Cockermouth. To get to the XC and DH trails, head out of Cockermouth eastwards on Main Street in the centre of town. This road will turn into Castlegate, then Castlegate Drive, which is a country road that heads towards Setmurthy. Continue for 3l m down this road and the DH trails are to your left. There are three access roads that turn left into the hill between Cockermouth and Setmurthy – each with great access to XC riding.

Facilities You won't find anything up at the trails, but Cockermouth itself is a popular town on the edge of the touristy Lake District, with plenty of shops and facilities, including bike shops.

Rough round-up Cockermouth and Setmurthy are two nearby towns with a joint XC and downhill region. There has been many years of investment put in by local riders, with plenty of reinforced areas and flowing lines etched out of the local terrain. There's a big mountain biking scene in the area so expect to see other riders, despite none of the trails being waymarked;

the area is a low-budget scene that doesn't advertise its existence at all. Don't expect this to be a fully catered-for site, but the are plenty of fantastic trails to ride.

Terrain There's plenty of unofficial singletrack, loads of bridleways and fireroads and tricky rock sections.

XC There are several loops of around 10-15 km with great climbs and perfect descents for those who love rooty, flowing singletrack. None of it is waymarked, but exploring and discovering is part of the charm of the area.

Downhill The DH trails are closer to Setmurthy and are nothing short of brilliant. The locals call it Minileithen because it rides like the Innerleithen Trail in Scotland, with loads of flowing berms, rock gardens, jumps and hefty drops. Not for beginners.

Dirt jumps/Freeride Although there is no specific freeride area, there's plenty to enjoy. The downhill tracks in Setmurthy hold some great runs for those of you who enjoy air time.

Conditions This is Forestry Commission land with dense forest and some beautiful open spaces which is definitely to be avoided after rain.

ⓘ **More info** 4Play Cycles (T01900 823377, 4playcycles.net) have maps to the trails, while there are plenty of videos online showcasing the downhill and XC trails.

⬇️35 Storthes Hall DH
🔘 🔘

Train station Stocksmoor
Nearest city Huddersfield
Sat Nav HD8 0WN

Location Located around 5 km to the southeast of Huddersfield is Storthes Hall downhill track. When leaving the centre of Huddersfield, take the A629 eastwards through Tandem and onto Highburton. Just after Highburton, you'll see Boothroyd Wood on your right. Take the next right (Thunder Bridge Lane), which is around 1 km after Highburton, then the next right (Grange Lane), and follow the road as it turns into Wood Lane. Park after 300 m, and go through the gap in the wall to your right, down the path and past the field to the start of the downhill.

Facilities Storthes Hall is a popular student accommodation venue, so there are plenty of good pubs and shops nearby.

Rough round-up This might be an unofficial site which is low-budget, but it still holds plenty of features including some pretty big jumps and drops, berms and more. All are short, but technically difficult, and definitely not for novice riders.

Conditions Some of the jumps have been reinforced with logs, but there is otherwise little addition to the natural terrain here, which is steep forest land.

⬇️36 Wassenden DH
🔘 🔘 🔘

Train station Brockholes/Slaithwaite
Nearest city Huddersfield
Sat Nav HD9 4EU

Location Wassenden DH is in the north of the Peak District, halfway between Holmfirth and Saddleworth on the Holmfirth Road. From either east or west, take the A635 through the Peak District. Midway through, take the small road to the north (Wassenden Head Road) signposted to Meltham, and after 200 m turn off to the left for the start of the downhill trail.

Facilities As this is a track in the middle of the Peaks, you won't find any facilities, so bring your own or carry on up Wassenden Head Road for supplies from Meltham. There are shops at the finish line though in Marsden.

Overview This is a fantastic singletrack ride all the way down to Marsden in the north – a journey of around 5 km through spectacular and empty moorland (Wassenden Moor) and passing Wassenden and Butterley Reservoir. You can uplift using a car but you'll obviously need someone to pick you up from Marsden, a loop of around 8 km by car.

Conditions This is open moorland so expect it to be almost unrideable after heavy rain. There are some rocky sections – it's not too steep overall – and there is a large possibility of meeting fell-walkers nearer the reservoirs as this is part of the popular Kirklees Way. Otherwise it's a fantastic day out and a few laps of this will make most riders' days.

FORESTRY COMMISSION

⟨↘37⟩ Stainburn

⊗ ⊕ ⊙ ⊙ ⊙ ⊙

Train station Burley-in-Wharfdale
Nearest city Manchester
Sat Nav N/A
Opening times The trails are open 24/7, 365 days a year and are free to use! You can also join Singletraction as a member for £15 and this money goes towards the upkeep of this and other sites.

Location Stainburn is roughly midway between Shipley and Harrogate in Yorkshire, and is an area of Forestry Commission land – around 18 km from Leeds. When travelling from Leeds, head north on the A660 from the city centre in the direction of Ortley. Turn right at the A658 towards Harrogate, after 300 m (and crossing the river) turn left on to the B6161 towards Leathley and Farnley. Follow this road for 1.5 km, then turn left at a small lodge just after a humped back bridge towards Farnley. Follow this road for 2.5 km to Farnley Village, then take the first right onto the B6451. Follow this road for 3 km through Farnley, past the farm and down to Lindley Wood Reservoir. Stay on this road and Stainburn car park is 500 m after the reservoir on the left as you go round a sweeping left hand bend.

Facilities/Overview Singletraction (the people behind Stainburn, Wharncliffe, Guisborough, Silton and Dalby) have worked with the Forestry Commission to produce a fantastic site, and Stainburn Forest's trails have been built with care and attention to the forest, with one purpose-built trail and several natural routes, all waymarked. The guys from

Singletraction have also worked on the Norwood Edge trails (just over the road), linking Stainburn with some great, natural singletrack. This is a great place for serious riders to head, though it should cater for all tastes (though families and complete beginners may wish to try elsewhere first). There is plenty of XC riding elsewhere in the forest, and there is a constant stream of trail additions and improvements being made. Well worth a journey.

XC This is a predominantly XC trail centre, with an orientation towards downhill. There are three waymarked trails, none of which are particularly

> Lowdown

☺ Locals do
Become members of Singletraction and get involved with dig days.

Take food and drink with them.

☹ Locals don't
Build anything illegally.

Worry too much about meeting other forest users. There aren't many people out here.

✔ Pros
One of the UK's most feature-full sites.

✖ Cons
In the middle of nowhere with no facilities.

Constant building and evolving. Which can also be a plus!

The North Stainburn

long, but they were created so that you could hit them over and over again and still find new features on each descent. As mentioned earlier, the Norwood Edge trails feature routes that have aimed to stay more natural than the Warren Boulder Trail at Stainburn (a purpose-built and man made, obstacle strewn route of around 4 km). It's definitely a case of quality over quantity but that just adds to the fun of the riding here as it encourages riders to try moves over and over again to clean sections as they don't have to worry about the 50 km that they still have to ride!

Downhill There are no dedicated DH runs but there are plenty of short DH sections on the XC routes. The Descent Line Trail is a short, but action packed route with rocks, roots, berms and jumps but by no means, solely DH, although well worth a try.

Freeride There are no specific areas for freeriders, though the Warren Boulder Trail should have enough features for those who like to be in the air. The pump track should keep a few skills riders happy too.

Easy Try the Black Route and cut out at waymarked 12 to loop back. It'll loop you back to the start quicker and give you an indication as to whether you want to try the whole route.

Hard The Warren Boulder Trail is a must.

Not to miss The Warren Boulder Trail should be on every rider's wishlist.

Remember to avoid Heading there after recent rainfall.

Nearest Bike/Hire shop Chevin Cycles is the nearest bike shop, in nearby Otley (chevincycles.com, T01943 462773).

Local accommodation Dowgill House in Otley is a Georgian House with fantastic rooms, T01943 850836, dowgillhouse.co.uk.

Eating The nearest place to get supplies would be Otley. Take supplies with you as there are no facilities on site.

ⓘ **More info** Stainburn has been built by Singletraction, the group behind Dalby Park and Silton Forest. Check out their site at singletraction.org.uk.

↘38 Temple Newsam

🔵 🔴 ⚫

Train station Cross Gates
Nearest city Leeds
Sat Nav LS15 0LN for Temple Newsam
Road, the bottom of the trails.

Location Temple Newsam is one of
the most celebrated historic houses
in the country, situated just on the
edge of Leeds. The trails are more aptly
described as being south of Coulton, in
Avenue Wood. Exit the M1 at junction
46 and take a left at the roundabout
onto the A63. Head straight over the
first roundabout but at the next, take
the second exit left (Selby Road, the
B6159), and follow this road until the
first lights then take a left onto Colton
Road. Go down here, straight over the
mini roundabout, then right at the
fork, and carry on for 600 m. There's
a turning to the right with a gravel
car park at the end. This is the start of
the trails.

Facilities There are plenty of facilities
back at Selby Road or at the bottom of
the trails. This is an inner-city area so
there are shops everywhere.

Overview This is a great example
of when mountain bikers and a city
council come together to make good
trails. This downhill area was built in
2004/5 and is perfect for beginners
and good riders alike. Not strictly a DH
trail, it is wide enough to be used as
4X, has jumps and log drops (though
all rollable), berms and a very flowing,
gravelly surface. For those that like
XC the track is loopable by riding
back to the top. Definitely worth a
look in if you're in the area, and for
those wishing to learn, it's also one of
the main haunts for the local riders,
though it can be a little rough at the
wrong time as it's not the best area
in Leeds.

Conditions This is a purpose-built
trail with a sandy, gravelly base which
drains really well. It's not strictly
singletrack (though there is some
around), but more like a downhill
fire-road with jumps. It's in need of a
bit of love but the trails are still good
enough to ride.

ⓘ **More info** For all Leeds mountain
biking info, MTB Leeds is the place to
head and they have a great website at
mtbleeds.co.uk

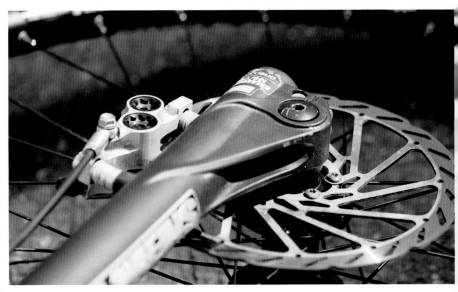

⬆40 Woodbank DJs

🅧🅒 🄳🅙

Train station Bredbury/Stockport
Nearest city Stockport/Manchester
Sat Nav SK1 4JR

Location Woodband Memorial Park and Vernon Park are next door to each other in the village of Offerton, on the east edge of Stockport. Leave the M60 (Manchester Ring Road) at junction 27 and drive south on the A626 (St Mary's Way) for around 500 m. At the next major junction take a left onto Spring Gardens, then left into Turncroft Lane. Go to the end of this lane, and the entrance to the park is in front of you as the road bends sharply to the right.

Facilities Both parks are well-kept Victorian parks with a museum and extensive gardens. There are cafés and facilities but the DJs are unofficial so there are no facilities on site.

Rough round-up There are some impressive, unofficial dirt jumps at both sites, though you'll have to ask local riders to find the exact location. You can also ride around looking for them as Vernon Park isn't huge. Many local riders here combine a day messing on the jumps with a leisurely stroll down the river Goyt (Woodbank turns into river-side countryside to the southeast). Perfect for some gentle XC riding.

Conditions This is well-maintained park land with areas of outstanding natural and cultivated gardens and fauna. There are no specific riding areas in the parks, but it is tolerated.

ⓘ **More info** Stockport Council's website has a page for both parks, stockport.gov.uk.

⬆39 Wiswell Wood

🅧🅒 🄳🅗 🄳🅙

Train station Whalley
Nearest city Blackburn
Sat Nav BB7 9DR

Location You'll find Wiswell Wood to the northeast of Whalley village, around 4 km south of Clitheroe and 8 km northeast of Blackburn. Leave the M65 at junction 7 and follow the A680 to Clayton le Moors, then north towards Whalley. At the end of the A680, you'll come to the junction where that road meets with the Burnley Road (the A671); here, turn left onto the A671, then immediately right into Portfield Lane – almost as if you were going straight across the junction – and then another right onto Clerk Hill Road. Head up here for 500 m and Wiswell Wood starts at the copse of trees just off the road on the left. Park at the old schoolhouse and head for the red phone box for the start of the trails.

Facilities There's not a great deal up at the woods and fields, but nearby Whalley has plenty of shops and facilities. Take supplies with you.

Rough round-up These are some fantastic downhill trails, packed with features such as rock gardens, purpose-built gaps and drops next to the dry-stone walls down the trails to keep the local riders happy. This is a very popular mountain biking area, so expect to see lots of other riders who should be happy to share the secret XC trails that criss-cross the fields around the area if downhill isn't your thing. There are the beginnings of northshore being built and many of the heavily eroded areas have been reinforced. Help with building the trails is always appreciated.

Conditions This is a popular and large spot out in the open with the chance to drop into some dense woods, though felling often changes the area and the trails without warning. Avoid in high winds or after heavy rain.

ⓘ **More info** The Woollybacks Mountain Bike Club regularly ride at Wiswell Wood, and have a page dedicated to the site (with maps and advice etc), see thewoollybacks.co.uk.

⬎41 TNF Grizedale

🎿 🚻 Ⓝ 🚴 🅿️ ⛰ ☕ 🏨 🚻 🔧

Train station Windermere
Nearest city Preston
Sat Nav LA22 0QJ
Opening times 1000-1700

Location The Northface Trail is part of an incredible set-up at the Grizedale Visitor Centre, slap bang in the middle of the Lake District. Leave the M6 exit at junction 36 and take the A590 towards Kendal, then the A591 towards Windemere, then Ambleside,

and turn off here on the A593 in the direction of Coniston, then the B5286 towards Hawkshead. Go through the village and at the T-junction pick up the brown signs towards Grizedale, which is around 3 km over the hill from Hawkshead. You can park at either the Moor Top car park, or carry on to the Grizedale Visitor Centre, just off this road on the right.

Facilities/Overview As you can tell from the name, the main trail at

Grizedale has been heavily backed by The North Face, alongside some investment from the Forestry Commission. Grizedale has a fully stocked Visitor Centre, which is a multi-million pound venture featuring a bike shop, bike hire, café, restaurant, bike wash and plenty of helpful information. The Visitor Centre is also the HQ of the Forestry Commission, so you can expect every facility here to be perfect! As mentioned, TNF Trail is the main trail but there are many more routes to explore.

XC Riders travel here for The North Face Trail – a fun-filled 10-mile red-graded run, which has plenty of wood to ride over, as well as some fun uphill sections that disguise the ascent. However, the singletrack straight from the Visitor Centre lulls you into a false sense of security as much of the route is fire-road, and far too much considering it's the flagship route here. That said, it's a great run when it you get off the roads. There are two more

red runs for the serious riders and five blue runs for the family.

Downhill There are no specific DH tracks here, though the end section of the North Face Trail is quite good fun and you can self uplift by driving to the Moor Top car park.

Freeride No freeride.

Easy The entire trail is relatively straightforward, but there are many sections for groups of differing abilities. You'll find fire-road for the kids and some trickier singletrack for the little ones.

Hard You'll enjoy Under The Boardwalk; the two long sections have narrow line for the confident and a fun 360 loop.

Not to miss The boardwalk sections.

Remember to avoid If you're extremely experienced you might find it frustrating.

Nearest Bike/Hire shop Grizedale Mountain Bikes (T01229 860369, grizedalemountainbikes.co.uk) are based at the Visitor Centre and hire out a selection of bikes depending on your needs. Prices range from £15-£45 for a full day.

Local accommodation The Grizedale Lodge B&B (T01768 482155) is next door to the Visitor Centre, while the Forestry Commission website has a downloadable PDF of fantastic, affordable accommodation in the area.

Eating The café is set into the forest so the views are superb. They also have a takeaway hatch if you don't want to stop for too long! Open 1000-1600.

ⓘ **More info** Try forestry.gov.uk/thenorthfacetrail, or call the Visitor Centre on T01229 860010.

> Lowdown

☺ Locals do
Throw in a detour to make it a bit more challenging. Check the map and some of the bridleways.

Gun down the singletrack sections.

☹ Locals don't
Jump – it has a distinct lack of kickers.

✔ Pros
Great family run out.

Incredible infrastructure with the new Visitor Centre set up.

✖ Cons
Almost half the route is forest road, and there's no specific DH track.

Not built for downhill, so DH riders may get bored.

⬎42 Whinlatter Forest

🅧 🅓🅗 🅝 🅜 🅞 🅐 🅐 🅖 🅐 🅟 🅞

Train station Windermere/Workington
Nearest city Carlisle
Sat Nav CA12 5TW

Location Whinlatter Forest Park sits
on the B5292, just outside Keswick,
and is yet another fantastic Forestry
Commission initiative in the Lake District.
Take junction 40 from the M6 and head
west towards Keswick on the A66. Carry
on through the town of Keswick in the
direction of Cockermouth, and at the
village of Braithwaite turn on to the
B5292 Whinlatter Pass. Head along here
and turn off at the Forestry Commission
car park.

Facilities At Whinlatter you can
find a Visitor Centre, toilets and the
Cyclewise Shop & Bike Hire (T017687
78711), stocking clothing as well as
offering bike hire facilities and courses.
The Siskins Café is open 1000-1700
all week offering great home-cooked
food. There's also a Go Ape facility for
you to monkey around on.

Rough round-up This is a well-run
centre with some of the longest
purpose-built trails in the Lakes, with a
12-mile, red-graded trail.

Terrain Whinlatter Forest
boasts beautiful, steep slopes
with commanding views over
Bassesnthwaite Lake. The going is
fantastic, purpose-built singletrack that
works in all weathers thanks to a shale
surfacing and reinforced areas over
any potentially boggy ground.

XC As you would expect, there are
plenty of unofficial routes shooting off
in every direction here, but the two
main routes are the Altura Trail and
the Quercus Trail. The Altura is a 19-km
red trail with 15 km of pure singletrack
featuring berms, jumps, tabletops
and plenty of rock features. It's more
picturesque than sister trail TNF at
Grizedale, having better views over the
lakes, and packs in more singletrack
compared to TNF's forest road, yet is
less popular. Quercus is a blue-graded
trail that's a little bit tamer than it's red
cousin, but will still push intermediate
riders to their limits.

Downhill The last section of
Altura features a swift downhill
that adventurous beginners to
intermediates will love.

Dirt jumps/Freeride Both loops
have jumps, berms and some more
technical sections but there are no
specific dirt sculptures for freeriders.

Conditions Predominantly hard-
packed singletrack, with some stony
and gravel sections. Walkers and
horseriders are asked not to use the trail
so it's pretty much ours alone!

ⓘ **More info** Take a look at the
Forestry Commission site for any other
info that you need: forestry.gov.uk.

JARVIS GOODYEAR

⛰43 Wooler 4X

Ⓧ Ⓓ Ⓝ Ⓚ

Train station Cathill
Nearest city Newcastle-upon-Tyne/
Edinburgh
Sat Nav NE71 6QP

Location Wooler 4X is a national-standard 4X venue at the north end of the Northumberland National Park and near the border with Scotland. When driving from the south, approach Wooler on the A1 from Newcastle-upon-Tyne, then take a left just after Warenford on the B6348 heading to Wooler. When driving from the north, take the A68 from Edinburgh and turn off at Saint Boswells on the A699 to Kelso, then the A698 Coldstream, then the A697 south to Wooler.

In town, head for the Haugh Head Garage, 1.5 km south of Wooler on the A697, which is the hub for the 4X venue and also hires and sells bikes.

Facilities Haugh Head Garage is a petrol station and bike shop in one, and the place to head to buy a ticket for the 4X venue – which is around 600 m to the northeast of the garage, but closed to the public unless pre-paid to use. There's nothing at the 4X course so it's worth buying supplies here.

Rough round-up The 4X course has had plenty of national-standard competitions held on its banks, and there are plenty of other jumps, gaps, tabletops and some northshore up at the same venue, all built by the enthusiastic and hard-working Cheviot Hill Riders (aka Team CHR). You can pay per visit to the 4X course, of pay a yearly membership fee. Helmets are obligatory.

Terrain The 4X track is a purpose-built surfaced track dug into the side of a hill which drains well.

XC Thrunton Woods is the local XC spot. Call in to Haugh Head Garage for details or check the website for stats and directions.

Downhill Start at the top of Wooler Common for downhill riding (signposted at the top 'Technical Steep Downhill Track'), and go through two gates to the top of the hill, and Wyndy Gyle is another popular DH trail in the area.

Dirt jumps/Freeride The 4X track will be enough for the freeriders among you. It has plenty of jumps and the DH trails in the area are worth a look as well.

Conditions The 4X track is all-weather, while the other spots around Wooler are a mixture of average to poor drainage areas, culminating in what the CHR riders call Slymefoot Slidings on Wyndy Gyle, a boggy and slippy downhill (hence the name).

ⓘ **More info** Cheviot Hill Riders have a brilliant website with all the info on their favourite local haunts at team-chr.co.uk.

⛰44 Yeadon BMX track

Ⓧ Ⓓ

Train station Guiseley
Nearest city Bradford/Leeds
Sat Nav LS19 7UR

Location Easily found, Yeadon BMX track is at the northwest end of the Leeds Bradford Airport in Yeadon, itself around 5 km northeast of Bradford, and 9 km northwest of Leeds. Take the A658 from Bradford, following signs for the airport. Take a left in Yeadon onto High Street (if you go under the railway tunnel, you've gone too far!), then right onto Cemetery Road. The BMX track is just after Yeadon Tarn (the lake), on your right.

Facilities Yeadon is a small town with plenty of shops and amenities and a short ride away.

Rough round-up This is a brilliant BMX track with loads of berms and jumps to get some good dirt jumping or freeride practice on, and a popular spot for the local Leeds/Bradford scene. It has just been resurfaced to make the park that little bit better. It's not not worth a huge journey, but worth a look in for nearby riders and perfect for those learning as everything is rollable.

Conditions This track doesn't have the best drainage in the world but is fine to use shortly after rainfall. It's a flat area so it's not perfect for 4X, but fun to practise on.

Bike Park Wales
[FORESTRY COMMISSION]

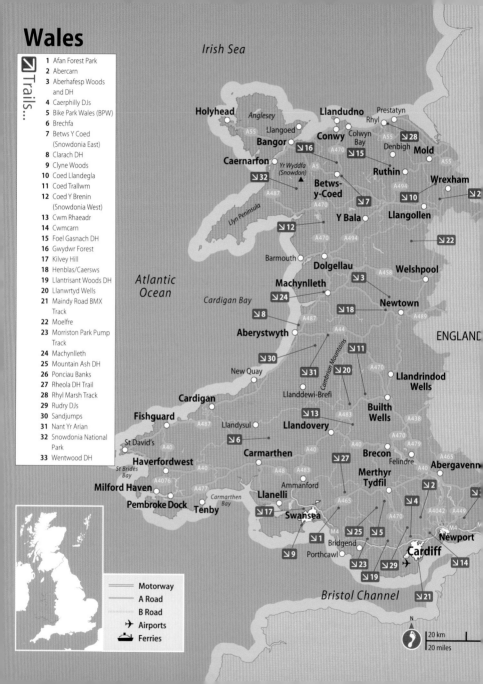

Wales is largely responsible for being the place that kick-started the trail centre experience in the UK. The original centres of north Wales have shaped how and where we ride today. Not that it was ever a case of age before beauty; the original centres sparkle in the shadows of the Snowdonia National Parks Mountains and still cut it today. Add to this the many new centres that have opened over the years throughout Wales and what you get is a strong scene as diverse in its riding styles as it is in its landscapes.

The craggy, rocky and rugged beauty of the north combine with the strong industrial past of the south to make an interesting tour of what, in real terms, is a relatively small country. Luckily for us it is has a big heart and lots to offer the mountain biker.

Culturally, visitors can learn about the heavy industrial past that typifies many regions, and even go down a former working mine at the Big Pit, Blaenafon Torfaen. It is also a pleasure to hear the most widely used Celtic language, Welsh, spoken by the natives and also visit the many beautiful beaches along the Pembrokeshire coast.

As a mountain bike destination Wales seems to serve two distinct markets – the day trippers from the many nearby English towns and cities and those on long weekend or week breaks who tend to base themselves around one or two centres. Look slightly beyond this and you will find a country that offers a great variety of terrain across the different disciplines of biking, from the family holiday to the thrill-seeking downhillers. Wales has got it covered.

Local scene

It might be a bit of overkill to say that mountain biking has saved the Welsh tourism industry, but the sport is definitely bringing in a new generation of visitors to this spectacular corner of the world. From Snowdonia in the north to the Welsh borders, down to the remote, incredibly picturesque valleys in the south, Wales is absolutely chock full with world-class riding spots. And the Welsh know it. Some of the best trail-builders are from this area, the riding scene here is super-strong, and with every passing year the trails get more varied, more interesting and the maps grow larger. Long may it continue.

Top: Winning in Afan!
Above: The Severn Bridge – gateway to the good stuff.
Previous page: Machynlleth. [JUSTIN SULLIVAN PHOTOGRAPHY]

Coed y Brenin. Always good for a 'fork in the road' gag.

Hubs

There are spots of fantastic rides all over the country, but broadly speaking, the XC areas in Snowdonia have the most heritage (Coed y Brenin is widely hailed as the first purpose-built UK trail centre), and with the addition of Machynlleth in the south and Gwydyr Forest and Betws y Coed to the northeast of the National Park, the riding here is still first class. Meanwhile, there are plenty of stand-alone spots such as Moelfre, Aberhafesp and Brechfa, as well as the incredible riding to be found near the seaside resort of Aberystwyth (the Sandjumps trails are a sights to behold). But it's the south Wales spots of Cwmcarn and Afan that now pull in the majority of outside riders to the country. Why? Because they could compete with any trail centre in the world for views, facilities, variety, XC riding, and, in Cwmcarn, downhill tracks.

❺ Best rides in Wales

Wales has a wealth of world-class riding spots, and virtually every one mentioned in the following chapter is worthy of a long journey. But we reckon the following should comprise your 'must visit' list:

❶ Cwmcarn, page 190

Nestled away from the terraced housing below it is Cwmcarn, hiding some incredible XC runs that snake the contours of the valley and the DH runs cut straight down the steep banks. The investment has done wonders making it an incredible spot to ride.

❷ Afan Forest, page 172

With some of the best, flowing singletrack in the whole of the UK, a forest that will take your breath away, and some of the best facilities you'll find at a bike park, it's not hard to see why this rates as our favourite spot in Britain.

❸ Coed y Brenin (Snowdonia West), page 186

Claiming to be the 'home' of UK mountain biking with the first ever purpose-built riding centre, we urge you to take a trip to the edge of the Snowdonia National Park for spectacular views and spectacular riding.

❹ Bike Park Wales, pages 176

The newest gem in Wales has so much on offer. For the downhill lover it's a site you should definitely visit, with some extensive XC to take you back to the top of the DH runs. Don't go to Wales without trying BPW first.

❺ Coed Llandegla, page 182

Otherwise known as One Planet Adventure, Coed Llandegla hosts some superb XC trails that challenge the most experienced downhill riders, and keep a few freeriders smiling as well.

↘1 Afan Forest Park

◉ ◉ ◉ ◉ ◉ ◉ ◉ ◉ ◉ ◉ ◉

Train station Maesteg

Nearest city Swansea

Sat Nav SA13 3HG

Opening times The trails are open 365 days of the year and the only closures are due to forest operations (details of which you can find on the website mbwales.com). Opening times change seasonally but never differ too much. All trails are free to ride but you will have to pay for parking – £1 per day.

Location Afan and Glyncorrwg are easily found, around 15 km to the northeast of Swansea. Exit the M4 at junction 40 and drive north on the A4107 – Afan Valley Road. The Visitor Centre is brown-signposted from the motorway (though make sure you take a left at the first roundabout) but if you're worried about getting lost, go 8 km along the A4107, then turn off at Cymer heading north on Sunnyside Terrace torwards Glyncorrwg. From the A4107 there are signs for either Afan Forest Park, and in Cymer follow Glyncorrwg Mountain Bike Centre.

Facilities/Overview Afan Forest Park is affectionately known as 'little Switzerland' and it offers two Visitor Centres and start/finish points at Afan Argoed and Glyncorrwg. Afan is better suited to the day tripper with Glyncorrwg taking on the flagship role. With eight trails (Rookie, Blue Scar, Blade, Skyline, Whytes level, Y Wal, Penhydd and W2), a bike park and more all-weather singletrack than any of the other Welsh mountain bike centres, this is a must for any keen trail rider. The forest block is also one of Wales' largest and the trails really

DAN MILNER

> **Lowdown**

◉ **Locals do**

Ride the fun bits on the Whytes level before cutting across to the skyline descent.

Relax in the Drop Off café afterwards.

◉ **Locals don't**

Always follow the waymarked routes. There's plenty of routes to find in the forest.

Ride when it's chucking it down.

◉ **Pros**

All-weather riding surface.

Range of difficulty make the forest welcoming to all levels of rider.

Very friendly atmosphere at the centres and on the trails.

◉ **Cons**

Won't satisfy the diehard downhillers or freeriders due to lack of uplift and stunts (though Cwmcarn isn't too far away).

Can be quite exposed when the weather closes in.

do get you into the thick of it. The trails are of a similar style – flowing singletrack – but it is a great riding venue for all bikers as there are as many thrills on the way down as there are views on the climb up. With a stunning Visitor Centre, a bike-friendly attitude, a stable mineral soil (that holds up in all weathers) along with plenty of smaller irregular pieces of rock which combined with the exposed roots, make this one of the UK's best sites.

ISOBEL CAMERON/FORESTRY COMMISSION

XC When visiting Afan Forest, you'll soon find that the trails are predominantly aimed at the XC rider, with long climbs and contouring flowing descents. Inexperienced riders should start with the short blue trail (Blue Scar) and longer Penhydd route (this is a red-graded route) out of the Afan Argoed centre. Technically proficient riders will love the speed they can achieve on the W2 run (which combines The Wall and the Whytes level trails). For those looking for a more tranquil, scenic experience the skyline trail at 46 km is the longest and has long forest road stretches linking singletrack sections where the great vistas can be taken in.

Downhill Although there are no downhill specific trails, many of the descents offer plenty for the downhill rider. Many riders quote the final descent of The Wall as their favourite.

Freeride Afan Forest now has a dedicated bike park for the freerider. Graded black, it has some easier sections to it for the inexperienced rider to try. There are 5 different routes to take through the bike park with berms, jumps and many small drops.

Easy The Rookie trail has been designed for new riders and families, with wide trails and great views. It's a good route to build up confidence.

Hard Starting at either centre the W2 trail is a challenge, linking both the Wall and the Whytes level trail you will ride some 43 km which takes in all the best sections of singletrack in the valley. Whichever way you ride it you will have a café at the half way point and somewhere to have a cup of tea and recall your tales after.

Not to miss The Wall final descent should be done by all who visit the forest park. Oh, and it is possible to uplift the wall final descent using your own vehicle on the public road.

Remember to avoid The long forest road ride along the old railway at the start of the wall – tag onto someone who knows the shortcut!

Nearest Bike/Hire shop Afan Valley Bike Shed is located underneath the Afan Forest Visitor Centre, but there's also Skyline Cycle (T01639 850111) based at both centres.

Local accommodation
If you're travelling in a large group, it's worth trying out the superb log cabins at Bryn Bettws (T01639 644037) situated on the side of the Wall trail and near the bike park. There are also a number of bike-friendly B&Bs in the area perfect for individuals and small groups, as well as camping and caravan spots with electric hook up available at the Glyncorrwg Mountain Bike centre.

Eating Both Visitor Centres offer food although the bike-friendly sized meals in the Drop Off café are not to be missed. The nearest supermarket is in Port Talbot so best to stock up before you drive up the valley.

ⓘ **More info** Afan Argoed Centre (T01639 850564), Glyncorrwg Centre (T01639 851900 or mbwales.com). There are also bike maps available to purchase in the Visitor Centre, or download them from afanforestpark. co.uk.

N2 Abercan

Train station Risca
Nearest city Cardiff
Sat Nav NP11 7EU (roughly)

Location You'll find Abercarn next door to Cwncarn, which is around 9 km north of Newport. Exit the M4 at junction 28 and head north on the A467. Drive past Risca and Crosskeys and head towards Abercarn. Park in the village where you can.

Facilities Snacks and meals are available at the Cwm Carn Forest Visitor Centre during opening hours (see the Cwmcarn page). Evening meals are available in local pubs and restaurants; try the Cross Keys pub.

Rough round-up This downhill track is largely overshadowed by its big brother (and next-door neighbour) Cwmcarn, but the all-weather course here is perfect for those who like their trails a bit more low budget and loose. You can also find some great XC if you head out on the many kilometres of singletrack that criss-cross the woods here or jump on the comp circuit by checking out Dragon Downhill. Many local riders here like to hit the Twrch Trail of Cwmcarn and then head off into Abercarn's unofficial singletrack.

Conditions This is an all-weather site that has been cut through the hill with plenty of switchbacks etc, into the brilliant Welsh forest.

ⓘ **More info** dragondownhill.co.uk.

Opposite page: Abercan.

N3 Aberhafesp Woods and DH

Train station Caersws
Nearest city Welshpool/Shrewsbury
Sat Nav SY16 3HT (for Aberhafesp village centre)

Location Aberhafesp Woods are located around 3 km northwest of Newtown, itself between Welshpool and Aberystwyth in mid-Wales. When driving from Shrewsbury, take the A458 to Welshpool, then the A483 to Newtown. Head north through the town, then take a left onto Milford Road (the B4568) to Aberhafesp. To get to the woods, carry on through the village and after 600 m, take a right, then first right, then first right again and the woods are at the top of this hill.

Facilities Aberhafesp has a few local shops and a pub.

Rough round-up While nearby Henblas Downhill is a popular venue for the comp scene, Aberhavesp is a more mellow venue with plenty of XC to be had in the singletrack throughout the woods, while there are a few DH trails that the locals have added to and strengthened over the years.

Conditions This is very remote land with staggering views and un-populated paths.

N4 Caerphilly DJs

Train station Aber
Nearest city Cardiff
Sat Nav CF83 1LB

Location The extensive dirt jumps in Caerphilly are to the east of the town, which is itself around 5 km to the north of Cardiff. Leave the M4 at junction 32 heading north on the A470 to Pontypridd. After 3 km, take the A468 to Caerphilly town centre. Head through the centre on Nantgarw Road, then take a right onto Castle Street (you'll have to loop around the Castle) then after 200 m take a left onto Van Road. Head down here, past the Goodrich Pub, go straight on at the roundabout and after 1 km, the Coed Parc y Van Forestry Car Park is on the left. The DJs are around 200 m up a dirt track to the right (then right again) off the car park.

Facilities The Goodrich Pub does a mean bit of grub, otherwise central Caerphilly has plenty to offer.

Rough round-up In 2012 the Van Road Trails Group signed a 10-year contract with the Forestry Commission Wales to manage the dirt jumps and trails. This means that the public-access dirt jump site is only going to get more popular with the local mountain bike scene. With this new contract the dirt jumps can be changed at any time, but currently it's a pretty extensive site with a lot going on with fast berms, table-tops, gaps and jumps of every size. The DJs are built with everyone in mind (there are easier lines for less experienced riders) and it's a great place to really progress your own riding. A must for local riders and it's probably worth a trip if you aren't too far away.

Conditions This is a well-maintained site, with a clay-hard packed base all set in an open clearing of forestry commission land. A great set up. Please don't ride them when they're wet, and be sure to fix any damage.

⬐5 Bike Park Wales (BPW)

Train station Pentre Bach
Nearest city Cardiff
Sat Nav CF48 1RA

Opening times Bike Park Wales is open 1000-1800 (weekdays) and 0900-1800 (weekends) during the summer and 0900-1700 during the winter. The car park gate shuts an hour later in both summer and winter to make sure that you don't get locked in. It's £5 for the day to ride or £30 to use the uplift for the day – this includes your £5 riding charge.

Location Bike Park Wales is situated around 5 km south of Merthyr Tydfil and is the newest bike park in Wales. Leave the M4 at junction 32 and drive north on the A470 for around 20 km until you reach a roundabout with the

A470 carrying on ahead of you and the A4060 to your right. Take a left at the roundabout and you will see a large sign for Bike Park Wales. Drive up this road and you will soon reach the Visitor Centre.

Facilities/Overview BPW is one of the newest bike park in Wales and is very close to being one of the best facilities around as well. It's a park that's built by riders, for riders so it's got their best interests at heart! The Visitor Centre has all the information you need as well as maps of the trails themselves – trails which cater to every ability, whether you're a DH enthusiast or a family out for the day. There's a lot on offer here with bike hire, bike shop, café and, if you'd like

ANDY LLOYD

> Lowdown

⊙ Locals do
Pre-book the uplift to take full advantage of all the trails.

Progress quickly with the range of routes here.

⊙ Locals don't
Ride without protective gear.

Disrespect the park. They don't leave litter and they treat others with a smile.

⊘ Pros
A park built by riders for riders, so they know what riders like to ride.

Every day uplift allows you to get the most riding in possible.

⊗ Cons
Uplift can book up quickly.

some tuition, coaching. There is also a daily uplift that runs, but it's best to book this online as spots can run out quickly.

Downhill The downhill trails here are pretty extensive and everyone can try their hand at varying degrees of descent. The hardcore riders amongst you will probably be attracted towards the black runs at Bike Park Wales. That said, a lot of the runs here have tight rock sections, drop offs, jump trails and more, to cater for every level of riding.

XC If you're not using the uplift at Bike Park Wales then you will probably be using the climb route quite a lot. This route links the bottom of the trails to the top (where the uplift will drop you off), but if you're really keen on good XC riding, it's best to head for Afan Forest.

Freeride There's no specific freeride area at BPW but the features on many of these runs will appeal to those of

you that like being in the air more than you like being on the ground. There's also a pump track for riders wanting to progress their bike handling skills.

Easy The green trails are perfect for families and riders that need to build up their confidence before taking on some of the harder runs.

Hard Plenty of the black runs here will test even the more experienced of you out there. There's even a pro line to try out!

Not to miss A well earned meal in the Woodland Café. You'll be riding so much that the food will be a treat.

Remember to avoid Going all out on a hardtail. There are trails for most bikes but the hardtail is the least forgiving bike here.

Nearest Bike/Hire shop There's a bike shop on site at that will fix any problems you have, as well as selling

you the odd clothing item here and there. Bike hire is also located in the same shop with a range of bikes that suit every type of riding. Both can be contacted by calling T07730 382501.

Local accommodation Gethin Lodge (T02920 883781) is less than a mile away from the bike park and has secure lock-up for bikes as well as a bike wash; another location designed for bikers by bikers. Castle Hotel (T01685 386868) is the nearest hotel to the park for those of you that prefer to keep away from self catering.

Eating The Woodland Café on site serves breakfast, lunch and snacks every day, and is open 1000-1700 weekdays and 0900-1700 on weekends in the summer (0900-1600 all week during the winter).

ⓘ **More info** For any info on the park itself, prices or closures, check out the Bike Park Wales website, bikeparkwales.com.

ISOBEL CAMERON/FORESTRY COMMISSION

Train station Llandovery

Nearest city Swansea

Sat Nav SA32 7SN

Opening times The trails are open 365 days of the year, day and night, and the only closures will be due to forest operations. You can find details of these on the website mbwales.com.

Location Brechfa is the name given to the open countryside near the town of Abergorlech between the towns of Carmarthen, Lampeter and Llandeilo, around 30 km north of Swansea and to the west of the Brecon Beacons. Head all the way to the end of the M4 (junction 49), where it turns into the A48. Keep on this road for around 10 km, then head towards the National Botanic Garden on the B4310 (also in the direction of Nantgaredig). Continue on this road to Brechfa (a total journey of around 12 km). Abergorlech is another 6 km along this road with the Forestry Commission Car Park clearly signed to the left.

Facilities/Overview The XC and DH trails at Brechfa have caused quite a stir in both their design and their construction, traversing through stunning mixed woodland of ash, beech and conifer, the routes are fast and flowing and sure to bring a grin to any rider from the novice to the experts – all these factors make this one of the best mountain bike venues in Wales. The Gorlech red route will challenge the experienced cyclist and peak adrenaline levels while the green and blue Derwen trails starting at Brwrgwm car park are gentler, but

still flow amazingly well and are great for novice mountain bikers. Brechfa is a shale area and the trails have been built using this shale mixed with the soils to give a really smooth, hard and fast trail surface that never gets muddy – it does get wet though.

Downhill The descents on the blue and red trails, especially the final descent of the red, have earned popular following among the downhill crowd due to their speed, features and flow. Despite this, there are no official trails in Brechfa forest, but even the most hardcore downhill rider will have fun.

XC The waymarked trails in Brechfa make it a fantastic cross country riding area as they take you through stunning forest. There are also plenty of trails to be found away from the waymarkers, all you have to do is go exploring. Brechfa is a different style trail to its Welsh counterparts, with a

ISOBEL CAMERON/FORESTRY COMMISSION

much smoother trail surface and more obvious descents with features to maintain flow.

Freeride The obstacles that have been designed into the XC trails such as tabletops and step up jumps, natural wallrides and northshore obstacles makes up for the lack of a designated freeride area. The additions make these trails fun for all to ride.

Easy The green Derwen trail is an easy start for all riders and has an extended blue loop to push you that little bit further. The blue descent back down to the green trail is one of the best in the forest.

Hard Starting in Bwrgwm it is possible to follow the black trail out from the car park and link it into the red route before returning back following the black waymarkers. This will however be one big ride, around 45 km with five climbs. Anyone completing this will be feeling it for days to come, but it takes in all the best sections and has some amazing views.

Not to miss The food (well earned) at the Black Lion!

Remember to avoid Riding too far out on your first visit. You're a long way from help so keep it in mind!

Nearest Bike/Hire shop You won't find a bike shop in the Brechfa Forest area so have all supplies on you – food and tools. The nearest shop with a good range of stock for repairing high end bikes is Summit Cycles in Aberstwyth (T01970 626061).

Local accommodation
There are a few B&Bs but try local bike enthusiasts Carl and Ivy at Bike Brechfa (T01558 685811) who can accommodate you and guide you around Brechfa's hidden corners.

Eating You'll do well to beat the food in the Black Lion (T01558 685271) in Abergorlech where the red Gorlech trail starts.

ⓘ **More info** Aberystwyth Tourist Info (T01970 612125, mbwales.com) and bikebrechfa.co.uk.

> **Lowdown**

❶ Locals do
Ride most of the more challenging optional sections on the trail.

Always take in the blue descent as part of their rides.

❷ Locals don't
Hang about – the style of the trail helps develop fitness, skill and speed.

❸ Pros
Pretty, rural part of Wales with some of the best riding out there.

Best beginner green and blue trails for novices and kids that contain real mountain biking singletrack.

❹ Cons
Limited facilities on site.

The shale can be slippery when very wet.

↘7 Betws Y Coed (Snowdonia East)

◎ ◉ ◎ ◎ ◎ ◎ ◎ ◎ ◎ ◎

Train station Betws y Coed
Nearest city Chester
Sat Nav LL24 0AE for the Visitor Centre

Location Betws Y Coed is a popular, touristy village (often called the Outdoor Capital of Wales) on the northeast edge of the Snowdonia National Park and is the park's official gateway. When driving from the west, coming in on either the A55 from Chester or the A5 from Shrewsbury, turn onto the A470 which leads directly to Betws Y Coed.

Facilities The Snowdonia National Park Visitor Centre is the gateway to the national park and well signed from Betws Y Coed town centre. It has a café and all the amenities you could wish for. However, where the trails start (at the forestry car park), there are few facilities, so take your supplies on the short ride from Betws town.

Rough round-up Betws Y Coed is a beautiful alpinesque village, much

of which was built in Victorian times. It is also the principal village of the 1200 sq km Snowdonia National Park and situated where the River Conwy meets its three tributaries flowing from the west – the Llugwy, the Lledr and the Machno. Surrounded by mountains with cascading waterfalls, hill-top lakes, river pools and ancient bridges, it is clear why Betws is such a popular destination. With all this rugged beauty and terrain it wasn't long before bikers caught on and started riding in the area and the forestry commission developed a purpose built trail first at Gwydwr Forest to the north, and later added the Penmachno and Mynydd Cribau trails.

Terrain The trails here benefit from some incredible views as they're set in some of the most beautiful forest in the UK. With everything from technical riding through to gentle meanders, some would say this is quite an old school place to ride – something that can often be a plus!

XC There's two main routes here, The Marin trail and Penmachno routes (either 25 km or 30 km loops), and they both have an honesty box at the start. The Marin trail takes in a lot of the forest as the majority of the climbs are on forest road and tracks, allowing you to take in the incredible scenery. The descents take in tight singletrack, that is technical and rocky as well as open and flowing lines through dark forest and exposed ridgelines. The Penmachno trail is similar to the Marin trail as it takes in plenty of scenery but also throw in stream crossings and elevated wood sections. Interestingly, the geology in this region is ancient, with some of the oldest rocks in the world found here; again this translates well into the trails, with many rocky sections that make for great singletrack.

Downhill There is no specific DH track here, but head north into Gwydwr Forest and you'll find plenty of unofficial trails.

Dirt Jumps/Freeride The challenge of the hidden DH trails, which are very technical, are the only outlet for freeriders. Betws Y Coed does not offer the freerider any features itself.

Conditions The XC routes are hard-packed dirt singletrack. The area is popular with walkers but well known as a mountain biking centre so expect to see plenty of bikes.

ⓘ **More info** Snowdonia National Park Visitor Centre, T01690 710426, mbwales.com or betws-y-coed.co.uk.

SNOWDONIA-GUIDES.CO.UK

⛰8 Clarach DH

XC DH FR

Train station Aberystwyth
Nearest city Aberystwyth
Sat Nav SA43 3LN (to Cardigan Bay Holiday Park)

Location Clarach is just to the south of Cardigan Bay Holiday Park, a huge expanse of caravans on the coast around 1 km north of Aberystwyth. Heading into Aberystwyth from the west, you'll be arriving on the A44. Just before arriving at the town centre, take the A487 back out of town in the direction of Machynlleth. After 800 m take a left onto the B4572 and after about 1 km you'll see Cardigan Bay Caravan Park signposted off to the left. Head down here, park at the site, and ride into the woods to the south of the caravans.

Facilities Cardigan Bay Holiday Park has plenty of facilities and amenities, though perhaps a little inflated in price. Aberystwyth is a short ride away and full of shops and students!

Rough round-up This is a downhill site with a few short, but feature-full trails through the woods. The views over the bay area are beautiful, and there's plenty of XC riding with drops, jumps and flowing lines for the freeriders. Add in Nant Yr Arian nearby, plus the impressive Sandjumps (not to mention Machynlleth up the road), and there's plenty of first class riding to be had in this old seaside resort. Plus it's a very happening town with a lively university.

Conditions This is forest land next to the sea, with spaced trees and great soil for building features. Plenty of chicken lines or decent jumps for the brave, including a road gap.

⛰9 Clyne Woods

XC DH FR

Train station Swansea
Nearest city Swansea
Sat Nav SA3 5AS

Location You'll find Clyne Woods to the southwest of Swansea, just north of the Mumbles. Leave the M4 at junction 47 and head south towards Swansea centre on the A483. After 4 km, take a right onto the A4216 heading to Cockett and Black Pill. After 2 km, take a right into the coastal road (Mumbles Road, the A4067) and head towards Black Pill. Just after the Shell Garage on your right, follow the brown bike sign off to the right and park at either Clyne Valley Country Park (here at sea level), or climb up Derwen Fawr Road, then take a left onto Ynys Newydd Road (signed to the recycling centre), and take a left just before into the higher Clyne Woods car park (though this is locked at night).

Facilities Nearby Black Pill is the place to head to for shops and amenities, but the sea level Clyne Valley Country Park has hot and cold snacks available.

Rough round-up You probably wouldn't travel that far to session Clyne Woods, but for local Swansea riders, this makes a welcome change to other, bigger trail centres nearby, and features some impressive dirt jumps, northshore, a load of freeride drops and bombholes, and some feature full (if not short), DH trails. Alongside this, the new pump track was introduced to Clyne Woods recently, something that is popular with all levels of mountain bike rider. All set in some spectacular scenery.

Conditions During winter, expect it to be muddy, but it generally drains fairly well, and is a mixture of woodland and cleared, DJ area with solid, buildable land. Be sure to fix any casings on the DJs.

ⓘ **More info** The MTB Pigs is a Swansea-based mountain biking club whose website contains info about Clyne and other local XC routes, mtbpigs.co.uk.

⊾10 Coed Llandegla

Train station Wrexham General/
Wrexham Central

Nearest city Chester/Wrexham

Sat Nav LL11 3AA

Opening times The trails are open 365 days a year and you can ride them at any time. The only time there are trail closures are usually down to forest operations so check the website before leaving. The café and bike shop have varied opening times from Tuesday through to Sunday but are closed on Mondays. All trails are free although there is an all day car park fee currently of £4.50.

ONE PLANET ADVENTURE

Location Coed Llandegla Forest is located right next to the A525, only 10 km west of Wrexham. When driving from the northwest, take the A483 south from Chester towards Wrexham then take the A525 west, signposted towards Ruthin. When driving from the Ruthin area, take the A525 east towards Wrexham. Coed Llandegla Forest is signed from the road.

Facilities/Rough round-up

Coed Llandegla, otherwise known as One Planet Adventure, has an incredible set up with four well-maintained XC trails featuring plenty of technical riding with a green, blue, red and black trail to test all abilities. There's an excellent Visitor Centre with the One Planet Café, bike shop and workshop for all your mechanical, thirst and food needs. Due to its proximity to Chester and some of the northwest cities, it's hugely popular. Perfect for families too or for those who simply want to have a lovely meander in the forest.

Downhill In keeping with most of the Welsh trail centres Llandegla does not offer any specific downhill runs, but it does have plenty to keep the downhill rider entertained. Used by many pro riders to have a fun blast while keeping the fitness levels up, Llandegla throws berms, tabletops and plenty of whoops that will keep you manualling and jumping through the fun black sections. Not suited to long travel DH bikes though.

XC You'll find that all four of the XC routes at Llandegla are suitable for the XC rider as even the most technical black sections can be rolled through safely at moderate speed. The trail lengths range from short family loops of 5 km, to 12 km for the blue, 18 km for the red and the black at 21 km.

Freeride There is no specific freeride area but if you're a freerider looking to develop your skills here, you should check out the black runs as they hold various jumps of different sizes –

perfect to learn and progress on. There are no big obstacles here so more skilled riders won't be challenged, but for the majority there is plenty of fun to be had. Dirt jumpers and pure freeriders looking for drops might like to take a trip back towards Wrexham, where Bwlchgwyn Quarry (just off the road, in the town of Bwlchgwyn) has some decent terrain.

Easy Follow the novice (blue) trail around the loop and back to the centre. Too easy? Take the intermediate (red) loop as well after lunch.

Hard Take the black route. Each black section is a loop branching off the intermediate trail, so if you enjoy it, loop back around and hit the section again.

Not to miss Those pumpy, swoopy black sections.

Remember to avoid Not contributing. The parking fee is put back into the trails: please pay.

Nearest Bike/Hire shop The One Planet bike shop (T01978 751656) at the Llandegla Visitor Centre stocks many parts and accessories and you can hire bikes from them. Elsewhere there is a good shop in Chester, The Edge Cycleworks (T01244 323580) which stocks a wide range of brands.

☺ **Locals do**
Socialise at the centre, a great place to chat mountain biking with your fellow rider

Session the black runs.

Learn to manual over the wooden northshore bridge.

☹ **Locals don't**
Always follow the waymarked routes. It's great to find your own shortcut.

Try and out-jump local builder Jason Rennie (he set the world long jump record here at 134 ft!).

✔ **Pros**
The trails are enjoyable to all.

Very relaxed vibe.

✖ **Cons**
You will have to stay elsewhere and commute.

Some doubletrack can be quite boring for the more experienced.

Local accommodation
If you're after a place to stay you are better off looking towards Wrexham or Chester as Llandegla has nothing on site. Both Wrexham and Chester have a wide range of accommodation on offer. In Wrexham try Windings (T01978 721114) for bed and breakfast. For reasonable prices, just to look at the range of accommodation in Chester, look at visitchester.com.

Eating The One Planet café in the log cabin-style Visitor Centre is the place to eat when you're hitting the trails. Run by enthusiastic bikers, they know exactly what you need. Also home to an award-winning bacon sandwich.

ⓘ **More info** One Planet Centre (T01978 751656), Chester tourist info (T01244 402111), Wrexham tourist info (T01978 292015, coedllandegla.com).

Wales Coed Llandegla

⟨↘11⟩ Coed Trallwm

Train station Llanwrtyd
Nearest city Cardiff
Sat Nav LD5 4TS

Location Coed Trallwm is situated around 6 km north of Llanwrtyd Wells, right in the heart of Wales. When driving from Llanwrtyd, take the A483 northwest out of town and in the direction of Beulah. Here, just before you cross the river into the village, take a left on the road signposted to Abergwesyn. Just 5 km up this road the Coed Trallwm Mountain Bike Centre is clearly signed on the right.

Facilities The mountain bike centre has a café with a log-burning stove and serves hot and cold drinks alongside food. It currently closes in the winter

but do check with their website before heading there (see below). They also provide riders with several delightful, self-catering cottages that are available to rent, sleeping from between 2-10 people. If you don't wish to stay overnight, remember that you have to pay £2 to park your car, but this gives you complete access to ride the forest.

Rough round-up This is a privately-owned area with some fantastic singletrack for riders of all abilities (although there are no trails for complete beginners), plus some fantastic facilities and incredibly beautiful cottages available for those looking for a weekend – or longer – retreat. The forest holds three waymarked trails: blue, a gentle 4 km loop with a 95 m climb and descent;

red, a little tougher than the blue but the 140 m climb is all worthwhile as it holds some beautiful singletrack; and black, a 5 km, 155 m tough climb with some spectacular views at the top. The trails are well made and packed full of features, and the area is a great stop-off for the fantastic riding in nearby Llanwrtyd Wells and the varied and natural Elan Valley singletrack. There is also more unofficial riding above and around the Trallwm site but not waymarked.

Conditions This is a well-maintained site, but still quite raw so it can be muddy in the winter.

ⓘ **More info** Call the Coed Trallwm Visitor Centre on T01591 610546, coedtrallwm.co.uk.

Top riding tips Josh Bryceland

Josh Bryceland is the 2007 and 2008 UCI World Cup Jr Downhill Champion as well as the winner of the 2014 UCI World Cup Downhill. Here are his 5 tips for better riding and five spots to try them out on…

❶ Drops

Most people lean back heavily. They lift the forks up and hope to land on the back wheel. Really though you want to soak up the drop, so if it's about a foot, you try and push the bike into the floor. Ride towards the drop, get over the back wheel and compress into the bike before you've left the ground. As you leave, extend your legs and arms and push the bike into the floor as quick as you can. If it's a bigger drop, compress before the drop like before, then stay in that position with the bike and push the bike to meet the floor. Best place to learn them? I reckon a really good place to try them out is at the skills training centre at Fort William. They've got really good drops of all size.

❷ Cornering

Common mistakes are probably where you don't commit or if you brake while you're in the turn. I reckon it's best if you do all the braking before the corner, then just lean in to it, commit, and look as far out of the turn as possible. If you look at the middle of the corner, you're not committing to the turn as much as if your look all the way to the end. Try it, it really works! A place that has good corners is Llandegla in Wales. There's a cross country trail with loads of berms all the way round it that's amazing to lean into and bank it.

❸ Jumps

In downhill, the most common mistake is when people just launch off a booter and just pull up on the bars. What you want to do is look for a jump, roll at it a few times, judge the speed and let the jump do the work. Try and land with both wheels at the same time, keep you eye on the landing and try and get your wheels parallel to the landing. I never use my brakes when I'm in the air, but I always have, finger on each brake lever at all times. Cwmcarn is perfect for practicing 'cos there's a track with some cool small jumps at the top and they get bigger as you go down.

❹ Braking

A common mistake is people just locking up the back wheel because they're only using one brake. Remember you should have two levers, and the front brake works just as much if not more than the back brake. So you want to use both evenly. Also try braking as hard and as late as possible. If you just use your back brake you'll simply skid as you come into the corner, if you use both you'll be more in control. A good place to try this out – where there are loads of steep sections – is Hamsterly 'cos it's pretty steep at the bottom so it's all about being good on your brakes.

❺ Save energy and keep focused

A lot of people burn themselves out 'cos they can't save their energy on longer routes like at Fort William. Any downhill course over two minutes long – unless you're incredibly fit – you can't ride the top sections and push on it. If you're riding a really long course, and you're pedalling, remember to breathe a really deep breath, and save some energy at the bottom because you won't make up on a short pedalling section what you lose if you're tired and bouncing off roots and rocks and getting messed up in the trees. Have a sit down on an easier section, and take some deep breaths. If it's smooth give your hands a quick shake and get back into it! A good place to try this out? Try Fort William's DH track – it's really long, and is proper knackering.

ⓚ ⓓ ⓝ ⓒ ⓖ ⓐ ⓔ ⓕ

Train station Talsarnau
Nearest city Welshpool
Sat Nav LL41 4YA

Opening times The trails are open 365 day a year and the only closures on trails will be due to forest operations. Details are usually posted on the website, mbwales.com. All trails are free to ride but you will have to pay a fee for parking your car. It's £4 for a day, £2 for three hours and £1 for one hour. All money helps the upkeep of the trails.

Location Coed Y Brenin nestles in the heart of the Snowdonia National Park. Leave the M6 and take the M54, heading west past Telford, the A5 around Shrewsbury and then the A458 through Welshpool. Once you've past Welshpool, head for Dolgellau on the A470 (it's signposted), then at the village turn north on the A470 where after 7 km there's a well-signed right into the Coed Y Brenin Visitor Centre.

Facilities/Rough round-up For many years this was the UK's flagship trail centre, and the trails at Coed Y Brenin have led to the evolution of many new venues across the country. Its name means 'forest of the kings' which is an apt moniker for this large block of forestry containing over 21,000 acres. The area is a rugged former volcanic region with many mineral deposits that have been mined for years. For those interested there is a geology trail from the fantastic multi-million pound Visitor Centre. For the biker though, this means it there is an incredibly hard-wearing rocky surface to rip through the forest on. The trails hug beautiful, river-carved valleys with technical rock features and climb out over untamed mountain tops.

Mountain biking is huge in Coed Y Brenin and the whole region has really taken to the development of the bike centre and its trails. When you add the drama of southern Snowdonia's mountain views and the very real possibility of seeing the magnificent red kites circling overhead, it makes for a great day in the saddle. Although many of the trails have been recently re-named, many insist on calling the trails by their old names. So you don't get too confused on the hill, the Red Bull trail is now known as the Tarw (Welsh for bull), the MBR route remains and the old Karrimor trail is now affectionately known as The Beast!

XC You'll soon understand why Coed Y Brenin is classed as an XC riders mecca – it's the original British cross country trail centre. There are nine trails in total with the added extra of

ISOBEL CAMERON/FORESTRY COMMISSION

a skills area. Coed Y Brenin has one green trail, two blue, three red and three black, clearly showing that there's something here for every ability of rider. The longest route in the park is the well loved and aptly named, Beast. At 38 km, it's a trail that will test even the most experienced rider, so make sure you're fully stocked up with supplies before you go!

Downhill Coed Y Brenin doesn't cater to the downhill rider as all trails are built with gentle gradients and there's no uplift. However, downhillers often rider here on trail or cross country bikes though as the terrain offers some technical challenge and the loops offer a good days riding away from the downhill bike.

Freeride Built in 2013, Y Ffowndri is a new addition to the trails here and is the perfect place to hone your bike skills before taking on one of the longer routes. There's a pump track here with hip jumps, double rollers and berms but it's the technical rock lines here that will really get you used to the mountain trails. Not perfect for those of you who are budding freeriders looking for a day full of jumps – it's not going to be a park for you.

Easy If you really consider yourself a novice, then the best trail for you will be the family trail (Yr Afon). It's a gentle 11 km ride and perfect for beginners. The Minortaur loops are blue-graded and short as well if you fancied a little bit tougher of a ride but not as long.

Hard The only really physically challenging route is the black trail 'the Beast' at 38 km long and with a ride time of between 3-6 hrs depending on

fitness, it will leave you ready for some coffee and cake back at the café.

Not to miss The chance to ride on an all-weather surface stone path! They're fantastic.

Remember to avoid Forgetting any spare parts or tools you might need. A puncture can mean a very long walk back!

Nearest Bike/Hire shop Beics Brenin is the bike shop that's on site. They also hire bikes out to the public so call in here for hire, spares and repairs (T01341 440728).

Local accommodation There are a number of places to stay near to the forest, such as Tyn-Y-Groes Hotel (T01341 440275) which has warm beds, good meals and quality ales, as well as having a secure lock-up for bikes. If you want to stay closer to the trails you can cycle to them easily from the Ferndale (T01341 440247) which can accommodate up to 24 people and is bike friendly and reasonably priced.

Eating There's a café on site that serves good food to hungry bikers and

can keep your energy levels topped up. Their venison burger has venison that comes from the forest park itself! In Dolgellau, try Y Sospan (T01341 423174), once the town courthouse and jail, now serves food all day.

ⓘ **More info** Coed Y Brenin Visitor Centre (T01341 440742), Dolgellau Tourist info (T01341 422888) or try mbwales.com

---

> **Lowdown**

☺ **Locals do**
Wear many layers in the winter, as it can be cold on the hill tops.

Test their rock-riding skills in the bike park first to give them a taste of the trails.

☹ **Locals don't**
Ride much else other than XC.

Use super lightweight tyres – they will tear and puncture.

✔ **Pros**
Unique stone pitching throughout the trails, interesting to ride and weatherproof.

Area is very bike friendly.

Trails will satisfy every level of XC riders

✘ **Cons**
Won't satisfy the diehard downhillers or freeriders due to lack of uplift and features.

Cwm Rhaeadr

Train station Sugar Loaf/Llanwrtyd
Nearest city Cardiff
Sat Nav SA20 0SR

Location Cwm Rhaeadr can be found roughly 64 km north of Swansea, pretty much in the middle of South Wales. Follow signs for Cilycwm from the A483 (near Llandovery). Once in Cilycwm village continue northwards towards Llyn Brianne Reservoir until signs for Cwm Rhaeadr are seen.

Facilities Predominantly XC trails originally built by local master trail builder and pro-rider, Rowan Sorrell. It's a single red-graded trail around 7 km in length and climbs up to great views of the Tywi Valley, before dropping back down through the Douglas Fir forest. Apart from the great trail, there is not much on offer in terms of infrastructure.

Rough round-up While this is only a relatively small area of Forestry Commission land, the trails have been designed by and for mountain bikers. It's a great forest ride with technical sections and holds something for everyone. The climb up takes on a lot of fire roads, but the route down will leave you smiling and wanting more.

Terrain Steeper and mostly singletrack with technical section with variable surface types.

XC With tabletops, berms and drops all across this XC loop, it's an incredibly fun trail. However, this has been designed as an all-abilities trail so even beginners can roll over all the obstacles, while experts can go as hard as their talent allows. The trail starts and finishes in a small forestry car park, from there it's a long gentle climb up the forest road until you reach the singletrack which steepens and switches back up the steep hill side. This takes you to the highest point and the views out over the valley and waterfall are stunning. From here, there is an option to leave the waymarked trail and follow the bridleway out onto the Mynydd Mallaen for a much longer ride. Sticking with the main trail, it's a fun blast all the way back to the car park with berms, jumps, bombholes and loose shale. Whilst in the area, it is worth riding some of the natural trails up at Llyn Brianne.

Downhill Some parts of the descent have some nice DH riding, but there's no set DH trail.

Dirt Jumps/Freeride Like the DH aspect, there is no jump and park area. That said, there are several lines through the trail that incorporate tabletops, medium steps and drops.

Conditions The XC routes are hard-packed dirt singletrack designed specifically for mountain biking and usually in very good condition.

ⓘ **More info** Cwm Rhaeadr has its own website on the Forestry Commission website forestry.gov.uk, while mbwales.com is always the place to head.

ALEX GANN

⬃14 Cwmcarn

Ⓚ ⑪ ⑩ ⑪ ⊚ ⊚ ⊚ ⑦ ⑪ ⊙ Ⓐ
⊖ ⑦

Train station Risca

Nearest city Newport

Sat Nav NP11 7EU

Opening times The trails are open
365 days a year, day and night. The only
closures are due to forest operations
and details are posted on the website
mbwales.com, all trails are free. Uplift
pass £26-£29.50 per day depending on
whether you use it at the weekend or not.

Location Cwmcarn is a small town
to the northwest of Newport in South
Wales. It's easily found off the M4 as
well. Exit the M4 at junction 28 and
head north on the A467, past Risca
and Crosskeys towards Abercarn. The
Cwmcarn Visitor Centre is found by
following the brown Forest Drive signs
off to the right.

Facilities/Rough round-up Cwmcarn
Forest drive is an incredibly pretty little
valley that's tucked away from the
terraced housing below it, and it is up
here that you find excellent trails that
either cling to its contours or dissect
them diving down steeply to the valley
floor. With Cwmdown, which is perhaps
the most efficient uplift service currently
operating in the UK, you'll be able to
make the most out of the hill. The terrain
here is made up of steep-sided valleys
while the soil is excellent; loamy and
buff on the lesser known local trails and
super hardpacked on the main routes
ensuring it drains very well. This makes
Cwmcarn a great place to get out on the
bike when the weather isn't so kind.

XC There are two main XC trails at
Cwmcarn, one being the Twrch trail

and the other being Cafall. The Twrch trail is suited to those with some previous off-road experience and high level of fitness as the climb is quite tough. The Cafall trail is similar to the Twrch trail as riders will need good fitness to deal with the tough climbs and the steep, technical descents. There's also plenty of other XC trails to find if you explore in any direction, but these two waymarked trails are enough to keep you going.

Downhill One of the extreme runs that will test you to the limits of your ability is the Y Mynydd downhill track. It's super fast with some big lines and has the availability of smaller, easier jumps. One fact is constant though: everything is rollable. At 1.9 km, it's probably not suited to the total beginner, but anyone with some previous downhill experience will get plenty of thrills out of this course. Either ride up the Twrch to the start or use the Cwmdown uplift service for plenty of runs.

Freeride There's a small freeride area at the top of the Twrch trail with some drops, tabletops and berms. Many freeriders will be found sessioning the bottom section of the downhill course perfecting their jumping skills.

Easy For complete novices and young children, make use of the Brecon-Monmouth canal which is perfect for gentle rides. Riders with off-road experience should take in the Twrch trail.

Hard Those wanting a challenge would be best trying the Pedalhounds trail, a new trail at Cwmcarn. A quick run that ends where the uplift begins!

Not to miss Cwmcarn boasts probably the best uplift service currently running in the UK. Cwmdown can transport up to 40 riders on a weekend. A full day ticket is between £26-£29.50 but you can expect anything up to 13 runs! Online booking at cwmdown.co.uk

Remember to avoid Accidentally hitting the infamous quarry jump on the DH course.

Nearest Bike/Hire shop For those of you needing basic spares and supplies on the hill, the Visitor Centre will be able to supply you with what you need. For more urgent repairs and hire go to Martin Ashfield Cycles in Risca and for specialist parts try Sunset MTB in Cardiff.

Local accommodation
For B&B, try the bike-friendly Coed Mangu Guest House (T01495 270657) situated in the village at the foot of the forest drive. The forest drive has a campsite with electrical hook up. For those looking for a more cosmopolitan stay, nearby Cardiff and Newport offer plenty of accommodation for all budgets.

Eating Snacks and meals are available in the Ravens Café during opening hours (0930-1600 Saturday to Thursday and 0930-1530 Friday). Evening meals are available in local pubs and restaurants; the Cross Keys has simple bar meals or try Vittorio's (T01633 840261) in Newport for a good restaurant meal.

ⓘ **More info** Cwmcarn Forest Drive (T01633 850864), website mbwales.com.

⊕ **Locals do**
Have lots of secret trails – you'll never find them all!

Use the Cwmdown uplift service to get the most out of their days and get some extra descents in.

⊖ **Locals don't**
Always park at the centre; many incorporate the centre's trails into longer rides, parking elsewhere.

Go straight for the black runs, they take on the reds first to build up confidence.

✔ **Pros**
A centre that offers all kinds of riding, XC/DH/FR.

A great local riding scene with lots of trails.

✘ **Cons**
You'll wish you had three bikes.

Theft of bikes and bike gear can be a problem from the car park.

CHRIS MORAN

Wales Cwmcarn

⬇15 Foel Gasnach DH

⊛ ⊛ ⊛ ⊛ ⊘ ⊙ ⊛ ⊙

Train station Colwyn Bay
Nearest city Chester
Sat Nav LL15 2DN (Cyffylliog)

Location Foel Gasnach is a much loved, remote downhill area around 10 km west of Ruthin, deep in the Welsh hills, to the east of Snowdonia National Park. Heading west from Chester on the A55, or from the A5 from Shrewsbury, turn off towards Ruthin on the A494 (from either north or south). At Ruthin, head north on the A525 in the direction of Denbigh, and then after 1.5 km turn off to the left heading towards Bontuchel first, then Cyffylliog. At Cyffylliog, take the second left, heading southwest, and carry on down this road for 2 km, then take the first right at the crossroads just after the red phone box. Stay on this road and take the first left after a large turn-around.

Facilities Cyffylliog has a small shop and the Red Lion Pub, but in terms of facilities by the trails, there are none. The downhill tracks are in the middle of nowhere so it's best to take your own supplies.

Rough round-up This is easily one of the best downhill sites in Wales and has been built in conjunction with the Forestry Commission as well as a hardcore team of local riders. Fantastic due to the ability to do self-uplifts (as long as you have a vehicle and a spare driver!) and loved by more advanced riders. Definitely not for beginners due to large drops, big gaps and the presence of danger at every turn.

Do remember that to ride here you will need to join the FDHR club – this costs £10 for the year, trails are open 7 days a week and the money goes into their upkeep.

Terrain When it comes to unofficial singletrack, there's plenty to explore and discover, but the majority of the routes here are fire-road if you want to do some exploring.

XC There is XC riding to be had but this is downhill territory so you'll pretty much only see full suspension rigs.

Downhill There are four downhill trails here, each one with a 100 m vertical drop and each a very technical few minutes of your life with steep sections, big jumps and even bigger drops. Foel Gasnach was formed after the loss of the infamous 'Scouse' track in Nannarch. In general the trails are

rooty and can be pretty slick in the wet. It is possible to do a lot of runs in a day here and there is a good local scene. The track (and club) are run along with the Forestry Commission and have plenty of comps on through the summer and autumn.

Freeride There's no specific freeride but it's certain that freeriders will enjoy the large drops and impressive gaps.

Conditions The downhill here is largely in Forestry Commission land, very remote, and very prone to bad conditions after rain. However, there has been a huge amount of time invested in bridging problem areas and making the tracks weatherworthy, but still best avoided after periods of rain.

ⓘ **More info** foeldhriders.com has all the info you might need.

16 Gwydwr Forest

⊗ ⊕ ⊖ ⊙ ⊚ ⊛ ⊜ ⊝ ⊞

Train station Betwys y Coed
Nearest city Chester
Sat Nav LL26 0LB for Llanrwst town centre

Location Gwydyr Forest is only around 1 km southwest of the town of Llanrwst, which is on the northeast edge of the Snowdonia National Park. From the west, coming in on either the A55 from Chester or the A5 from Shrewsbury, turn onto the A470 which heads directly to Llanrwst. Once in town, head over the river and towards the national park on the B5106 (clearly signed to Snowdonia), then as you near Gwydyr Castle turn left up a minor road into the forest and take the first forest road on your left. The Marin Trail is clearly waymarked from here, and parking is available at Nant Cottage, the start of the trail.

Facilities For supplies, the town of Llanrwst is your best bet, or nearby Betws Y Coed has a fantastic mountain bike and forest Visitor Centre.

Rough round-up Gwydyr Forest is home to the Marin Gwydyr Trail, as well as a whole host of unofficial singetrack routes, fire-roads, bridleways and some secret downhill trails. In addition, some of the loops take in the Betws Y Coed area, and the two mountain bike centres are inter-twinned and an absolute must for lovers of beautiful XC riding.

Terrain There's plenty of unofficial and waymarked singletrack, but also a fair bit of fire-road and bridleway.

XC The Marin Gwydyr Trail is a 25 km loop with a 450 m climb/descent that has some technical and rocky riding with stunning views and was one of the first purpose-built trails in the country. Even if forest road isn't to your taste, the singletrack is very good and a novice cyclist should be able to complete the loop perhaps walking the odd section in around 2-4 hours.

FORESTRY COMMISSION

Wales Gwydwr Forest

Downhill Gwydyr Forest is littered with a lot of steep and technical flowing trails, and because of this it's long been a stomping ground and training place for much of North Wales' downhill contingent. It is important to realise that these are not officially recognised, so you will require some local knowledge to find them.

Dirt Jumps/Freeride The freeriders of you out there won't find any specific features but some of the hidden downhill trails should keep you happy.

Conditions This is a well-maintained route, with plenty of shale and rock that drains well, and is almost an all-weather area.

ⓘ **More info** The Forestry Commission website (forestry.gov.uk) has a page on Gwydyr Forest; try Beics Betws in Betws y Coed, T01690 710766, while Llanrwst has lots of info on its site, llanrwst.net.

⊻17 Kilvey Hill

🚲 🚶

Train station Swansea

Nearest city Swansea

Sat Nav SA1 7AP (roughly – it's an access road for the tower, no postcode)

Location Kilvey Hill can be found to the east of Swansea city centre. Leave the M4 at junction 45 and take the Neath Road (A4067) south towards Swansea. Go straight on at every

CHRIS MORAN

roundabout until you reach the football stadium on your left, from here take the brown signs for the Marina (first exit on the roundabout just after the stadium, straight on at the next roundabout, second exit at the next, then take the first left after this roundabout into Pentrechwyth Road), and first right off this road into the Kilvey Hill car park and start of the sculpture trail.

Facilities Swansea is a major city with plenty of amenities and shops.

Rough round-up When it comes to inner-city riding, this 193-m-tall descent is one of the best out there, and the views from the top are brilliant – Swansea city centre, docks, bay, Neath, Port Talbot etc… However, it can be popular with other users.

Perhaps this is why the trail – while technically a DH trail – has been adapted (largely by the Swansea student riding population) into more of a freeride trail with plenty of jumps and features that'll please those who love to be in the air. Worth checking out Kilvey and Clyne Woods if you're in the area and for local riders this is one of the best city sites in the UK. There is an access road up to the tower (head into Pentrechwyth and take a right up the hill), but it is for 4x4s only, and the gate is often locked.

Conditions Best avoided after heavy downpours despite how well the hill drains.

ⓘ **More info** Check out the Swansea Mountain Bike Club, mtbpigs.co.uk.

Wales Kilvey Hill

N18 Henblas/Caersws nr Newton

Train station Caersws
Nearest city Welshpool/Shrewsbury
Sat Nav SY17 5JE

Location You'll find Henblas around 8 km to the west of Newtown, itself between Welshpool and Aberystwyth in mid-Wales. When driving from Shrewsbury, take the A458 to Welshpool, the A483 to Newtown, and then the A489 before turning off onto the A470 towards Caersws. 3 km after along the same road, you'll hit Pontdolgoch, here pass the B4568 to Llanwnog, but take the next right (just before the train tracks), and then the second right. Henblas is at the top of this hill.

Facilities You can buy supplies from the local shop in nearby Pontdolgoch, otherwise, bring your own.

Rough round-up Henblas (or otherwise known as Caersws) is a private downhill track situated at Henblas Farm. It's a series of three downhill trails that make full use of the fantastic natural terrain and have been added to and built up by the local mountain bike scene. There are regular monthly uplifts run by the landowner and the trails are of expert standard (though with some chicken lines), and are home to the Caersws Cup Downhill series. Expect steep, rugged, and technically demanding runs. Has an uplift service during the race days.

Conditions A great place to ride, with three downhill runs and tons of different sections on each so that you could make up a different trail every run. The ground always tends to be drier here than surrounding areas: Cearsws seems to have its own microclimate. A super efficient uplift and a good mix of roots, fast trail, jumps and technical sections means it's a great place to spend the day. Uplifts can be organised with the landowner, you will need a group of 15 or more to book the day. To arrange an uplift day call T07977 987755.

N19 Llantrisant Woods DH

Train station Pontyclun
Nearest city Cardiff
Sat Nav CF72 9XA for Lanelay Road

Location Llantrisant Woods can be found to the west of the town of Llantrisant, itself around 10 km northwest from Cardiff. Leave the M4 exit at junction 34 and take the A4119 towards Llantrisant. Take a left at the first roundabout onto the A473, go over the next roundabout, then take a right at the next roundabout towards Talbot Green on Lanelay Road. Immediately take the first left up a dirt track. You'll find the trails up here.

Facilities There are plenty of shops and facilities in nearby Talbot Green and Llantrisant but you will have to bring your own supplies to the forest.

Rough round-up These downhill trails are very popular with local riders and have plenty of armoured sections, good jumps, and decent lengths (expect rides of around 3 minutes for good riders). The top sections are fantastic singletrack through dense forest, while the mid and lower areas open out into fast, feature-full lines of flowing jumps and fire-road sections. Well worth a visit.

Conditions This is a well-maintained site, with potentially muddy upper sections but well-drained lower, gravelly areas. Lots of roots make it slick in the wet. Best ridden in the dry when the trails are running fast, as the hill is not too steep. Many riders trail ride here and come down the downhill routes as part of a longer XC ride.

ⓘ **More info** Good trail cam action of Llantrisant can be found on YouTube.

↘20 Llanwrtyd Wells

Train station Llanwrtyd
Nearest city Swansea
Sat Nav LD5 4BA

Location Llanwrtyd is a quaint little village in the middle of Wales around 15 km north of the Brecon Beacons. The town sits on the A483 and can only be reached via this main thoroughfare from either the northeast or the southwest.

Facilities/Overview Llanwrtyd Wells' fame has changed from a mineral springs resort to the world capital of crazy escapades such as the bog-snorkelling world championships, a peculiar but brilliantly entertaining event that has now sprung an off-shoot – the bike bog snorkelling event, all thanks to the Green Events Company. Those aside, there is plenty to make this town stand out; rolling hills and rugged mountains, spectacular passes and gentle valleys, open pastures and thick forest, trickling streams and, perhaps most interesting – the Mid-Wales Beer Festival.

Rough round-up The riding from Llanwrtyd is situated mostly around the town itself. Some trails are waymarked and featured on trails maps that can be collected from town, other routes are not and will require headwork and a sense of adventure. Nearby Coed Trallwm has three short forest trails and a lovely café (see Coed Trallwm, page 184). Many riders base themselves in Llanwrtyd then head over to the excellent Elan Valley singletracks. The

best way to learn the multitude of tracks here is to combine your visit with an event such as the Red Kite Mountain bike bash or the Real Ale Wobble. See the Green Events website for more details, green-events.co.uk.

Terrain As the trails are in open country, you'll notice that there's a lot of bridleway riding. That said, it can get very soft if it's been raining.

XC This is a place that's perfectly suited for even the most purist of cross country riders as so many of the trails follow old bridleways and paths and it really does have a different feel to the other Welsh trail centres. There's no better way to explore than to book into the Real Ale Wobble. This is held once a year and is a non-competitive event based on having a good time. Half pints of ale are provided at check

points and the route is marked out so that hopefully even the most inebriated will find their way home.

Downhill Although there are numerous big hills and mountains around Llanwrtyd Wells, there are no downhill trails and no downhill scene in the surrounding towns.

Dirt Jumps/Freeride There are no trails or facilities suited to freeriders.

Conditions Some of the trails around the town tend to be in open country and can be quite soft going if the weather has been particularly wet.

ⓘ **More info** Green Events put on most of the activities, green-events.co.uk; Llanwrtyd Wells Visitor Centre (T01591 610666), website mbwales.com.

N21 Maindy Road BMX Track

Train station Cardiff
Nearest city Cardiff
Sat Nav CF24 4HL

Location Leave the M4 at junction 32 and head into Cardiff on the A470. After 3 km, you'll pass through the suburb of Maindy. Turn left into Maindy Road and the BMX track will be immediately on your left, clearly visible from the road. Maindy Road is just to the north of Cardiff city centre so easily found from any direction.

Facilities Plenty of shops and amenities can be found in Maindy itself.

Rough round-up This BMX track has gone under renovation in recent years thanks to the expansion of the leisure centre site adjacent. It's a tight track which you can pump all the way round, either gapping all the jumps or rolling them. Good for those just learning and wanting to perfect their bike-handling skills before hitting proper dirt jumps. Blackweir dirt jumps are nearby, but unofficial, so ask at Maindy for directions and local riders should give you directions.

Conditions This is an inner-city site which is half concrete – the drop in and some corners – and half dirt jumps. It drains well but still avoid in the rain.

N22 Moelfre

Train station Gobowen
Nearest city Oswestry
Sat Nav CV32 7UA

Location Around 10 km to the west of Oswestry, just inside the Welsh border

is Moelfre – an area of outstanding natural beauty. From Shrewsbury (itself off the M6 and M54), head northwest towards Oswestry on the A5. At Oswestry, take the B4580 heading for Rhydycroesau on the border with Wales. Carry on a further 5 km on this road and turn to the right signed Moelfre. There's plenty of XC trails but the downhill should be fairly obvious being cut into the side of the open fields to the northeast of the village.

Facilities There's not a lot here in terms of shops or amenities so it's best to take your own supplies.

Rough round-up This is one of the best downhill tracks in the UK, and has helped shape champions Gee, Dan and Rachel Atherton (as well as being home to numerous NPS DH events). The trail is around 3 minutes long for a decent rider, and cuts through open fields where features have been built to accommodate dips, gulleys and jumps. There are plenty of chicken lines, and good jumps (including a large drop at the top section) to challenge good riders and the high-speed open fields and natural corners and undulations are fantastic for all levels. There's also a 4X track for those of you who feel the need for some competitive racing. You're also able to uplift if you have a car and a spare driver!

Conditions This is open land with no trees, good -fast-draining top layer, and some rocky, gritty sections. Very fast.

N23 Morriston Park Pump Track

Train station Llansamlet
Nearest city Swansea
Sat Nav SA6 6AJ

Location You'll find the Morriston Park Pump Track about 8 km north of Swansea city centre. Leave the M4 at junction 45 and head south on the A4067 until you reach the second roundabout. Take a right onto Chase Road and follow this road – it will turn into Pentrepoeth Road and then Clasemont Road (this is also the A48). About 100 m after the mini roundabout, you will see a small lay-by. Turn off to the left before Llwyn Yr Eos, this is the north entrance to the park. Park up and walk about 50 m into the park and the pump track will be on your right.

Facilities There is nothing at the pump track itself but there are plenty of small shops nearby, and Swansea city centre is a short drive away.

Rough round-up This isn't the best, most well maintained pump track you'll find but it's great for local riding. Situated just behind a hospital, the pump track is in the north end of Morriston Park. Whether you're an experienced rider or not, this pump track is a great place to hone your bike handling skills.

Conditions There hasn't been any major work on the pump track so expect it to get muddy after bad weather.

⬊24 Machynlleth

⊗ ⊕ ⊙ ⊘ ⊗ ⊖

Train station Machynlleth

Nearest city Welshpool/Shrewsbury

Sat Nav SY20 8EB

Opening times You'll find the trails open 365 days a year, day and night, with the only closures being due to forest operations. You should be able to find all details about this on the website mbwales.com. All trails are free although there is a pay and display car park in Machynlleth centre and an honesty box at the ClimachX Trail.

Location Machynlleth is a town on the southwest edge of the Snowdonia National Park, just a few kilometres inland from the Irish Sea and close to Coed Y Brenin. From the east, head in from Shrewsbury, take the A458 towards Welshpool, then continue towards Machynlleth, all well signposted as they're the biggest towns in the area.

Facilities/Overview The town of Machynlleth is the ancient capital of Wales and is now well known for its Centre for Alternative Technology and the town's eco friendly slant on modern living. Don't look for major chain stores here – nearly every one the shops and stores on the high streets of Machynlleth, Aberdyfi and Tywyn are owner-occupied traders and businesses. As British towns become more and more like clones of each other, it is a refreshing change walking around Machynlleth. There are 4 main trails to hit when heading to Machynlleth, although the fourth – the ClimachX trail – can be found in nearby Dyfi Forest. The three waymarked trails (Mach 1, 2 and 3)

are suitable for riders who enjoy the steadier form of biking. Mach 1 is the shortest at 16 km, and graded blue, with Mach 3 being the longest at 30 km, and graded black. The thrill seekers amongst you will do better to head up the Dyfi valley to the ClimachX Trail in Dyfi forest. This 16 km

loop is packed with fast sweeping singletrack and the final descent just keeps on flowing.

XC The three Mach trails will get you out into the hills but you're better speaking to the local riders about where to go for great natural XC riding to really make the best of the Dyfi valley. The Mach trails (1,2 and 3) are all waymarked from town, with 1 being southwest from town heading out on the A487 towards Aberystwyth, while Mach 2 and 3 are on the same road in the opposite direction.

Downhill There are no DH-specific trails in the area although on a short travel suspension bike you can have a lot of fun on the ClimachX trails descents.

Freeride There are no freeride-specific trails here although the 'Eye of the Needle' drop on the ClimachX Trail would challenge some of the best riders.

Easy The Mach 1 trail is blue graded and the easiest of the lot with some tarmac sections and some staggering views.

Hard The 30-km Mach 3 is the toughest of the bunch with the most technical DH section in 'The Chute'.

Not to miss The pleasant town with its no-chain policy.

Remember to avoid Trying to open a Starbucks here.

Nearest Bike/Hire shop Dolgellau Cycles, at nearly 18 km away, is the nearest bike shop (T01341 423332) after The Holey Trail shut down.

Local accommodation There's a range of accommodation available in this popular tourist town. The Dyfi Guest B&B, T01654 702562 is very bike friendly.

Eating You'll notice a distinct lack of commercial chains so expect quality local produce, and while you'll pay a little more, it's so much better. Try the Maengwyn Café (T01654 702126).

ⓘ **More info** Machynlleth Tourist Info (T01654 702401), website dyfimountainbiking.org.uk.

JUSTIN SULLIVAN PHOTOGRAPH

> **Lowdown**

😊 **Locals do**
Have a lot of experience riding natural XC in the Dyfi Valley

Loop back up the forest road to ride the final descent of the climax again.

😕 **Locals don't**
Head out on the bike after heavy frost – it makes the trail very sticky.

✓ **Pros**
Healthy living, alternative, bike-friendly town.

✗ **Cons**
Limited riding without a local rider or local knowledge.

N25 Mountain Ash DH

Train station Merthyr Tydfil
Nearest city Cardiff
Sat Nav CF45 4LJ (roughly)

Location Mountain Ash is a small town located on the A470 between Cardiff and Merthyr Tydfil. Exit the M4 at junction 32 and head north on A470 in the direction of Merthyr Tydfil. Head past Pontypridd, then at the first roundabout take a left onto the A4059 heading in the direction of Aberdare/ Mountain Ash. After 4 km take a left into the forest access road signposted Lletti Turner Woods. Park at the bottom before the metal access gate (if you want to be sure of being able to exit), or head up the road for 150 m to the car park from where the trails start.

Facilities You won't find any facilities on the trails themselves, but there are plenty of shops and amenities at nearby Mountain Ash.

Rough round-up This is a fast downhill track without many obstacles (although there's always room to change) that's rocky in parts and challenging. Well worth a journey and especially worth it if you're in the area and want a fast, smooth DH day out. Park on the road at the bottom and then either ride up the forest road to the top or push up the trail to section it bit by bit. This is a working forest though and the trail is subject to closures.

Conditions The top section is rooty, but there are plenty of rocks around and some very slippery slate. This is Forestry Commission land, and rarely used except for other riders.

N26 Ponciau Banks

Train station Wrexham
Nearest city Wrexham
Sat Nav LL14 2LA

Location Ponciau Banks BMX Track is in Rhosllanerchrugog, 4 km southwest of Wrexham in Ponciau Banks Park. On the A483 from Wrexham or Oswestry, take the turnoff for Rhosllanerchrugog (the B5605 – Wrexham Road), then take a right onto Aberderfyn Road and finally a left on Clarke Street. Go to the end of this road and turn right into School Lane. The BMX track will be on your left.

Facilities Rhosllanerchrugog is a small town but it has plenty of shops and facilities and the park is right centre.

Rough round-up After receiving a grant from the council, this track was resurfaced in 2013 and has been growing in popularity ever since. This is a beautifully sculpted pump track that's great on a mountain bike or a BMX and will polish up those jumping, manualing and pumping skills in no time. Some of the jumps are quite advanced but most will have a great time riding this track. It's been designed to be ridden in several different styles and directions. It is situated about 10 minutes from Llandegla trail centre so can be incorporated into a trip there.

Conditions The resurfacing of this track has made it a lot smoother to ride and the extra bonus of good drainage means that it's rideable after bad weather.

ⓘ **More info** There are normally training sessions run on the track so check with brena.john@wrexham. gov.uk before going.

N27 Rheola DH Trail

Train station Neath
Nearest city Swansea
Sat Nav SA11 4DU (roughly)

Location You'll find Rheola DH trail to the south edge of the Brecon Beacons, around 18 km to the northeast of Swansea. From the M4, exit at junction 43 and head towards Neath on the A465. Carry on this road for around 10 km, hitting the town of Blaengwrach and then Glyn Neath. Take the left after the McDonalds and head back on to the B4242 Glyn Neath Road. Head back on yourself on this road for 4 km, and the entrance is on the right just before the village of Pentreclwydau.

Facilities It's best to head towards Glyn Neath or Resolven for any supplies or amenities. Rheola has no shops selling sustenance.

Rough round-up Rheola's one DH trail has hosted many rounds of the British Downhill Series and also the National Championships. It is a technical downhill course that is overall quite fast but has a few slower, tricky sections. This is a rough trail with lots of exposed rock so make sure that you've got good bike control. There are potential uplift days when there are comps on (check the website), otherwise this is a push-up area, well worth a visit for good riders while learners and intermediates might find other trails in the area more rewarding.

Conditions Exposed rock and roots give good riders a challenge. This is a beautiful area with few intruders so expect to see few people save for other riders.

ⓘ **More info** dragondownhill.co.uk

S28 Rhyl Marsh Tracks

Train station Rhyl
Nearest city Liverpool
Sat Nav LL18 2AD

Location The Marsh Tracks can be found on the north coast of Wales, in the heart of Rhyl and is around 25 miles west of Liverpool. Travelling west on the A55, exit at junction 27 and head north on The Roe, which then turns into St Asaph Road. When you reach the roundabout, take the second exit onto the A525, heading towards Rhyl, then a left at the next roundabout onto Rhuddlan Road and continue until it turns into Vale Road. Just before you drive over the railway tracks, take a left onto Marsh Road and the tracks can be found at the end of the road.

Facilities There is nothing on site at the moment but there are plans to add a café. Nearby Rhyl has plenty of shops and amenities.

Rough round-up Rhyl Marsh Tracks is an interesting facility for local riders. There is a BMX track (based on the exact design of the 2012 Olympic track), a road bike track and, the latest addition, an MTB track. It has all been made out of recycled materials and has been placed on an old tip so it's a very green site! With fast berms, tabletops, rollers and more, it's able to ridden by all level of rider, although experienced riders will be able to get some air. It's not worth a long drive but for local riders it's a must, and for those that want to test themselves on an Olympic standard track, it's worth it too.

Conditions The BMX track has great drainage so is rideable quickly after heavy rain, but the MTB track will need more time before it's rideable when bad weather has left its mark.

ⓘ **More info** For all info and opening times, check out marshtracks.co.uk or their Facebook page (Marsh Tracks).

S29 Rudry DJs

Train station Aber
Nearest city Cardiff
Sat Nav CF83 3DP

Location Close to the Caerphilly DJs are the Rudry Dirt Jumps – both around 5 km to the north of Cardiff. Exit the M4 at junction 32 heading north on the A470 to Pontypridd. After 3 km, take the A468 to Caerphilly. Head through the centre of town on Nantgarw Road, then straight onto Bedwas Road (the B4600). After 1 km you'll hit a roundabout, take the last exit, then the first left (both signed to Rudry). Head down here for 2 km then turn off Starbuck Street just after the houses. The dirt jumps are just up this road in the copse of trees to the right.

Facilities Caerphilly is the place for shops and amenities, although there is a small shop on Starbuck Street.

Rough round-up These are some low-budget dirt jumps built near the famous Caerphilly public access jumps. They are smaller than Caerphilly and would suit those looking to learn. Definitely worth a visit for those in the area, or for those overwhelmed by Caerphilly.

Conditions A hard packed base all set in a small clearing of trees. Please don't ride them when they're wet, and be sure to fix any damage.

S30 Sandjumps

Train station Aberystwyth
Nearest city Aberystwyth
Sat Nav SY25 6DN (Miner's Head pub)

Location Sandjumps are located on the edge of a disused lead mine around 10 km to the southeast of Aberystwyth, mid Wales. Driving west towards Aberystwyth, head on the A44 until you reach Ponterwyd. At Ponterwyd (10 km before Aberystwyth). Take the A4120 south towards Devils Bridge, then at Devils Bridge take another left onto the B4343. Head down here for 4 km, then take a right at the T junction in the direction of Ysbyty Ystwyth. After 1 km turn off to the right at Pontrhydygroes, then after 500 m take a left off this road (at the stone cottage) heading back towards the river. Follow this road to the end. The dirt jumps are just there on the right.

Facilities There's a pub back in Pontrhydygroes, otherwise this is open land remote from most facilities.

Rough round-up These are some fantastic dirt jumps fashioned from the black sand deposits left by the old lead mine. There are a huge variety of hips, gaps, doubles and drops scattered around the area, and perfect for beginners all the way through to pro riders. If you're in the area already then a detour is a must, or for those of you that love dirt jumps, a long journey might be worth it!

Conditions The jumps are made of a black sand deposit, and drain well, but as always, avoid in the rain and please fix any broken landings.

⟪↘31⟫ Nant Yr Arian

Ⓚ Ⓑ Ⓜ Ⓖ Ⓐ

Train station Aberystwyth
Nearest city Aberystwyth
Sat Nav SY23 3AD (for Ponterwyd)
Opening times The trails are 365 days
a year and the only trail closures will be
down to forest operations. You can find
details about this on mbwales.com. All
trails are free, though parking is £1.50 for
up to 2 hours or £3 for over 2 hours.

Location Nant Yr Arian is located
around 13 km east of Aberystwyth in
mid-Wales. Assuming you're driving
from the west on the A44, pass
through the village of Ponterwyd.
After 2 km take there's a bus-stop
(for the 525 bus), the car park entrance
for the trails directly opposite.

Facilities/Overview The Bwlch Nant Yr
Arian Visitor Centre is new to the forest
and has all the snacks, refreshments
and amenities you will need for a day
in the forest. Aberystwyth is the nearest
town, a 15-minute drive away and is a
coastal resort surrounded by three hills
with a busy student community and
some 50 pubs that retains a friendly
community feel. Nant-yr-Arian forest
sits high on the mountains just inland
from Aberystwyth, and offers stunning
high-level wilderness riding with
trails heading out into the epic
scenery of the Cambrian Mountains.
This is perfect for those who like their
riding rigged; just remember to be
prepared for everything from river
crosses, to technical rocky descents,
to mountain climbs.

XC The three main trails here –
the Pendam trail, Summit trail and

Syfydrink trail – offer up some true all-mountain riding and run across exposed moorland through some tight, technical singletrack. Pendam is a short (9 km) blue-graded taster trail, Summit is the longer singletrack (16 km) slog, while Syfydrin is the expert and gruelling trail at 35 km long. Summit and Syfydrin are both graded red.

Downhill There are no official, waymarked downhill trails in Nant Yr Arian, but head to Summit Cycles in Aberstwyth and they'll be able to give you some local knowledge of where to find good downhill runs.

Freeride Like the downhill routes, there are no specific freeride spots here. However, there are some features on the trails that will keep the freeride-minded of you interested. Also, there's the impressive sand jumps at Pontrhyfendigaid, a disused quarry.

Easy Start on the Pandam area to get your bearings and legs back if it's been a while since you were in the saddle!

Hard There are plenty of hard lines to explore on the Syfydrin trail.

Not to miss The incredible views from the top of the Summit trail.

Remember to avoid Travelling here when the weather is anything but perfect.

Nearest Bike/Hire shop The excellent Summit Cycles (T01970 626061) are based in Aberystwyth and sponsor the 'Summit Trail' at Nant Yr Arian.

Local accommodation
The George Borrow Hotel B&B is a mere 1.5 km from the Visitor Centre and are very biker friendly (thegeorgeborrowhotel.co.uk, T01970 890230).

Eating In Aberystwyth, The Honoured Guest (T01970 617617), a Chinese restaurant, isn't the best restaurant but it's a pretty cheap and cheerful place to find food, otherwise, there are limited supplies.

ⓘ **More info** mbwales.com, or Summit Cycles has a trails section at summitcycles.co.uk – these two sites are a great source of information.

> **Lowdown**

🙂 Locals do
Ride in groups.
Go hell for leather on the Syfydrin trail.

🙁 Locals don't
Ride the Syfydrin trail without appropriate protective gear.

✅ Pros
Varied trail riding and vibrant seaside town.

❌ Cons
Limited facilities for non xc riders.

⟍32 Snowdonia National Park

ⓚ ⓜ ⓖ ⓐ ⓔ ⓕ

Train station Llanrwst/Betws y Coed

Nearest city Chester

Sat Nav LL55 4EU (to Pete's Eats, Llanberis)

Opening times The trails in Snowdonia National Park are open all day, every day and are free to ride. Some of the new downhill trails you will have to pre-book and pay for uplift, but the majority of trails in the National Park are free to ride.

Location Snowdonia National Park (Parc Cenedlaethol Eryri in Welsh) is a protected parkland area of some 2170 sq km in the northwest corner of Wales and is famous for the country's highest mountain – the 1085 m Mt Snowdon. When driving from the west, either the A5 (travelling from Shrewsbury in the south), or the A55 from Chester and drive towards the town of Llanberis. This is in the northwest corner of the park and home to the local mountain bike, climbing and social scene nearest the mountains. Llanberis is on the A4086 between Capel Curig in the west and Caernarfon in the east.

Facilities/Overview Snowdonia, an area of outstanding natural beauty, is hugely popular for all lovers of the outdoors and is incredibly vast! There are plenty of cafés and Visitor Centres dotted around the immense national park, and each town is a picture-perfect tourist hub, with all amenities you'd need. It houses centres that hold some exceptional mountain bike trails, Gwydyr Forest Park and Coed Y Brenin to name two. There's almost too much here to go into in any detail.

There's an astounding amount of XC riding to be had in the area, as well as numerous downhill tracks – some with the ability to have uplift if you've got a car. You have to remember that this area is popular with other mountain users so you will have to be mindful – clashes do happen. Please ride with respect. For those looking for purpose-built trail centres, Coed Y Brenin centre north of Dolgellau is the place to head. See page 186. There are other waymarked XC routes too, most notably Gwydyr Forest (featuring the Marin Trail, Myndd Cribau and Penmachno waymarked routes), along with plenty of unofficial singletrack to explore and self navigate around.

XC For true XC riding there are a number of guide books specifically on long routes in the National Park, available at the local bike shop. We suggest Best MTB Trails in Snowdonia, 25 routes for Llanrwst, Betws-Gwydyr, Coed Y Brenin, Llanberis and Conwy Mtn (bike-fax.com).

Downhill The three most popular trails are Moel Cynghorion, Moel Eilio and Snowdon itself. This is one of the most thrilling descents in the UK, with the trail being partly the bridleway back to Llanberis (which can be congested with walkers). It's a very rocky descent with big drops and slate surface in parts (which can cut both tyres and skin!). Locals often push up the Festiniog Railway track – which can take up to 2 hours – but the reward is a 1000-m descent of up to 20 minutes. For a more detailed

breakdown of location and expected terrain for all the routes, look on the Pete's Eats website (see below).

Dirt Jumps/Freeride There is no specific or purpose-built northshore or freeride area in Snowdonia (though there are some armoured bridges on the Mynydd Cribau route), but with such a huge area to cover there is an enormous scope for finding and sessioning some good spots, from road gaps to neolithic northshore to root jumps. Call in to Energy Cycles in Llanberis (T01286 871892) for some local hidden spots! Remember to call into Pete's Eats Café too – said by many to be the 'best café in the world' and an incredible source of local mountain biking information.

Conditions Everything from forest land, hidden singletrack through to high-speed open field running.

Easy There are many easy routes in the park, from fire-road to gentle country rides for the family.

Hard The black run at Antur Stigion is well worth a try if you're feeling brave.

Not to miss Trying out the downhill runs at Antur Stiniog.

Remember to avoid Not taking tools and supplies on a ride. The unofficial trails here can be long so take things with you.

Nearest Bike/Hire shop Llanberis Bike Hire (T01286 872787, llanberisbikehire.co.uk) is the best place to start as it's near Pete's Eats and the entrance to the park itself. They hire out bikes for £25 per day as well as hiring out a bike trailer for your own uplift!

Local accommodation
Hit The Hills (hitthehills.com) is a bike friendly place to stay, with food included but is more hostel-style accommodation than anything else. There is so much on offer nearby that it's worth looking into before booking.

Eating There are plenty of cafés to pick up snacks and hot meals when riding, but when outside of the National Park, we suggest Pete's Eats (petes-eats.co.uk) as they serve big meals at reasonable prices. Perfect for the mountain biker.

ⓘ **More info** Try checking outeryri-npa.gov.uk/visiting/Activities/Cycling – a site that lists several routes in Snowdonia National Park and will allow you to ride without breaking the law! Perhaps the best source of info on the region is Pete's Eats Café and don't forget to check out Artur Stiniog (anturstiniog.com).

> **Lowdown**

☺ **Locals do**
Pre-book the uplift to take full advantage of all the trails.

Adventure out into the woods to find unofficial singletrack.

☹ **Locals don't**
Disrespect other forest users – you will see other forest users!

✔ **Pros**
An insane amount of forest to explore

Friendly locals willing to reveal hidden trails.

✖ **Cons**
Far too much to explore in just one visit.

TOM CALDWELL

↘33 Wentwood DH

Train station Newport
Nearest city Cardiff
Sat Nav N/A

Location Just 15 km northeast of Newport, South Wales, is Wentwood downhill track. Exit the M4 at junction 24 and drive towards Chepstow on the A48. After 4 km exit to the left in the direction of Parc Seymour. Pass through the village and head out on the north road in the direction of Pen-y-Cae-Mawr. Head 2.5 km up this road, then take a right off the road into the Wentwood Car Park. For more detailed directions email Wentwood through the website address below.

Facilities You won't find many facilities on site, except for race days, when some hot and cold drinks and snacks will be served. This is a bring-your-own site so it's best to stock up in nearby Parc Seymour as it has plenty of shops and amenities.

Rough round-up Wentwood has seen plenty of competitions in its day and is one of the UK's premiere downhill destinations – perfect for riders of all ability. It's also out of the way, meaning you're unlikely to encounter anyone save for other riders. This is a fantastic locally-maintained rider set up, which is ran in conjunction with the Forestry Commission and a great example of what can be done when working together.

Terrain Mostly singletrack, with the DH trail being a mixture of reinforced bridges, purpose built jumps, and fantastic rootsy, and rocky, natural terrain. The top section is soil, with the bottom area being more rocky.

XC You won't find many XC riders here as there are no official XC routes. However, with so many natural trails, this is a great place for XC riders, you just have to find it, and the downhill trail compliments this set up. Perfect for any bike really.

Downhill There is one DH trail here, which is approximately 760 m of fantastic riding with plenty of chicken lines for those who aren't up for hitting the bigger jumps. There's a full description of the track on the Wentwood website (see below), but this is definitely worth a journey to session.

Dirt Jumps/Freeride There is no specific freeride area here but there's plenty on the DH track for freeriders to occupy their time with!

Conditions The XC routes are hard-packed dirt singletrack, while the downhill trail is purpose-built and well maintained. All are on a red clay base which gets very slick in the wet, so as always, avoid after periods of heavy rain.

ⓘ **More info** Wentwood has its own website at wentwooddownhill.co.uk, or the Forestry Commission has a Wentwood page at forestry.gov.uk.

Local riders
Rowan Sorrell

Bike Orange Blood 224, Alpine 160
Local spot Bike Park Wales
Club member Afraid not, there are so many riders in south Wales you don't need clubs.
Age 33
Note Rowan is Bike Park Wales co-owner

Where's the one place you'd recommend above all, for those coming to Wales?

RS Glyncorrwg, good trails and great centre.

Where has the best XC?

RS I'd have to say the Afan Forest park.

Where is the best Downhill?

RS Cwmcarn or Caersws – they're both good fun.

The best dirt jumps?

RS Swansea: the scene is going off there but invite only I'm afraid.

If you were to take a family out – say a cousin who's visiting with his kids – where would you head?

RS Head straight for Brechfa green and blue trails, they'd love it.

What secret stashes do you know about?

RS Plenty – but they are secret…

If you were a huge fan of cake and wanted to find the best trail with a foodie pit stop, where would it be?

RS The Drop Off Café in Glyncorrwg is the place to be.

Where, if anywhere, outside of your area do you often visit with your bike?

RS Redhills in the Forest of Dean.

Which websites have the best info on your local area?

RS If you want people to show you round the trails then try mtb-wales.com.

Which is the best shop to head to if you're in Wales?

RS Skyline cycles in Glyncorrwg – they have good mechanics, loads of stock and they're located bang on the trail head.

Rowan taking on a rock garden.

Southern Scotland

Kirroughtree. [FORESTRY COMMISSION (ANDY MCCANDLISH)]

North Sea

Motorway
A Road
B Road
✈ Airports
⛴ Ferries

peth
ewcastle
ateshead
Sunderland
19
Easington
Hartlepool
kton-
Tees
Middlesbrough   Whitby
lington
A19
North York Moors
Osmotherley
irsk Helmsey Pickering   Scarborough
Thornton-   Filey
le-Dale
A64
A19
Kirkham   Bridlington
esborough
A165
YORK   EAST RIDING
York   OF YORKSHIRE
ewood
Beverley
ds Selby   Kingston
A164   upon Hull
eld M62 M18 Barton-upon-Humber
NORTH LINCOLNSHIRE
Scunthorpe
Doncaster   Grimsby
A180   Nettleton
Waddingham
M18   Louth
Gainsborough   Market
ffield   Rasen
erfield   A1   A46   A16
NOTTINGHAMSHIRE   Lincoln Horncastle Ashby
M1   Mansfield   by Partney
LINCOLNSHIRE
mbergate   Newark-on-   Skegness
A46   Trent Sleaford   A16
rby   Nottingham A1   A17
Castle   Boston   Wells-next-
Donnington Melton Grantham Donnington   the-Sea   Cromer
ESTERSHIRE Mowbray Spalding Holbeach Sandringham Fakenham Erpingham
King's Lynn   Happisburgh
Empingham Stamford   A148   NORFOLK
Swaffham   A140
A47   Great
Norwich   Yarmouth

In the south of Scotland you will find the brilliant 7Stanes project dominating the scene. The project is a Forestry Commission initiative that created seven purpose-built trail centres all south of Glasgow and Edinburgh. They are perhaps the UK's most used riding centres and it's not hard to see why: each one has its own very different aspects and characteristics, the areas offer fantastic facilities such as cafés, bike shops and Visitor Centres, absolutely world-class trails, jaw-dropping views and careful, thoughtful layouts. Their website (7stanes.gov.uk) has a wealth of info including videos and maps, and an explanation as to the name (each trail centre features a 'Stane' or sculpture, and they hope you'll try and visit each one to complete your experiences). Roughly speaking, Ae Forest is the family-friendly but freeride-heavy site, Dalbeattie is great for riders who love the rockier side of things, Kirroughtree is another family-friendly area with incredible singletrack, Glentress is the flagship centre, being closest to Edinburgh, and features absolutely everything you could wish for, Glentrool is the perfect introductory 'Stane', Innerleithen is the full downhill set up and just next door to Glentress, Mabie is the place to head if you like northshore, while Newcastleton is the beautiful, empty, gentle giant of the centres. But of course, there are exceptions to these rules, and each centre has lots of diversity.

But southern Scotland has more to offer, and the absolutely stunning Jedburgh Forest (shortened to Jedforest Trails), are for fans of route-finding, proper old-school mountain biking, with the added bonus that you can ride back to England and possibly join up with some of the Kielder routes. Meanwhile, Drumlanrig Castle is simply a cut above. Its trails are first class, the setting is exactly as one would imagine for a Scottish Castle, and it is where the bicycle was actually invented! All in all, southern Scotland is perhaps the most exciting area in the UK for its impressively diverse range of mountain biking.

Local scene

It's easy to see that Scotland's strengths lie in its bona fide mountains (something a lot of the UK lacks), its tourist infrastructure, and in a few places (Fort William, Glencoe and Innerleithen) its permanent uplift operations. With Fort William being a regular stop on the downhill racing scene, the popularity of riding in Scotland is forever growing.

Compared to England and Wales, Scotland has an abundance of open space, yet its centres are situated fairly close together, making it possible to tour the whole country in a packed two-week break! One thing to remember is that, if you wanted to and had the nerve to, you can trek across miles upon miles of open land that's accessible to mountain bikers, making the available riding quite literally endless. We wouldn't recommend it if you are inexperienced as it's possible to ride for days without seeing a soul in some of the more remote ares of the country.

Hubs

Scotland has a great scene on both social and competitive levels. The hub sites of Innerleithen and Fort William are developing internationally competitive riders; indeed, Innerleithen is home to a Scottish Junior Downhill World Champion, Ruaridh Cunningham. At the trail centres, fed by the central lowlands where most of Scotland's population lives, there are regular meets between riders often organized through the many web forums. The larger centres really encourage a chilled riding experience where you can hang out in their onsite cafés and bike shops. There is both a Scottish Downhill and a Scottish Cross Country race series which are very popular and use the best venues in the country, see sda-races.com and sxc.org.uk. Probably the most extensively used Scottish website is descent-world.co.uk, which is more focused on the downhill side of the sport but the forums are full of trail meets too. There are companies who are making the most of the landscape by offering guiding services off the beaten track and then there is Dirt School, offering coaching to all abilities of riders, dirtschool.co.uk.

❿ Best rides in Scotland

For the most varied, wild, and exhilarating rides in the UK, Scotland is the place to head. Below are 10 of the very best centres.

❶ Glentress, page 220

Glentress is home to trails that range from family-friendly through to the toughest of the tough; all encompassed in a super-friendly vibe and some incredible facilities. It's not hard to see why this is classed as the most well-rounded trail set up currently operating in the UK

❷ Fort William, page 246

Fort Bill is infamous on the DH circuit and attracts many enthusiasts each year. And it's not hard to see with the trails on offer! There's also a great 4X track, some wonderfully challenging XC, and the UK's only gondola uplift.

❸ Ae Forest, page 216

This is prime DH territory featuring the 22-foot Coffin Jump and a host of other features. There's also the Omega Man trail, a twisting, turning free ride behemoth, which is perfect for a day's excitement.

❹ Drumlanrig Castle, page 232

Billed as the Afan of the north, there are some magical trails here, built by the infamous Rik Allsop. Add in the expected, amazing views and a cool vibe, this is one hell of a trail centre.

❺ Isle of Arran, page 254

If you're a fan of empty trails and staggeringly beautiful views, you'll want to head to the Isle of Arran. It's easily accessible and incredibly worthwhile.

❻ Innerleithen, page 224

With so much on offer, both marked and unmarked, it's possible to spend a day here and not hit the same line twice. It also offers more varied tracks than Fort William, making it a must-visit destination for riders in Glasgow and Edinburgh.

❼ Mabie, page 228

If you're a northshore lover, then the Dark Side, orange graded trail is 100% northshore, ready to test your skill and nerve. If you can spare a few seconds from staring at the 10 cm-wide sections, you'll see some incredible views.

❽ Golspie Highland Wildcat Trails, page 250

With as much fun riding up as there is going down, the only thing that will stop you from riding as much as you'd like to are the stunning views over the Moray Firth – just breathtaking.

❾ Laggan Wolftrax, page 258

The XC trails at Laggan are nothing short of absolute perfection. There might not be a lot on offer but the fact that they are so well-rounded just means that it's a great place to ride. If you include the bike park to your day, you won't go home disappointed.

❿ Middleden MTB Trails, page 263

Middleden is a shining example of what can be created when an MTB club and a countryside trust come together. There's not too much on offer but there are some fun trails that will test your technical riding. And it's not too far from Edinburgh.

FORESTRY COMMISSION (PETE LAING) · FORESTRY COMMISSION (JOHN MCFARLANE)

Local riders
Chris Ball

Chris Ball spent six years on the UCI Downhill circuit and is a former Scottish national Champ. He now coaches the Scottish youth and junior MTB Teams (leading to Ruaridh Cunningham to a gold at the Junior World Championships) as well as running a public coaching service named 'Dirt School'. See the fantastic dirtschool.co.uk for more info.

You've got friends visiting for just one weekend and they can go anywhere in Scotland. Name the one place you'd definitely have to take them.

CB   Scotland is small and compact enough to squeeze more than one trail into a weekend. Based in the Tweed valley, the trails at Glentress and Innerleithen are a must and could both be done in a long day or taken at an easier pace over a couple of days.

Which trail centre or resort has the best party scene or the best after-riding activities?

CB   For pubs you want to choose the trails nearest to the bigger towns. You can have a good night in Peebles – not far from Glentress – or Fort William, near Laggan and the Witches Trail. For a bigger night, to Edinburgh, only 25 miles from Glentress and Innerleithen.

Where did you learn to ride, and where would you send beginners to ride?

CB The great thing about Scotland is its variety. I learnt on the massive roots and rocks of Dunkeld, the flat out fast straights of Fort William and the tight technical forestry of the Tweed Valley.

There are more green and blue routes now than ever before so try the blue at Golspie for sandy trails and great sea views, or Glentress for a huge variety of all levels of trails.

Where's best for mixed ability groups?

CB Some of the larger centres like Mabie, Glentess, Drumlanrig and Laggan have a good mix of trails all near to each other. That way the group can stay together and everyone can enjoy the day. These sites also have cafés so riders wanting a shorter day can relax with a coffee whilst waiting for the others to return from their epic.

Where's the best place for views, sunsets, or just total rustic charm, etc?

CB Without a doubt, the summit of Golspie has to have the best views of any black route in the world. With the vast expanse of the North Sea out in front of you and the rolling green hills of Sutherland to each side, the scenery is incredible. With only the little town of Golspie below and the odd oil rig in the distance, there's nothing to disturb you up there.

In your opinion, which is the best downhill track in Scotland?

CB Fort William boasts the only World Cup track in the UK and gondola uplift too. The five minute plus track sorts the men from the boys and you can ride knowing that the world's best have battled for the elusive rainbow stripes on the very same dirt you're riding on too.

If you had friends visiting and they could only bring one bike – a hard tail – where would you take them?

CB Some of the smoother trails in the south of Scotland would be the best bet. Mabie, Ae forest or Dalbeattie would all make a good day out.

Where would you take kids to learn?

CB The Skills Loops at Glentress or further north at Fort William offer a great way to teach the basics in a safe environment. Glentress's Blue trails also give a great feeling of speed but with very low risk. The flow as the trails sweep through Tweed valley pine forest is unparalleled.

Where's the best place to avoid pedalling uphill? Where has the best uplifts? Would you avoid anywhere?

CB Fort William has uplift seven days a week in the comfort of an enclosed gondola but Innerleithen also runs uplift by bus a couple of times a month. Either are a good choice. Avoid using your own transport in Forests like Dunkeld as it has a negative effect on Forestry-run venues trying to grow the sport in a safe and planned manner.

Where's best for total variety?

CB For the best variety, try and road-trip to as many venues as you can. The 7Stanes trail network or Golspie, Learnie and Laggan are all grouped close enough that you'll find a huge variety, all within an hour or so of each other.

⬊1 Ae Forest (7Stanes)

🔵 🔴 🟠 Ⓝ 🔵 Ⓢ 🔵 🔵 Ⓜ
🔵 🔵 🔵 🔵 🔵 🔵

Nearest train station Dumfries.
Nearest city Dumfries/Glasgow.
Sat nav postcode DG 1QB.
Opening times The trails are open 365 days a year and are completely free to ride! You will have to pay to park your car, but it's a small price to pay for the facilities on offer.

Location Directly north of Dumfries is Ae Forest. When travelling from Dumfries, take the A701 towards Moffat and the A74(M). After 10 km there are signs for Ae off to the left. Head through the village and take a right towards the forestry commission site (signposted 7Stanes). The new trail head & car park is around 100 m down this road on the left (opposite Ae bike Shop & Café).

Facilities/Overview Ae Forest used to be one of Scotland's premier downhill spots, and was predominantly for higher standard riders and those who wanted to launch big airs down scary, big downhills. However, with the addition of family-level trails, a XC side to Ae emerged. With a café & a bike shop (which hires, sells & fixes bikes and equipment, is a Specialized Test Centre, has wireless internet, showers and bike wash), uplift service (on certain days), & car parking, Ae Forest has shown the reasons why it's the most well-rounded bike centre in the 7Stanes portfolio.

XC The green-graded Ae Valley Route is perfect for families and novice riders. It's a gentle ride with one sharp climb

thrown in between forest roads and plenty of singletrack. It's a 9-km loop with plenty of stopping points. The blue-graded Larchview Trail is a 13.5-km loop along a similar vein but with some northshore sections and some deeper forest riding. The red-graded Ae Line is named after the A-Line in Whistler, and shares similar attributes – good jumps, fast, technical riding and some good descents (including The Omega Man – see downhill). At 24 km of concentration, it's pretty tiring, but well worth a try.

Downhill This is prime DH territory, with the original course having hosted events for the past 10 years. There are three DH tracks – the original Downhill Course – a 1.6-km track with the 22-foot Coffin Jump and some other

hefty drops and jumps. Walk it first. The second is The Shredder, a DH run that's built for beginners. Tight berms to flat, open corners, to off camber sections and so much more, it's the perfect introduction to DH that all beginner riders will need. The third is the Ae Line Trail which holds some incredible DH towards the end of the trail and features tables, jumps, drops and gaps (there are several lines to take, depending on how big – or rollable – you want your jumps and drops to be). For uplift days, check with upliftscotland.com (should be around £32 for ten uplifts).

Freeride The Shredder is an orange-graded bike park for downhill riders but there's plenty in there to keep the freerider happy. There are plenty of tabletop jumps and even a road gap to practice all jumps on, but riders can also find plenty of northshore and jumps on the XC routes to be happy with.

Easy The green route here is commendable for getting families off the beaten track.

Hard The DH riding here can be fierce but the the Ae Line holds one of the best sections of trail in the UK.

Not to Miss The Omega Man section of the Ae Line trail. Incredible.

Remember to Avoid Trying the Downhill Course without checking out the drops beforehand.

Nearest Bike/Hire shop The Ae Bike Shop is part of the café that's on site. They hire out a range of XC and DH bikes for the day and also have a dedicated workshop and on site mechanics if your bike gets bashed on the trails or needs a service. T01387 860541.

Local accommodation
Ae Farm Cottages, Gubhill Farm, visitsouthernscotland.com has self catering cottages.

Eating The Ae Bike Shop and Café will be able to quench your thirst and fill your hungry stomachs 7 days a week at Ae Forest. If you don't want to use the café, you should take supplies from Ae (the shortest named town in the UK).

ⓘ **More info** The 7Stanes site is 7stanesmountainbiking.com, the Ae Bike Shop and Café can be found on Facebook and the uplift site is upliftscotland.com.

› Lowdown

☺ **Locals do**
Ride downhill to a ludicrously high standard.

Always walk up to and inspect a jump before hitting them

☹ **Locals don't**
Push up the Omega Man – there are always people coming down; use the special push up track to the side.

✔ **Pros**
No better classic downhill in the UK.

Quiet riding on weekdays in a tranquil setting.

✖ **Cons**
Uplift infrequent.

⬐2 Dalbeattie (7Stanes)

Ⓚ Ⓡ Ⓝ Ⓢ Ⓞ Ⓣ Ⓞ Ⓑ

Nearest train station Dumfries.

Nearest city Dumfries.

Sat nav postcode DG5 4QU.

Opening times Like other 7Stanes facilities, the trails are open 365 days a year and are free to use, although you will have to pay £3 to park your car.

Location Around 20 km southwest of Dumfries, overlooking the Irish Sea and the Lake District, is Dalbeattie. From the A74(M), exit at junction 17 or 18 (Lockerbie), and head west on the A709 towards Dumfries. Continue all the way into town, take a left onto Shakespeare Street, then right onto White Sands, and then left onto Galloway Street crossing the river. Carry on down this road (it turns into the A711 Dalbeattie road), to Dalbeattie, and the 7Stanes trails are clearly signposted as you approach town.

Facilities/Overview Dalbeattie has been a granite quarrying area since the 1790s, and the trails here take full advantage of this incredible natural asset with most of the routes being very grippy and all-weather draining. The trails have benefitted from being included into the 7Stanes portfolio as the site has broadened its trails to include something for every rider. For those riders who love to ride over tricky rocks, this is the place to be. Dalbeattie doesn't have a huge vertical drop, so no massive climbs or super-long descents (compared to other centres in Scotland), but still plenty of technical riding, and the infamous 'Slab' rock (read on...). Facility wise, there's not much up at the trails, though there is a bike washing area at the bottom. All the cafés and bike shops are located in Dalbeattie town, 1.5 km to the north of the start of the trails, Richorn car park.

XC For novice riders, there are green and blue trails to enjoy – the green Ironhash Trail being an 11.5-km loop that starts out on wide singletrack and takes you deep into the heart of the forest. The blue-graded Moyle Hill

Trail has again been upgraded from its once forest-road beginnings, and keeps some staggering views over its 14 km of gentle riding. The red-graded Hardrock Trail is the main attraction here with over 25 km of riding and the infamous 'Slab' – a 14-metre long boulder which many find incredibly intimidating to ride over. It's steep, riddled with lines, and only the confident rider who leaves the brakes off will pass. The 'Terrible Twins' are a similar feature further down the trail, and even though they're smaller, they are no less able to catch even good riders out (the features are graded black, but can be bypassed so don't increase the trail's overall grading). All the features on the trail are rollable should you not want to try them out.

Downhill No dedicated or specific DH trails here.

Freeride The skills area is 1.5 km of testing northshore and feature riding that most freeriders will love, though if it's pure jumps you're after, then other 7Stanes sites might be more in keeping.

Easy The Skills Area is the place to head in order to work out what standard of trail you should be hitting.

Hard The Slab, The Terrible Twins, and Volunteer Ridge are all technically difficult riding, and bravado-testing, bits of trail.

Not to miss The Slab.

Remember to avoid The Slab!

Nearest Bike/Hire shop MPG Cycles in Dalbeattie (T01556 610659) have bikes for hire, as do Gorsebank near the Dalbeattie trailhead – gorsebank.com, T01556 611634.

Local accommodation
The Belle Vue (T01556 611833) a bed and breakfast in the town or Maidenholm Forge Mill (T01556 611552) for a self-catering cottage.

Eating There are a choice of restaurants and pubs in Dalbeattie. Try the Sea Horse T01556 611173.

ⓘ **More info** For info on Dalbeattie try its official page on the 7Stanes site – 7stanesmountainbiking.com.

.

> **Lowdown**

☺ **Locals do**
Ride out of their comfort zone. This is challenging terrain but well worth pushing yourself for.

☹ **Locals don't**
Ride too slow. Attack the trail, as speed is your friend over the rocks.

✔ **Pros**
Plenty of interesting terrain that'll definitely get your rock riding up to scratch.
All-weather trails work in most conditions.

✘ **Cons**
Has been criticised for using lots of forest road.

Nearest train station Carstairs/
Edinburgh.

Nearest city Edinburgh.

Sat nav postcode EH45 8NB.

Opening times The trails are open all
day, every day, though it's best to check
with the 7Stanes website for closures. All
trails are free to ride but the car park is
pay and display (£1 for short stay, £5 for
the day).

Location Glentress is around 1 km to
the east of the town of Peebles, itself
around 30 km south of Edinburgh.
From either Edinburgh or from the
south approach the area from the A702,
turn onto the A721, then take the A72
towards Peebles. Carry on past the town
and Glentress is signposted off to the
left after 1 km.

Facilities/Overview With many
visitors staying for weekends or longer
breaks in the nearby bike-friendly town
of Peebles, it's no wonder Glentress is
often regarded as the best – and most
well-rounded – trail centre in the UK.
There's a fantastic Visitor Centre in The
Hub Café and Bike Shop, which hires
bikes (and nearby Peebles has plenty of
hire facilities). The terrain here is perfect
for every rider from the novice family
through to the best riders in the world,
and the area is hugely popular with
every level in between. It's a must-visit
spot for all riders.

XC It's advised to start in the skills
area as it has a variety of obstacles and
features that you might encounter on
the trails (with explanations of what the
feature is called, as well as tips on how

to ride it tips written on panels), and
should give you a good idea of what
colour trail you wish to go for. The green
routes are a mixture of 3.5-km or 4.5-km
loops, with the idea of getting families
into the forest as soon as possible. The
blue-graded route has some great,
flowing singletrack that finishes with
a long descent to the car park. The

red-graded run is the classic route, built
in 2000 by Pete Laing and added to
ever since. Plenty of switchbacks, tough
climbs, rock gardens and swooping
corners await. All the trails interconnect,
so there are bail-out areas, or you can
upgrade if you fancy something more
difficult along the way.

😊 **Locals do**
Head out on the trails early. Glentress can get very busy during holiday periods.

Ride at night – there's a regular meeting of night-riding with lights (see the Hub website for details).

😟 **Locals don't**
Share their shortcuts!

Leave anything behind on the trails.

✔ **Pros**
Perfect for families, beginners and intermediate riders.

Well managed, plenty of facilities and a great atmosphere.

✖ **Cons**
Die-hard downhillers will want to head to Innerleithen.

No uplift.

Southern Scotland Glentress (7Stanes)

Downhill While there are no specific DH trails in Glentress, there's still plenty of DH riding to be had, especially in the second half of the red route, which contains 18 jumps, 17 tables, 4 rock drops and 12 switchbacks. If you're after pure DH tracks, the sister to Glentress, Innerleithen, is the place to head.

Freeride There are 23 jumps packed into 650 m of trails so you can guarantee that freeriders will love it! There are plenty of random one-off launches, wallrides and northshore to test yourself on. You can start off small, and work your way up to the biggest of jumps.

Easy The skills area is a must and won't let you overestimate your skill level at Glentress.

Hard The black route is not to be approached light-heartedly.

Not to Miss Racing your mates down Spooky Wood is the perfect end to the day.

Remember to Avoid Paying for a round of cakes at The Hub Café by coming last!

Nearest Bike/Hire shop The Hub Café and Bike shop has bikes to rent.

Local accommodation
There are plenty of caravan parks nearby, like Crossburn Caravan park in Peebles – T01721 720501 and Rosetta Caravan Park in Peebles – T01721 720770. There's also Lyne Farmhouse B&B – T01721 740255 or Melrose Youth Hostel in Melrose – T0870 004 1141. All are good bike-friendly places to stay, but Peebles has plenty more and most are used to people coming to ride at Glentress and Innerleithen.

Eating The Hub Café on site stocks a lot of food that will satisfy the hunger of anyone, pre- or post-ride.

ⓘ **More info** The 7Stanes website is always the place to head for – 7stanesmountainbiking.com

◄4 Glentrool (7Stanes)

◎ ◎ ◎ ◎ ◎ ◎ ◎ ◎ ◎

Nearest train station Dumfries.

Nearest city Dumfries.

Sat nav postcode DG8 6SZ.

Opening times The café and Glentrool Visitor Centre (T01671 402420) are open 1000-1600 (1700 peak season). Trails are open 24/7 365 days a year and are free to ride.

Location Glentrool is a part of the Galloway Forest and is signposted off the A712 close to the A714 between Newton Stewart and Girvan. The trail head is at Glentrool Visitor Centre, about a mile from the village. The nearest train station is at Barrhill, around 18 km from the trailhead by main road.

Facilities/Overview If you're more suited to mellow, ambling rides and are looking to just get into the great outdoors rather than tackle some technical trails, then Glentrool might be the perfect place for you. Boasting excellent beginner and intermediate trails, Glentrool offers two green runs, mostly root-and-rock free and perfect

for the family. There's nothing higher than a blue run here, a run that consists of mostly purpose-built singletrack. There is a 218-m vertical ascent and a 2.8-km, meandering descent back to the Visitor Centre. Fast and swooping with bermed corners it is rated as moderate in terms of difficulty and length; however, the off-road smooth surface and long final descent make it easier for less experienced riders. All trails do take in the amazing scenery around the Loch Trool, giving great views of the area known as 'the Highlands of the Lowlands'.

XC The Green Torr is a relatively short XC loop, but the Big Country Route (waymarked) is a 58-km trail using forest roads set in some of Scotland's most spectacular countryside. At nine hours it will be your fitness, rather than your technical ability, that will be tested.

Downhill This is no trail centre for the DH enthusiast but those wanting speed will enjoy the blue ruin as it's relatively

steep and you'll need to know how to use your brakes effectively.

Freeride No freeride facilities available.

Easy The Glen trail is possibly the easiest at Glentrool and it takes you on an easy loop that leaves you back at the Visitor Centre. After that, you will be ready for the other green trail, which is longer at 14 km but offers the same degree of difficulty.

Hard With only one blue run on offer, the Green Torr run is your only option. The beauty of the obstacle-free surface and long descent, however, mean that riders who would otherwise not attempt this level of difficulty will be tempted to push themselves.

Not to Miss The Burns Stone, at the top of the blue trail, which overlooks Glen Trool and commemorates Robert the Bruce's first victory.

Remember to Avoid Travelling here on gusty days – the winds of Galloway Forest are legendary and make riding difficult.

Nearest Bike/Hire shop The Break Pad (T01671 401303) is a B&B and bike hire shop in nearby Kirroughtree. Open 1000-1700 each day and public holidays.

Local accommodation
Conifer Lodges (T0333 210 1055) has self-catering lodges and camping about six miles from the trails.

Eating The café located at the Visitor Centre is set on the river and has loads of picnic tables. A perfect place to take in their famous delicacy: a haggis toastie. The village doesn't offer much in terms of eating out, so you might want to get two of those toasties.

ⓘ **More info**
7stanesmountainbiking.com.

❯ **Lowdown**

☺ **Locals do**
Ride fast down the 2.8 km descent on Green Torr.

☹ **Locals don't**
Expect extensive downhill trails or technical singletrack.

Party into the night in Glentrool village.

✔ **Pros**
Amazing scenery.

Excellent trails for families and intermediates.

✖ **Cons**
Limited trails with only one blue run.

Visitor Centre and café closed through all of winter.

◎ ◎ ◎ ⑦ ◎ ◎ ◎

Train station Carstairs/Edinburgh

Nearest city Edinburgh

Sat Nav EH44 6PD

Opening times The trails are open all day, every day, and are free. If you're riding on an uplift day it'll cost you £32 per rider but this will allow you to get at least 9 runs in for the day!

Location Innerleithen is about 10 km to the east of the town of Peebles, itself 30 km south of Edinburgh. Travelling either from Edinburgh or from the south, approach the area from the A702 and exit at the A721 towards Blythe Bridge, then take the A72 towards Peebles. Drive past the town and head towards Innerleithen, then upon entering the village turn right into Traquair Road (the B709) and follow this road for about 1 km, then turn left at the T junction onto the minor road and Innerleithen car park is on the right-hand side. Innerleithen is clearly signposted from Peebles, and the 7Stanes area is signposted as soon as you enter the town.

Facilities/Overview Yet another fantastic 7Stanes facility, and one that was originally built for DH riders, though the inclusion of XC has changed this somewhat. Innerleithen has no easy routes, so for those of you with families, it's best to stick to nearby Glentress – this place is made for those who know what they're doing. As such, Innerleithen is a quiet, serious mountain biking destination, with good facilities in the village of Innerleithen but little at the trails. The geology here is also perfectly suited for

mountain bike trails with an excellent hard, stony soil that drains well, making this a great all-weather venue.

XC The Tarquir XC trail is both physically and technically demanding, so suited for experienced riders. There are many sections to this red route, allowing riders to cut out climbs if you aren't feeling particularly fit. You will, however, miss one hell of a view and some great bermy singletrack. Those who love natural riding will be spoilt with a plethora of paths on this and the surrounding hills, though none are waymarked so do require some exploration. The trails

here are generally very quiet compared to Glentress so don't expect to see too many other riders.

Downhill The downhill trails on Plora Rig of Innerleithen are infamous in the UK. While there might only be a reported four main marked runs, there are actually many other lines linking different sections, giving you so many DH options. You could spend a whole day on the hill and not hit the same line twice, not that you'd want to; many of the runs are steep and technical and require some learning. You should expect plenty of roots and

7 STANES CIC

Easy There's no stand-out easy route here as novice riders have nearby Glentress. However, the easiest route down the hill is 'Make or Brake'. All the jumps on this run are rollable and it is probably the least technical section on the hill.

Hard Book an uplift weekend at Innerleithen and spend a whole day mastering the DH tracks.

Not to Miss A run down Make or Break.

Remember to Avoid Heading here if you are sceptical of your ability to handle it. Glentress is nearby so go there first.

Nearest Bike/Hire shop Alpine Bikes (T01896 830880) can be found in the old church in Innerleithen and are well equipped for all the riders using the testing trails in the area.

Local accommodation

There are a few hotels and guest houses in Innerleithen such as the Traquair Arms Hotel (T01896 830229) or for self catering cottage accommodation try Cosaig Self Catering (T01896 830882).

Eating You won't find much at the trails themselves but the nearby town of Innerleithen has a host of bakeries and cafés. Don't forget to try both the award winning ice cream in the paper shop, the Traquair House Tea Rooms or Riverbank Restaurant (T01896 831221) for really good post-riding grub.

ⓘ **More info** The 7Stanes website has a wealth of info – 7stanesmountainbiking.com.

› Lowdown

☺ **Locals do**

Ride fast. Innerleithen has raised some of the world's fastest riders!

Section the downhills; it's a long push from the bottom back to the top.

☹ **Locals don't**

Hit the jumps when its windy: Caddon Bank has a wind sock at the top, just to warn you.

Ride without protection. There's a reason why it's tough to ride here.

✔ **Pros**

Great variety of downhill trails.

Technical riding.

Uplift available on some weekends.

✖ **Cons**

Not suited to novice or less confident riders.

Uplift only runs some weekends and is often oversubscribed.

tight turns through conifer trees (an Innerleithen trademark), which is what you'll find on the more natural style downhill runs. The trails all run down to the same finish with the bombhole jump which has seen many of the world's finest racers launching into the finish arena over the years. Uplifts are courtesy of upliftscotland.com.

Freeride Even though there's no dedicated free ride area at Innerleithen, the DH courses are graded orange for freestylers as they contain plenty of jumps, drops, berms and technical riding that'll get you in the air whether you want to or not. The final descent of the XC known as Cadon Bank which has a great flow again on anything other than a long travel DH bike, or riding across to the left and picking up one of the downhill routes.

↘6 Kirroughtree (7Stanes)

Train station Dumfries
Nearest city Glasgow
Sat Nav DG8 7BE

Opening times Similar to the other 7Stanes centres, the trails are open 24/7/365 days a year. You will have to pay for parking but it's only £1 for an hour or £3 for the whole day.

Location Just 40 km to the west of Dumfries and 4 km to the southwest of Newton Stewart is the 7Stanes facility of Kirroughtree. Exit the A74(M) at junction 17 or 18 and head west on the A709 towards Dumfries. Just before town, take the A75 Dumfries ringroad and stay on this road as it heads out west towards Newton Stewart. Turn off the A75 at Palnure (Cairnsmore Road) – signposted for the Visitor Centre – and

follow the road for approx 500 m then take the left hand fork, again signposted for the Visitor Centre. The road leads into the Visitor Centre car park and the start of the trails.

Facilities/Overview You'll notice that Kirroughtree is a little bit further out than the other 7Stanes sites but that generally means its trails are emptier. And what trails! The Galloway Hills are part of the largest tract of forest in the UK, and the site has some spectacular, purpose-built trails that intersect the area. The McMoab area is a must ride for all UK mountain bikers, while the trails themselves have gained a good reputation for their excellent contouring lines and the large granite rock features incorporated in the harder red and black routes. The surfacing used to

build the trails makes for a very artificial road-type surface, but the curves and lines make up for this, mixed in with the exposed areas of rock. There's a great Visitor Centre with a café and bike shop and everything you could wish for at the end of a day's riding.

XC Nothing short of pure XC country, with singletrack straight from the Visitor Centre and very little forest road anywhere on site. The green-graded route (Bargaly Wood) is a 6-km loop around the forest, though does use some minor public roads. The blue-graded Larg Hill is 10 km of easier trails that mirror the original red-graded run here, and there's nothing to stop you dropping into it to try it out. The blue-graded Doon Hill Extension is just that – a 4-km addition to the Larg Hill trail that takes you to a spectacular viewing point. The two major trails here, though, are The Twister – a red-graded 17-km loop that is close to singletrack perfection, with lots of flowing sections that join together through varied terrain and are what mountain biking should be – and the Black Craigs route which at 31 km includes the brilliant McMoab area, a large outcrop of grippy granite rocks (hence the name – Moab in the US is considered a haven for mountain biking), that have painted lines indicating the best routes through. This is a serious XC route with plenty of technical riding and tests for those with ability.

Downhill No specific DH trails here.

Freeride There's nothing that can be classed as freeride-specific, though the McMoab area would suit those who love northshore style riding, and there are plenty of jumps and drops around the trails. However, it might be best to head to another trail centre if you're looking for specific bike parks.

Easy The green routes are obviously the easiest but the blue routes are a better choice.

Hard McMoab is technically demanding, but incredibly rewarding with some unbelievable

views and a real feeling of being in the great outdoors.

Not to miss McMoab – one of the coolest trail features in the UK.

Remember to avoid Heading here if you want fast paced downhill and big drops.

Nearest Bike/Hire shop The Break Pad (thebreakpad.com, T01671 401303) is at Kirroughtree Visitor Centre where all the trails start. They hire a mix of bikes from kids to full suspension rigs and carry out repairs on site.

Local accommodation
The Break Pad has a B&B at Castle Douglas (T01556 502 693) with biker needs in mind, or Eskdale B&B (T01671 404195) is one of many bike-friendly stays in town.

Eating The Visitor Centre is the place to head for refreshments and is open 1000-1600 every day. Times can change depending on season.

ⓘ **More info**
7stanesmountainbiking.com.

> **Lowdown**

🌐 **Locals do**
Know the McMoab routes like the back of their hand.

🌐 **Locals don't**
Ride off the waymarked routes – these can be easily damaged by bikes.

✔ **Pros**
Good rock features and sinuous singletrack.

✖ **Cons**
Not as many good descents like other Scottish sites.

Ⓚ Ⓟ Ⓗ Ⓜ Ⓢ Ⓢ Ⓢ Ⓜ Ⓠ Ⓢ
Ⓢ Ⓟ Ⓟ

Train station Dumfries
Nearest city Glasgow
Sat Nav DG2 8HB
Opening times The trails are open
24/7/365 days a year and are free to ride.
Car parking is at the trail head and is £3
for the day.

Location Mabie is close to Dumfries,
roughly 4 km to the south of the city
centre. Leave the A74(M) at junction 17
or 18 (Lockerbie) and head west on the
A709 towards Dumfries. Continue until
you reach town and then take a left
onto Shakespeare Street, then left onto
Dockhead, right onto Pleasance Avenue
and then another left onto the A710
New Abbey Road, in the direction of
New Abbey. After 3 km Mabie 7Stanes is
signposted off to the right of this road.

Facilities/Overview Mabie Forest
is self-titled as the original mountain
biking venue in the southwest of
Scotland and was well-known for its
fantastic Phoenix Trail long before it
became part of the 7Stanes group.
With that amalgamation have come
good additions to the centre including
graded routes for all standards of rider,
and the longest northshore run in the
UK. Well worth a visit for all standards,
though fans of balanced, technical
riding will perhaps get the most from
the site, and fans of northshore will be
in their element.

XC If you're unsure about riding off-
road, the purple trail at Mabie is a 12-
km loop with a mixture of forest road
and B roads around the site. It's perfect

for dipping your toe in the water of off-road mountain biking. For those of you already assured in off-road riding, there's a skills area with blue and red-graded obstacles which will give you an indication of what the trails have to offer. The green-graded Big Views loop is a family trail that takes in some gentle climbs with some picturesque view point stops (hence the name). The Woodhead Loop (blue-graded) is a more technical version of the green route with some slightly trickier riding. The red-graded Phoenix Trail is the classic route here, a 19-km loop of natural and manmade singletrack that snakes through the incredible scenery offering you fantastic views and some flowing, twisting trails with plenty of rootsy sections and good jumps. It's classic old-school riding at its best.

Downhill No specific DH trails.

Freeride The orange-graded (some say double black diamond) Dark Side is a 100% northshore trail that contours along the hill and over rocks and stumps for 3.8 km. If you're anything

less than an expert rider, you shouldn't attempt it as it requires excellent balance and trails-like skills to ride. There is also a skills park with dirt jumps, and a mini 4X track that has rollable jumps and is a must for all visitors!

Easy The skills area is perfect for a warm up.

Hard The Dark Side is very difficult and not to be tried by novices.

Not to Miss Checking out the Dark Side – even if you don't want to ride it, it's worth a look!

Remember to Avoid Leaving your gloves on the wood burning stove at the Shed.

Nearest Bike/Hire shop The Shed, at Mabie Forest, is your hub for bike hire and food. See www.cycle-centre.com, T01387 270275.

Local accommodation
For a B&B within walking distance of the town centre, try the Glencairn Villas

(T01387 262467), or for self-catering, the Belmont Stables Cottage has secure bike storage (T01387 268032).

Eating The Shed in Mabie Forest is both a fantastic local-produce café (with log burner and home-made food), and also the bike rental centre.

ⓘ **More info**
7stanesmountainbiking.com.

› **Lowdown**

⊕ **Locals do**
Stun visiting riders with how well they ride on northshore.

Ride at night and on regular evenings organized by the Shed crew.

⊖ **Locals don't**
Ride the northshore clean in one go. It's that tricky.

Go hungry – the food at the Shed is superb.

✔ **Pros**
Traditional singletrack centre.

Great chilled, friendly atmosphere.

✖ **Cons**
No specific downhill routes.

↘8 Newcastleton (7Stanes)

Train station Gretna Green

Nearest city Edinburgh

Sat Nav TD9 0TD

Opening times The trails are open all day, every day and parking is free (at the Visitor Centre).

Location Newcastleton is nestled just on the north side of the Scotland/England border, around 30 km directly north from Carlisle. When driving from Edinburgh, head south on the A7 toward Harwick, then take the B6399 all the way to Newcastleton. For those driving from the south, exit the M6 at junction 44 and head north on the A7 over the border. Take a right into Canonbie and go through the village on the B6357 towards Newcastleton. From the village the 7Stanes site is clearly signposted.

Facilities/Overview This an immensely popular 7Stanes site, and is generally considered the entry-level trail centre, with a good choice of easy routes which don't have a huge vertical climbs (or drops) and have been carefully constructed for those getting into riding. That said, there's a great northshore section, plus a decent red route that can either be tackled by riders looking to get a fast bit of singletrack under their tyres

or those looking to push their limits. There aren't a great deal of amenities at the Newcastleton site itself, though the Dykecroft Visitor Centre (the trail head car park), does have toilets and changing facilities. There are plenty of cafés, restaurants and accommodation back in Newcastleton, a very picturesque borders town.

Downhill Despite having no specific DH trails here, the XC loops all feature long sections of downhill riding. Great for mid-level riders but good riders will not be taxed by the terrain.

XC You'll quickly realise that Newcastleton is all about flowing singletrack with a great collection of runs. The Linns route is ungraded as it's variable from section to section, although it's more like an overall blue route. It's a 100% forest road, 8-km loop that shares a climb with the red route. The Caddrouns route (a 6-km route in which the uphill sections are on forest road, while the descents are feature-full singletrack through the forest, ending with a 2-km ride down with plenty of bridges and swooping berms to try out) – perfect for the family or novices; the red route is a 16-km long run with fast, narrow singletrack, bridge crossings

FORESTRY COMMISSION (ANDY MCCLANDISH)

and boardwalks. The final descent of Swarfe Hill is so flowing that many riders will wish to repeat it immediately.

Freeride There is a northshore area of Newcastleton which has plenty of challenging riders for the level of mountain biker that the site attracts. If you're a northshore lover you may be better off at Mabie, but it's still fun. Other sites do have more jumps and gaps on the trails though.

Easy Caddrouns is the best run for riders who prefer gravity-assisted riding.

Hard Some of the northshore here is genuinely tricky, with skinny rides over decent drops.

Not to Miss The Hidden Valley area – it's packed with well-thought-out features

Remember to Avoid Getting stuck in The Bog.

Nearest Bike/Hire shop The closest bike hire is at Rock UK in nearby Whitaugh Park (3 km from trail head) – T01387 375394.

Local accommodation
The Liddesdale Hotel (T013873 75255), or the Sorbietrees B&B (T013873 75215) – both in Newcastleton – are bike-friendly places to stay.

Eating Head to Newcastleton and try the Olive Tree (T01387 375479)

ⓘ **More info** Check out the official website, 7stanesmountainbiking.com.

> **Lowdown**

☺ **Locals do**
Ride over to England to loop Keilder Forest if they want a longer XC ride.

Twin a ride at Newcastleton with some time in Mabie Forest.

☺ **Locals don't**
Forget to bring supplies.

Have a fully-catered Visitor Centre.

✔ **Pros**
Brilliant place for novice and intermediate riders to head.

You can ride to England and back!

✖ **Cons**
Not as challenging for good riders as the other 7Stanes sites.

No huge descents or challenging climbs.

231

 ⌐9 Drumlanrig Castle

⚙ ⚙ ⚙ ⚙ ⚙ ⚙ ⚙ ⚙ ⚙ ⚙ ⚙

Nearest train station Sanquhar/
Dumfries.

Nearest city Dumfries.

Sat nav postcode DG3 4AG.

Opening times The trails are open
24/7/365 days a year. There's a £6 charge
for riding which goes into the upkeep of
the trails. You won't begrudge paying it.

Location The iconic Drumlanrig
Castle is around 20 km north of
Dumfries, just off the A76. Leave the
M74 at junction 18 (from the south)
or 15 (from the north), head through
Dumfries and then north towards
Kilmarnock on the A76. Head through
the village of Thornhill, around 25 km
north of Dumfries and then a few
km after Drumlanrig Castle is clearly
signposted off to the left.

Facilities/Overview Situated
amongst the mightily impressive
7Stanes trail centres, you'd be
surprised to see a different trail centre
but Drumlanrig Castle has its own
treats on offer – a fantastic castle
(which was where the bicycle was
invented, and houses a bike museum),
a forward thinking estate with
plenty of facilities such as tea shops,
cafés and restaurants, sustainability
workshops, salmon fishing and plenty
more besides. And then there are the
trails – Rik Allsop has built some of the
most natural and flowing singletrack
in the UK around the estate, with
both complete novices and the most
expert of riders in mind. And if you're
done with the trails here and want
more, Ae Forest is 10 km away, while
Newcastleton, Mabie, Dalbeattie,
Kirroughtree and Glentrool are within
30 km.

XC There are so many XC trails here
it's literally an XC Valhalla, with perfect
introduction routes in the four green-
graded trails – The Policy (a 3-km loop
around the castle), Rocking Stone
(a 5-km loop through woodlands
and around the castle), Low Gardens

(an 8-km route past the loch and
river), and Burnsands (13-km ride to
Burnsands village and back). There are
two blue-graded trails – Copycat (a
9-km loop through the forest which
incorporates some of the easier riding
of the red-graded trail), and Secret
Forest (11 km of woodland riding).
Then there are the two serious routes
– the red-graded The Old School, a
20-km loop of classic, flowing
singletrack with plenty of roots, drops,
jumps and technical sections; and the
black-graded Magic Eight – 8 km of
testing riding which will push your
roots skills to the limit. All routes are
waymarked and within the estate
grounds, which makes for incredibly
pleasant riding, and some routes have
uncovered the old estate paths from
the Victorian era, when the estate
employed up to 80 path builders.

Downhill Despite having no specific
DH trails at Drumlanrig, the nature of
the trails means downhillers will find
something fun to ride and definitely
keep their bike skills up to scratch.
There is an uplift service but it runs very
infrequently. It's best to check with the
bike shop first to see if it's running.

Freeride There are no specific freeride
obstacles at Drumlanrig.

Easy Anyone looking for an easy ride
and a nice day out will find the green
routes to suit their needs.

Hard If you can handle the root-riding
of the red run, it's wise to move onto
the black run.

CHRIS MORAN

CHRIS MORAN

Not to miss A visit to the bike museum.

Remember to avoid Pushing your bike uphill to session the downhill bits. Avoiding riders is easier said than done.

Nearest Bike/Hire shop Rik's Bike Shed is on site (T01848 330080, and there's a Rik's page on drumlanrig. co.uk) and has a range of hire bikes from baby seats all the way to black trail worthy bikes.

Local accommodation Druidhall Farm has camping and caravan facilities, T0870 214 3271, or you can stay in self catering hostels like the Lotus Lodge in Wanlockhead, T01659 74544.

Eating The castle grounds has its own tea shop and the fantastic Old Stables has a couple of shops for you to buy supplies.

ⓘ **More info** Drumlanrig.com is the Estate website and has plenty of pages on the facilities and trails.

› Lowdown

☺ **Locals do**
Ride when it's wet – the roots are *even more* challenging, and there's a bike powerwash installed (and a shower block for riders) so getting muddy is no problem.

☹ **Locals don't**
Advertise their trails too much. This is one of the best-kept secrets in the UK.

✔ **Pros**
Brilliant, natural terrain, with incredible views and infrastructure.

Perfect family or multi-activity day out.

✘ **Cons**
Could have more high-end trails, and a DH track (though more trails are planned).

RICHARD NORGATE

Safety
Steve Ireland

Steve Ireland is behind the "Think Safe, Think 7" campaign. Here's how it breaks down:

❶ Before you leave the house

Make sure your bike is well-serviced and up to the trails you plan to ride. Make sure you're packing a good quality helmet, gloves, elbow and knee protection. If you're going on an XC route, have all the relevant maps with you, note any diversions or closures when you get to the trail centre, and make sure the route isn't above your fitness and skill level. Carry some first aid kit, and have some way of contacting the emergency services. Don't forget that a whistle is handy for when there's no mobile coverage. The distress signal is six whistle blasts or six torch flashes once every minute.

❷ Expect and anticipate

Dry conditions make tracks dusty and loose, wet conditions lead to mud. Anticipate other track users and beware of vehicles. Take special care at junctions. If you're in a group, always progress at the pace of the slowest member. Stay together.

❸ Here is where I am

Be aware of where you are at all times, use trail or ordnance survey maps and keep be aware of landmarks identified on these. Look out for emergency information posts on some of the more remote routes.

❹ Always stop to help others

Always offer to help someone if they appear lost or in trouble. Having someone to talk to can help a lot.

❺ Protect yourself and others

If you come across an accident don't put yourself or others in danger, assess the situation and immediate area, and warn other users to avoid further accident. Protect yourself and the casualty.

❻ Provide First Aid if you can

Assess the casualty and decide what to do. Remember A.B.C. (Airway, Breathing, Circulation – signs of life, blood loss). Be aware of spinal injuries – never move an injured person if they complain of back or neck injuries. Control any bleeding with pressure and elevation. Make the casualty warm and comfortable and place unconscious casualties in the recovery position if possible.

❼ Yell and tell

Consider options for safe return to trailhead or send for/call for help using 999 or the local emergency number. 911 on a mobile abroad gets you through to the local emergency services. Ask for Police (Mountain Rescue) and THEN Ambulance if not in easy reach of a route suitable for an ambulance If it's not possible to send for or call for help, use the international distress signal to attract attention (again – six whistle blasts/torch flashes repeated every minute).

S.10 Cathkin Braes

◎ ◎ ◎

Nearest railway station Burnside
(Strathclyde)/Busby
Nearest city Glasgow
Sat nav postcode G76 9EY

Location Cathkin Braes County Park
is located on the southern edge of
Glasgow, about 8 km south of the city
centre. Driving from Glasgow, head
south on the M74 and exit at junction
14 onto the A728. Continue on this
road and drive over the railway tracks,
the road will turn into the B766
(Carmunnock Road), follow this road
towards the town of Carmunnock and
take a left onto Windlaw Road. Take
the first right onto Gallowhill Road,
then the B759 (Cathkin Road) and
the trail car park will be on your right,
about 2 km up the road.

Facilities There's not too much
situated at the trails themselves but
Glasgow is only 8 km north, and the
town of Carmunnock has a few shops
and amenities.

Rough round-up Glasgow council
appointed Phil Saxena (of Architrail)
to build this track for the 2014
Commonwealth Games so that it
reached UCI standards. The track
is a 5.5-km figure of 8 loop that is
red-graded with blue and black
options so that the majority of riders
can test themselves. There are drop
offs, berms, rocky sections, steep
descents, tough climbs, boulders and
more – everything a Commonwealth
track needs. If you're in the North
of England or in Scotland, this is
a great opportunity to try out a
Commonwealth-standard track.

Conditions The terrain here is a mix
of ancient woodland with exposed
wide open spaces so it will be at
the mercy of the weather. As it's a
Commonwealth track, expect it to
drain well but the woodland will still
get muddy after adverse weather.

ⓘ **More info** The Glasgow Council
website has all info on glasgow.gov.
uk and Developing Mountain Biking
In Britain has plenty of info as well –
dmbins.com.

S.11 East Renfrewshire

◎ ◎ ◎ ◎ ◎

Train station Patterton
Nearest city Glasgow
Sat nav postcode N/A

Location East Renfrewshire covers
a large area just south of Glasgow.
All trails and routes can be accessed
via roads branching off the M77, the
motorway that flows south of Glasgow.

Facilities As the trails are spread out
over a large area there is no central
hub for these trails, let alone a Visitor
Centre. The trails themselves won't
hold many facilities, if any, so it's best
to take your own supplies with you.

Rough round-up Much like Highland
Perthshire, East Renfrewshire is an area
that encompasses a lot of woods and
routes. Because of this there are many,
many trails to mention, perhaps too
many to write down. Luckily, the local
council has produced a booklet that
shows off the 10 best trails in the area
to ride, and it's available to download
from eastrenfrewshire.gov.uk. The trails
vary in difficulty as to welcome every
rider, whether they be experienced or
novices. There aren't any downhill-

specific trails here but as it's a very
hilly area, the climbs are usually
accompanied by some great descents.

Conditions The trails take in a
combination of conditions but
mostly forest routes that are prone to
becoming muddy during bad weather.

ⓘ **More info** Your best source of
information is the council website –
eastrenfrewshire.gov.uk.

S.12 Jedburgh

◎ ◎ ◎ ◎

Train station Berwick-upon-Tweed
Nearest city Newcastle-upon-Tyne/
Edinburgh
Sat Nav TD8 6BE

Location Jedforest trails start from
the town of Jedburgh, which is just on
the Scottish Border, around halfway
between Newcastle and Edinburgh on
the A68. From either north or south
take the A68 and follow signs for the
town centre. There's a Towns Car Park
with tourist information next door –
they should be happy to give you a
free trail map.

Facilities There are no cafés or snack
stops on the trails, but all start and finish
in town so you can loop back to get
food or supplies for the next ride up
into the hills. The ease of riding back
into town and out again makes this
picture-perfect border town extremely
popular with mountain bikers.

Rough round-up If you're looking for
man-made singletrack that's built for
those looking for thrills, then 7Stanes
is probably more for you as Jedforest is
there for riders who want to get out on
their bikes and take in some stunning

Southern Scotland Jedburgh

235

countryside, with plenty of stopping points of interest. Some of the trails are ancient roman thoroughfares that the Jedburgh community have lovingly restored. This is a very historical area and the town is keen to preserve what assets they have.

Terrain There are plenty of man-made sections to the trails, to keep them flowing and to reinforce boggy sections etc, but essentially these are natural trails that sometimes piggyback on forest roads and even the odd bit of tarmac.

XC There are three main routes on offer here – the Dere Street Dash, a 10.5-km trail that takes in slightly steeper descents and more challenging surfaces; and two family trails that take in two loops of Lanton Wood. These two loops are perfect for family rides or for young riders looking to improve their skills on the berms and jumps. The main trail here is the red-graded Justice Trail, which combines technical riding with great views over the Oxnan and Jed Valleys and the Cheviot Hills in the distance. It is listed as being 40 km, which makes it a huge loop with all manner of singletrack adventures along the way, but in reality there are opt-out points at 5,10,15,20 and 30 km so you don't have to do the full trek if you start to get tired. That said, there are plenty of stops along the route should you wish to go the distance, including a castle stop and plenty of stream crossings.

Downhill and freeride No specific trails here for DH lovers. Best advised to head to nearby Innerleithen or Glentress.

Conditions As it's mostly natural riding, there can be a lot of mud around during the winter months. There's also a huge horse riding scene in the area too, though Jedburgh have built separate routes for riders in places.

ⓘ **More info** The Jedforest Trails have a great website with all the info you could need on their history, construction and the ethos behind the town, jedforesttrails.org.

Newmilns Bike Park

Nearest city Glasgow
Nearest train station Kilmarnock
Sat nav postcode KA16 9EB

Location The Newmilns Bike Park is around 32 km south of Glasgow and only 8 km east of Kilmarnock. It's located at Newmilns Dry Ski Slope so is relatively easy to find. Driving from Glasgow, head south on the M77 and leave at junction 6 heading onto the A77. Take a right onto the A719 and continue until you reach a roundabout. Take a left onto the A71 and drive for about 5 km, take a left onto High Street and the ski slope should be signposted from there.

Facilities As the bike park is part of the ski slope, there are plenty of facilities and amenities to be used at the ski slope itself, including a café for riders to refuel and continue riding. It'll cost you £2.50 to ride the trails but it's a small hit to the wallet for a long day's worth of fun!

Rough round-up This is a relatively small set up but incredibly fun at the same time. It's a great local downhill track with two main routes, a pump

track and dirt jumps. The first downhill track (named the A-Line mini) has tabletops, jumps, berms, drop-offs, rollers, rock gardens and the option of some northshore. The B-Line Mini has technical flat turns, off camber corners and a series of linked berms, nicknamed 'the Luge'. Both tracks have been created to really test and develop riders' skills. The dirt jumps aren't huge but are great to practice on. Experienced riders might get bored, but beginners will be able to become confident before moving onto bigger things.

Conditions There's been a lot of work going into the berms, making them into tightly packed soil, whereas the DH trails themselves are generally soil-based and can get muddy after bad weather. It's a site that has had a lot of work put into it so expect it to drain well, and ride fast.

ⓘ **More info** Extreme Valley Riders are the main bike club at the slope, so it's worth looking at their site before travelling – evriders.co.uk. Also check out the ski slope site skinewmilns.com.

Whitelee MTB Trails

Nearest train station Hairmyres/ Kilmarnock
Nearest city Glasgow
Sat nav postcode G76 0QQ

Location The Whitelee MTB Trails are located in the middle of a wind farm, just 16 km south of Glasgow. When driving from Glasgow, head south on the M77 and leave at junction 6, onto the B764. The Whitelee Visitor Centre will be signposted from here. It's a wind farm so it's pretty hard to miss!

Facilities There's already a Visitor Centre on site for anyone visiting the wind farm, a centre that holds a café and is a great hub for what will be a nice set-up when the new trails are finished.

Overview This site is going through a big development, and Whitelee Wind Farm have enlisted the help of Architrail legend, Phil Saxena. Despite the wind farm being a relatively flat area, there are plans to build two XC trails (both blue-graded with red sections) with rollers, drop-offs, jumps and northshore. There's a skills area to be built and a pump track as well for riders to get their bike handling perfected. All of the trails will make up just 4 km's worth of riding but it'll be packed into a small area and sounds like a lot of fun.

Aside from the development, there are already plenty of traffic-free routes that are used by riders.

Conditions The new development will be all purpose-built and so you should expect excellent drainage.

ⓘ **More info** Check out the Whitelee Wind Farm for more info – whiteleewindfarm.co.uk.

Central &
Northern Scotland

Fort William [JUSTIN SULLIVAN PHOTOGRAPHY]

Central & Northern Scotland

Motorway
A Road
B Road
✈ Airports
⛴ Ferries

Trails...

1 Aviemore
2 Carron Valley Trails
3 Comrie Croft Bike Trails
4 Contin Forest
5 Fort William
6 Glencoe
7 Golspie Highland Wildcat Trails
8 Glenlivet Estate
9 Highland Perthshire Trails
10 Isle of Arran
11 Kyle of Sutherland Trails
12 Laggan Wolftrax
13 Learnie Red Rocks
14 Mains Farm Trails
15 Middleden MTB Trails
16 Moray Monster Trails
17 Pitfichie Mountain Cycle Trails
18 Pollok Country Park
19 The Fire Tower Trail
20 The Kelpies Trails
21 Callendar Estate
22 Donkey Hill Dirt Track
23 Duchany Woods
24 Dunkeld DH
25 Kirkhill Mountain Bike Park
26 Loch Ard Forest Trails
27 Tetsmuir Forest

When riding up in northern Scotland, you are sure to find some outstanding terrain, in fact some of the best in the UK. If you like your riding empty, scenic and hardcore, then central and northern Scotland are definitely for you. The area is dominated by the famous Fort William, home to the UCI World Cup tour since 2000, host to the World Championships in 2014, and, at time of writing, newly confirmed the dates for the World Cup in 2015. It has the UK's sole full-time gondola uplift (much like one might find in the trail centres of Europe such as Les Gets and Schladming), Fort Bill has been at the forefront of UK riding for what seems like an eternity.

That said, this part of the country is also home to other outstanding gems, not least the stunning Kyle or Sutherland Trails. The sheer amount of man-hours that are going into building trails in this region is staggering, and if centres such as Golspie, Learnie Red Rocks and Kirkhill were to be found in southern or central England, they would dominate the local scene. In this part of the world, they are just yet another ultra-cool place to visit. Of course if you do get spoilt for choice, and actually over-ride many of the trails here, you could always pop over to the Isle of Arran where another level of interesting riding (in even less populated areas) is underway. If you find that this is too crowded for you, then I'm afraid a one-way ticket to outer-Mongolia with a bike, a shovel and the intention to dig your own trails is the only remedy.

Overview

It's not hard to see why the majority of riders in this area head to Fort William to test themselves and their nerves, but it's recommended that you stick around for longer than you had planned. You'll be surprised by Inverness as its ratio riding to population is incredible. Just take a 30 minute trip out of the city limits and you'll be spoilt for choice with Contin Forest, Learnie Red Rocks and much more available. Just a little more time on the clock and you can make it to Laggan Wofltrax, Aviemore and the windswept views of Golspie for some worthwhile riding. Further east and just north of Aberdeen, you'll find Pitfichie and Kirkhill Forest, and the link road between the two cities goes directly past Moray Monster Trails. It might not be an obvious destination but a trip to the two centres would reap huge benefits, and the staggering quality of the trails would only be matched by how empty they are. If you're inclined to do so, we suggest getting a sleeper train to Fort Bill and heading east from there.

For the riders situated around Glasgow and Edinburgh wanting to try something other than a 7 Stanes site, the Carron Valley Trails is the obvious choice, though if you can handle a small journey, a trip to the Fire Tower Trail on the way to Jura is a ride that will be rewarded by one of the coolest days ever, and remind you how much greatness is on offer in Scotland.

⟨↘1⟩ Aviemore

ⓧ ⓧ ⓧ ⓧ

Train station Aviemore
Nearest city Inverness
Sat Nav PH22 1QU (for Glenmore Lodge)

Location You'll find Aviemore on the A9 main trunk road through the highlands between Perth and Inverness. When driving from either city, head along the A9 to the town, then head along the B970 (Cairngorm Mountain should be signposted). Around 7 km from the town heading up the hill to the ski lifts, you'll come to Glenmore Lodge, home to the Scotland National Outdoor Training Centre, which can be used as a starting point for the riding and is home to the Glenmore Lodge Skills MTB Centre.

Facilities Aviemore is on par with Fort William as being one of Scotland's premier outdoor hotspots, with plenty of cafés, outdoor shops and supplies. Glenmore Lodge has a café and dining area, bar, and all sorts of adventurous facilities such as climbing walls, swimming pools and massage areas.

Rough round-up Aviemore – and its neighbouring mountain, Cairngorm – has been at the forefront of Scotland's winter sports industry for decades, so it is strange that they haven't embraced the mountain bike revolution as much as other centres such as Fort William. The omission is more startling as Aviemore's infrastructure includes numerous ski lifts, arguably the most scenic of the highland peaks, and Scotland's only funicular mountain railway, which would be perfect as a bike uplift. Perhaps this will change

in the near future, but currently there is only a skills loop and pump track at Glenmore Lodge (though small, and not permanently open to the public – call before heading there), and plenty of natural singletrack on the surrounding hills. You won't find any of the trails waymarked, reinforced or had any trail-building work to it. The reason for this is to keep the riding very natural and man-made-trail-free. Either way, the riding here is spectacular in its own right (and the town boasts two good bike shops), but it will involve route-finding, and possibly walking over boggy sections or muddy areas if there has been recent rain. If you want to know what riding was like in the highlands 15 years ago, before the advent of purpose-built trail centres and infrastructure to keep riders coming back for more, this is the place to head.

Conditions There are no purpose-built trails here, so the weather will determine what the singletrack conditions are.

ⓘ **More info** Despite the lack of waymarked trails, there is still a thriving mountain bike community. To go on organised rides, try Glenmore Lodge's website – glenmorelodge.org.uk, or you could try Bothy Bikes in Aviemore – bothybikes.co.uk.

Central & Northern Scotland Aviemore

FORESTRY COMMISSION SCOTLAND

Carron Valley Trails

Train station Camelon
Nearest city Glasgow
Sat Nav FK6 5JL

Location The Carron Valley Trails are found next to Carron Bridge, a small village around 10 km to the west of Falkirk, and roughly half way between Edinburgh and Glasgow. Travelling from Glasgow, head out on the M80 towards Stirling and exit at junction 5 heading towards Denny on A872. Go through Denny and take the B818 west in the direction of Fintry, and after you pass through Carron Bridge look for a turning to the left around 2 km further along the road. From Edinburgh, head northwest on the M9 towards Stirling, then take the M876 to Denny and follow the directions as above.

Facilities You won't find much at the trails except for a car park, which is open from 0730 until 1800 in winter and from 0730 until 2100 in the summer and is pay and display. Food and drinks are available from either Carron Bridge (10 km) or Kilsyth (10 km) so take supplies with you if you want to eat, drink and ride.

Rough round-up With its close proximity to Glasgow, Stirling and Edinburgh, Carron Valley is extremely popular with mountain bikers since the early 2000s, and the trails here have been built with year-round riding in mind. There is one waymarked trail – the Red Trail, a 10.5-km loop which branches out here and there and consists of four different styles of riding to suit virtually everyone.

Terrain The land here is Forestry Commission-owned, but the trails were largely built by the Carron Valley Development Group, who have poured thousands of man-hours in to the area and created some amazing purpose-built trails.

XC The four sections of the Red Trail are: Pipe Dream – an uphill section with drops and snippets of downhill to get you warmed up for the rest of the route. Next is Eas Dubh (the Black Waterfall) which holds some stunning views. It's best to take them in before trying out the tricky, rocky descent that is Kelpie Staircase, just before the switchbacks of Birling Boghills. Then comes the swooping lines of the Cannonball Run, and finally The Runway – a feature-packed descent with fun-park style obstacles such as banks, wallrides and tabletops.

Downhill The trails here will hold some treats for downhill enthusiasts but there are no specific DH tracks.

Freeride Again, there's plenty to keep freeriders happy here, but no specific bike park or northshore areas.

Conditions This is a mixture of forest land with plenty of all-weather surfacing and rock features.

ⓘ **More info** The Forestry Commission site has all the info on routes and the surrounding area – forestry.gov.uk.

Central & Northern Scotland Carron Valley Trails

ⓘ ⓟ ⓞ ⓞ ⓞ ⓞ ⓞ ⓞ ⓞ ⓞ
ⓞ ⓟ

Train station Perth
Nearest city Perth
Sat Nav PH7 4JZ

Location Comrie Croft is a four-star independent hostel, itself around 25 km west of Perth on the A85, and plays host to the Comrie Croft Bike Trails. When travelling from Perth, head west on the A85 and just after the town of Crieff, take a right into the hotel grounds. If travelling form the south, head north on the M9, then the A9 towards Perth. Take a left onto the A822 towards Crieff, then the A85 towards Crainlarich and the hostel is on the right off the main road.

Facilities This is nothing more than an impressive set-up – Comrie Croft Hostel is a 4-star, 70-bed building with communal lounging areas, laundry, drying, games room, café, bike wash and snack stop. There's also a bike shop on site that hires out bikes, repairs bikes and sells bike gear, next door to an eco campsite, toilets, route maps, showers and high-pressure bike wash.

Rough round-up This is another great example of how work between local riders and a forward-thinking landowner can help the mountain biking community by providing fun trails and a great atmosphere. They also organise regular races (the Hairy Coo), and have everything on hand for a good day or weekend out. Perfect for those who can already ride and fancy something more chilled than

CHRIS MORAN

the 7Stanes areas, or who just want another angle on highland riding. With the eco campsite, the emphasis here is on sustainable tourism and enjoying the countryside.

Terrain As it's in the heart of Perthshire, expect staggering views, waterfalls and open moorland.

XC Comrie has a lot to offer in terms of trails with a skills park to test your handling skills before hitting the trails themselves. There's a blue-graded trail that is suitable for novice riders, kids and families. At only 4 km in length it's not the most demanding of rides but the gentle uphill is met with a fun downhill section on the way back – that's possible to be lopped if you're really enjoying yourself. There are two other trails that start from the same point – the left-hand turn takes you down the (new for 2013) red run, which passes over some rocky sections with some twisting sections before leaving at the quarry. The right-hand turn takes you down the black route, which isn't too difficult but still requires good bike handling skills with rocks, roots and steep slopes littered all over the place. The alternative is to use the Croft as a launchpad into some of the available XC riding in the surrounding hills and

Strathearn Valley. There are lots to choose from, with varying degrees of difficulty (for example, you could head to Comrie Village on an green-graded 5-km loop, or do the Loch Tay route – a 35-km expert trail), and Comrie Croft have handily drawn quite cute maps showing each of the tens of routes available.

Downhill: There are no specific DH tracks here, but the Comrie Croft trail does feature a descent with plenty of obstacles to keep most riders happy.

Freeride The disused quarry is ever-expanding and always holds fun for the freerider. The skills park is not for the freeride dedicated.

Conditions The majority of the trails here have been built to work in most conditions. However, expect the longer, unofficial XC routes to be bogged after heavy weather.

ⓘ **More info** Try the fantastic Comrie Croft official website – comriecroftbikes.co.uk.

Central & Northern Scotland Comrie Croft Bike Trails

⟨↘4⟩ Contin Forest

Nearest railway station Dingwall/ Conon Bridge
Nearest city Inverness
Sat nav postcode N/A

Location Contin Forest is between the towns of Contin and the larger town of Strathpeffer, itself around 22 km northwest of Inverness. from Inverness take the A9 north, then the A835 towards Conon Bridge and on to Contin. Just past the village, around 200 m past the 30 mph speed limit sign, take a right where there's a Forestry Commission Scotland sign in green. At the top of this road is a car park and the start of the Torrachilty Cycle Trail.

Facilities There are no facilities at the forest but nearby Contin has shops and Strathpeffer is the bigger town in the area and home to Square Wheels (see below).

Rough round-up The main route here is a 16-km, combined blue-graded and ungraded trail which follows the River Blackwater with the 1046-metre-high Ben Wyvis in the distant view, and is a perfect family route. The ungraded section is a 12-km natural-singletrack route with some reinforced northshore-style wood over the boggier sections, and is home to the hardy 24-hour enduro race; The Strathpuffer 24 (see strathpuffer.co.uk for entry details). Call into Square Wheels in Strathpeffer to get directions and more details on the competition route and others in the Contin Forest. The guys that run Square Wheels have

waymarked some of the routes there and have maps available in the shop.

Conditions This is natural terrain with rock drops, rootsy sections and some difficult moss-sections that make the ridge rides quite scary. Great in the dry or when icy though!

ⓘ **More info** The Cycling Scotland website has more info on the forest at cycling.visitscotland.com, or try Square Wheels in Strathpeffer – squarewheels. biz, T01997 421000.

Central & Northern Scotland Contin Forest

245

Train station Fort William/Banavie

Nearest city Inverness

Sat Nav PH33 6SW

Opening times The trails are open all day, every day and are free to ride. The Gondola is open nearly all year (it's closed for a month between November and December for annual maintenance) but times change depending on the season. Normal hours are 1000-1700 but in the summer months they're open 0930-1800. A day ticket will cost you £14.50 and that could equate to 8-10 runs if you're very good! It's best to check with the website for concessions and age price ranges, and it's best to check with the website before leaving as many of the trails are often closed for competitions and/or maintenance.

Location Fort William is based on the banks of the Loch Linnie in western Scotland, roughly mid way up the country. Driving from any direction, the A82 is the major road into the town. Head north east on the A82, driving in the direction of Inverness, and follow the signs for Aonoch Mor/Nevis Range Gondola after 3 km.

Facilities/Overview Where to begin? Fort William is the easily the most famous UK mountain bike centre, mainly due to the hosting of World Cup races since 2002 (and the stand-alone World Championships in 2007). It's home to the UK's only gondola uplift and has arguably the best infrastructure – a Visitor Centre, cafés, restaurants and more. You're spoilt for choice with purpose-built DH tracks, an incredible 4X track, world champs-standard XC courses, and hundreds of kilometres of singletrack stretching in every direction over the highlands. Fort William town (affectionately known as Fort Bill), is the self-proclaimed Outdoor Capital of the UK, and filled with outdoor types. Hiring a bike and getting some bike-friendly accommodation is the easiest thing in the world.

Downhill The downhill at the Nevis Range is commonly known as simply the Fort William Downhill. It's a world cup standard track so don't take it lightly! Despite not having particularly steep sections, the combination of

high speeds, big rocks, holes on the upper slopes and the pure physicality of the course itself makes this track a real test for riders and bikes. The top of the course is very exposed so can be difficult in very windy conditions. It constantly wins the riders award for best DH and is for very good riders only.

XC The Witch's Trail is the main XC trail at Fort William and has many strings to its bow. It's a mixture of 7 different sections, all varying in difficulty. There have been two new sections built for 2014 – one green graded and one blue graded – both are easy descents that have been built to get novice riders more confident in the trails. There are a further 40 km of trails in the forest ranging from easy, low level forest tracks and disused railway lines to technical purpose built single track. The Cour Loop is an 18-km, blue-graded loop designed to get riders out into the incredible scenery. The red-graded 10 Under The Ben is a 17-km enduro test with some really tricky sections, specifically at the Nessie descent. The World Champs loop is a classic red-graded 9-km loop with one big uphill and a corresponding DH trail that the UCI World Cup uses as a race route.

Freeride The 4X track here was the first ever venue for the format in the World Cup so it's easy to believe that some call it the best in the UK. Situated at the bottom of the gondola, it's perfect for those wishing to get in the air, while at the base of the station is a skills area to see if you can handle obstacles that you'll encounter on the Witch's Trail. There is also a dedicated dirt jump area near the quarry with three lines ranging from beginner to expert with good progression throughout the sets.

Easy The skills area is perfect to discover what grade of trail you'd be comfortable on.

Hard The Fort William Downhill is simply one of the best, and trickiest runs in the world, never mind the UK.

Not to miss A trip up to Ben Nevis. It's Britain's highest mountain and beautiful in good weather.

Remember to avoid Taking a run down the DH track without walking it first.

Nearest Bike/Hire shop Alpine Bikes (T01397 704008, alpinebikes.com) can be found at Fort William holding a fully stocked workshop. They also hire out a fleet of bikes for every ability level.

Local accommodation
Unless your stay coincides with the UCI Mountain bike world cup, you're not going to have any problems finding somewhere to stay in Fort William. The Cruarchan is a well established and friendly hotel (T01397 702022) and B&Bs like Burntree House (T01397 701735). There's so much you will always be able to find something to suit your needs.

Eating The Pinemartin Café Bar is situated at the bottom of the gondola, while the Snowgoose Restaurant Bar is at the summit. Both serve home-cooked food to many hungry riders. There are also plenty of places in the nearby town; Crannog Seafood Restaurant is situated on the Lochside, and is well known for it's locally sourced fish from an area renowned for the quality of its fishing waters (T01397 705589).

ⓘ **More info** The official website is.ridefortwilliam.co.uk or try bike. nevisrange.co.uk for more info.

NICK BAYLISS

> **Lowdown**

😊 **Locals do**
Section the downhill as it's a very full run.

Wear protective gear.

😠 **Locals don't**
Go up the the gondola in high winds. The top station is always worse than the car park.

Just ride trails in the Nevis Range. There are some excellent trails in the Fort William area.

👍 **Pros**
Great facilities and town.

You can ride courses that the world's best ride on.

Stunning setting when the weather is good.

👎 **Cons**
Can have long periods of bad weather.

⊕ ⊕ ⊕ ⊕ ⊕ ⊕ ⊕

Train station Bridge of Orchy/
Fort William
Nearest city Glasgow
Sat Nav PH49 4HZ

Location Glencoe is another of
Scotland's permanent ski resorts, and
can be found around 30 km south of
Fort William on the A82. Driving from
either the north or south, take the A82
trunk road between Fort William and
Glasgow and you'll see the ski centre is
clearly signed as you go over the high
pass of Rannoch Moor.

Facilities Glencoe might be a fully-
functioning ski resort in the winter but
there isn't too much in the way of a
base lodge. The nearby Clachaig Inn is
a brilliant, traditional pub which also
has accommodation and a thriving
calendar of events (clachaig.com).

Rough round-up Glencoe has a
technical and steep, black-graded
downhill run, that some claim is even
more difficult than nearby Fort William's
track – you can gain access to it by the
chairlift (tickets cost £25 for adults and
should get you enough uplifts to fill
your day with riding). Alongside the
black run is a red route that has gained
a lot of praise from both DH and XC
riders as it's suitable for both bikes. It's
starts at the top of the chairlift and takes
you down a track of jumps, bumps and
berms. In addition, there are a wealth
of XC routes in the surrounding hills,
including a fantastic 7-km descent
down to Kinlochleven. The Glencoe area
is a satellite of the mighty Fort William
mountain bike centre (it is in the same

council district of Lochabers) and
many of the XC routes around
Glencoe are on the Fort William
website (ridefortwilliam.co.uk).

Terrain This is some of the steepest
terrain in Scotland, and a highland moor
mostly bereft of trees from Rannoch
Moor upwards. It's wise to expect
rocky, shaley descents over granite
and heather tracks. You also have the
option to descend past the base at
Glencoe to sample some lovely forest
to the east and west of the ski lifts. It is
possibly the most hardcore of all the
Scottish resorts, and has a fabulous,
outdoor history, much of which is
shown in photographs on the walls of
the Clachaig Inn. The area has a rugged
beauty that is almost unique, even in
Scotland, and the incredible colours
of the valley have been used in many
recent films including the recent Harry
Potter and the Prisoner of Azkaban.

Conditions Much of the XC riding
at the moment is forest road before

descending into singletrack offshoots
to various villages. It's the one
thing that lets Glencoe down when
compared to 7Stanes and Fort William.

ⓘ **More info** glencoescotland.
com is the main place to visit for all
info on XC routes in the area, as well
as having links to accommodation.
Glencoemountain.com is the official
website when looking for chair lifts
and all resort information. Fort William
has suggested XC routes as well as
nearby bikeparks and other places of
riding interest at ridefortwilliam.co.uk.

↘7 Golspie Highland Wildcat Trails

⊕ ⊕ ⊕ ⊕ ⊕

Train station Golspie/Dunrobin Castle
Nearest city Inverness
Sat Nav KW10 6TH (for the town car park)
Opening times The trails are open 24/7 365 days a year and are free to ride

MORVEN MUNRO'S/SCOTTISHWOODLANDS.CO.UK

Location Roughly 60 km north of Inverness, the most northern purpose-built trails in the UK are the Highland Wildcat Trails. Driving from Inverness, take the A9 north along the coast and the road will lead you directly through Golspie. You'll find that there are three starts to the trails – the first is from the Towns Car Park and clearly waymarked (though it starts with the red-graded uphill), or you can get back on the A9 heading north out of Golspie and take the first left (signposted for Backies), or the second left (Queens Drive, also signposted to Backies), for either of the other two car parks which will save some uphill climbing (though you'll always have to go and get the car at some point!).

Facilities/Overview Golspie trails have a number of attributes – they are the most northerly purpose-built trails in the UK, they were designed by

Pete Laing (the man behind much of Glentress's incredible trails), and they have absolutely jaw-dropping views over the Moray Firth and North Sea, with only the odd castle to disturb your vista. The great thing about Golspie is that it's kept nice and simple with three main trails – a blue, a red and a black. All start in Golspie, and climb 367 m to the top of Ben Bhraggie (pronounced Ben Vraggy), and then whizz back to town. There are no facilities on the actual trails, but since they start and finish in town you get to use Golspie's plentiful shops and amenities.

XC You'll quickly discover that the one thing all three routes have in common are that you'll need to do some proper climbing from Golspie to access all the fun stuff. But this is where the genius of the place comes in. There has been as much care gone into the getting up as the coming down and

Central & Northern Scotland Golspie Highland Wildcat Trails

> Lowdown

⊕ Locals do

Take supplies with them.

Stop to admire the view from the Duke of Sutherland monument at the summit.

⊗ Locals don't

Ride up when it's windy – it's an exposed place.

⦿ Pros

Empty trails, great views, and fantastic singletrack.

All-weather surface (limestone) drains exceptionally quickly.

✖ Cons

Far from most UK towns and cities.

Weather can be bad for days on end.

with plenty of features to distract you on the ascent, you'll be summiting in no time. At over 7 km, it's actually the longest stretch of purpose-built uphill singletrack in Scotland! The Blue Trail is a 6.5-km route from either town and has views all the up and all the way down, while the Red Trail is a tasty 7.5 km of rollable jumps, plenty of flowing singletrack and the views from the blue trail. The Black Trail is basically the same as the red though when you get to the top of the hill there's an additional loop around the summit with lots of big jumps, technical sections and additional climbs and descents. You can also head off towards Dunrobin Castle for plenty of unofficially singletrack and forest road, though these aren't way marked or part of the official Highland Wildcat trails.

Downhill Golspie isn't billed as a downhill centre as the loops are aimed at getting you to the top of the hill and back down again. That said, downhillers will certainly find something interesting to ride.

Freeride The Black Trail should have enough to keep freeriders happy as there are no specific freeriding areas.

Easy The Blue Route is a brilliant bit of riding to keep most novices absolutely enthralled.

Hard The Black Trail has a few shortcuts but is still a tiring ride, though packed with enough interesting features to make it a classic.

Not to miss The swooping descents on brilliant, purpose-built track for all abilities.

Remember to avoid Forgetting to take your camera! The views are stunning.

Nearest Bike/Hire shop Bicycle Bothy (T01408 621658) is the nearest shop to the trails.

Eating The Theme Tea Rooms in Dunrobin Castle is worth a visit, as it has a steam-powered Fire Engine from the 1800s in the dining room! If you're wanting something less extravagant then Coffee Bothy is a classic local café.

Local accommodation
Bhraggie House (T01408 633857) is very bike friendly and is based near the trails.

ⓘ **More info** The Highland Wildcat Trails have an official website with downloadable route map – highlandwildcat.com.

Nearest railway station Inverness
Nearest city Inverness
Sat nav postcode AB37 9EX (Glenlivet Estate Office)

Location Glenlivet mountain bike centre is located in the Carn Daimh Forest, near Tomintoul, itself around 65 km south east of Inverness. When driving from Inverness, take the A9 south until it forks, and take the A938 to the left. Continue on this road until it joins the A95, drive along this road for nearly 6.5 km and turn off onto the A939. This road leads to the Estate Office, which is signposted.

Facilities Despite only having two trails here, there's a lot of facilities on offer. The Coffee Still Café is the main hub of the trails, serving food and drinks six days a week (closed on Mondays) and also acts as the bike hire and shop – only when the café itself is open. You can buy trail maps from the Visitor Centre for £1.

Rough round-up The Glenlivet Estate is famous for historically being illicit whisky distilling country where smuggling was rife, so keep an eye out for more than just mountain bikers! Aside from that the trails here are set in some pretty spectacular scenery – another thing to keep an eye on.

XC There are two main trails here; the blue trail is a 9-km, family and novice friendly route that holds a few climbs but tops it off with some rewarding downhill sections, including exciting features. The Red Trail is a 22-km route that takes you to the top of Carn Diamh before throwing you down the Glenlivet descent – 6.5 km of singletrack, packed with features and jumps! It also holds some black-graded features for those of you wanting something extra.

Downhill There are no downhill-specific routes here but even the most downhill-focussed riders will gain some joy from the Glenlivet descent on the red trail.

Freeride Much like the downhill trails, there's nothing that's built for the freerider here. There are plenty of jumps on the Glenlivet descent but it's not worth a trip if you're only looking to get airborne.

Conditions As the trails are in Cairngorms, the weather can get bad. That said, the trails here are kept in good condition but can be tough to ride after bad weather.

ⓘ **More info** Check out the Glenlivet Estate website (glenlivetestate.co.uk) for maps and phone numbers.

Highland Perthshire Trails

CHRIS MORAN

Nearest city Dundee
Nearest train station Pitlochry
Sat nav postcode PH16 5BX (for the Pitlochry Visitor Centre)

Location The Highland Perthshire Trails can be found just south of the Cairngorms National Park and is roughly 110 km north of Edinburgh. Travelling north on the A9, pass through the town of Perth and head for the town of Pitlochry. Just before reaching the town, you will need to take a right turn onto the A924, which leads you into the middle of the town, where the Visitor Centre is signposted.

Facilities As the trails here cover as vast area of land, you won't find anything specific to mention at each trail. There's a Visitor Centre in Pitlochry that will give you all the information on the nearby trails, but there are so many routes to explore!

Rough round-up There really are a lot of trails here, some might say too many! With routes that travel and start at different forests in the area, every level of rider is catered for here with green routes for families and novice riders, up to black routes for even the most experienced of riders to take on. DMBinS has a great break down of all the routes in the area for download – dmbins.com/riders/where-to-ride/34_highland-perthshire-trails. The Highland Perthshire trails are another great example of mountain bikers and landowners coming together to form some great trails. Just remember to respect the trails when you ride there.

Terrain Nicknamed 'Big Tree Country', you can imagine that you'll be dealing with a lot of forest riding. And you'd be only partly right. With the amount of routes here, you'll be riding through forests, glens, lochs and more. You'll find that it's all natural XC trails around the southern Highlands in Scotland so expect a mix of muddy trails, root filled runs and rocky sections.

XC The best known routes are through Glen Tiltin and Blair Atholl but with so many routes and trails on offer it's hard to find a place to begin. Every level of rider really is catered for in the southern Highlands, and trails vary in length and difficulty, depending on what you're looking for. The best site to check out is dmbins.com, where they break down routes by difficulty.

Downhill There aren't any downhill specific trails in the southern Highlands. That said, there are a lot of descents on many of the XC trails here that will keep the downhill lover smiling. There's no doubt that you'll find a lot of downhill riding in these parts.

Freeride Much like the downhill section, there's nothing freeride-specific but with the broad choice of routes, and the amount of routes, on offer, freeriders are sure to find something to keep themselves happy.

Conditions The Highlands can be susceptible to some pretty adverse weather conditions and so the trails here can be affected. As they are all natural XC trails you should expect them to get fairly boggy after heavy rainfall.

ⓘ **More info** First port of call should be to the DMBinS site – dmbins.com – to download all route cards. There are many other Highland Perthshire sites to look at but we suggest highlandperthshire.org.

⊗ ⊗ ⊗ ⊗ ⊗

Train station Ardrossan
Nearest city Glasgow
Sat Nav KA27 8DP (for Brodick centre)

Location The Isle of Arran can be found off the west coast of Scotland and is accessible by car-ferry from Ardrossan to the Island's capital of Brodick. Alternatively, there is a summer-only service which runs from Claonaig on Kintyre to Lochranza in the north of the island. You can take a car over to the island to just jump on the ferry with your bike as all the main trails start from Brodick. The island itself is only 20 km long and 10 km wide with one main ring road, so it's hard to get lost!

Facilities Brodick is a small fishing village with an imposing castle overlooking the bay and hits most

GERARD TATTERSFIELD

visitors as a stunning, picturesque place that is akin to going back 50 years in time. The rest of the island is similarly picturesque, with many remarking how Arran is a condensed version of Scotland: incredible hills, beautiful lochs and some awe-inspiring views over the sea. There are also some fantastic, old-school B&Bs, village shops and roadside cafés.

Rough round-up The Scottish Tourist Board and the Arran Bike Club have both done an outstanding job in promoting the island as a cycling paradise. With some brilliant trails already built, and scope to build more, the island is set up to create a 7 Stanes-style, island-wide trail network and centre. Twin that with the fact that the terrain is so incredibly suited to bike riding – with enormous, empty and ancient mountains rolling down to the sea, and the island's quiet ring road, which will get you to supplies in the form of a small

village within every 3 km – and you'll soon discover that Arran is a brilliant mountain biking destination.

Terrain The rugged mountains here are some of the oldest in the world and it's serious granite country, with gorged valleys and awesome, empty Glens to match. It is, in a word, unspoiled. These mountains are beautifully complimented by the forests and rugged moorland to the South of Brodick, more ideal mountain bike country.

XC There are two blue-graded routes here with the Castle trail being a perfect run for beginners and novice riders. It loops around Brodick Castle and the surrounding hills, with views back to the mainland and over to the majestic Goatfell and Cairsteal Abhail mountains. The blue trail takes in more of the island and throws you into some more technical singletrack. The red trail starts at the Ferry Terminal and heads uphill to Corriegills and the Clauchland Hills Forest, where there's plenty of tough singletrack and stunning views, before the descent on the other side of the hill down to the bay of Lamlash with its Holy Isle dominating the horizon. The loop back descends into Brodick for a total of 18 km. The black route uses some of the same trails, but an additional loop into Glencoy and miles of forest singletrack above Lamlash and Whiting Bay makes this an awesome full day's ride at 35 km in length. There are many more routes available, please check on the Arran Bike Club website for more ideas.

Downhill There are no specific DH trails here, but the hills are just under 900 m high and covered in granite-strewn trails so there's plenty to explore.

Freeride No official freeriding trails here but there's scope to build something on the island.

Conditions In a period of severe weather, Arran can be exposed, but otherwise it's generally mild and sheltered with palm trees lining the shore. As a rule of thumb, there are not too many horse riders, dog walkers and ramblers to contend with.

ⓘ **More info** The Arran Bike Club can be found at arranbikeclub.com, while the official Arran Tourist Board site is visitarran.com.

🔽11 Kyle of Sutherland Trails

Nearest train station Culrian/Invershin

Nearest city Inverness

Sat nav postcode IV24 3DP (now closed Carbisdale Castle)

Opening times The trails are open all year round and are free to use.

Location The Kyle of Sutherland actually consists of two trail centres next door to each other, Balblair and Carbisdale, and within riding distance to each other. Take the A9 north from Inverness and then take a left onto the A836 signposted towards Bonar Bridge. Just before Bonar Bridge, in the village of Ardgay, look for signs to Culrain, and take the back roads to Culrian where there are signs for Carbisdale Castle Youth Hostel. Alternatively, stay on the good road to Bonar Bridge, take a left onto the A836, then another left onto the A837 towards Rosehall. Pass through Rosehall and then after 1.5 km take a left off the road heading to Doune/Birchfield/Achnahanat. Then take the next left and this road heads to Birchfield, then Carbisdale Castle, then Achnahanat in that order. To get to Balblair, simply head west on the A836 from Bona Bridge and turn right after 1.5 km signed to the Forestry Commission car park.

Facilities/Overview With the Kirk of Sutherland Trails being a long way for even the majority of Scottish riders, and they are not very big (Balblair has a total of 13 km of trails, while Carbisdale is really one 4-km trail with some extensions), so there has to be a good reason to entice people this far north. In fact there is: Rik Allsop, the trail designer at Drumlanrig, has designed Balblair's fantastic Black route, and the amount of features that have been packed into that – and the other trails – is awesome. Before the closure of Carbisdale Castle, this site boasted many facilities, now it's just down to the trails, the way marked routes and a map you can find online.

XC Balblair holds two routes: the blue – a 3-km uphill slog that's tame in comparison to its black-route brother. It'll still hold your interest as it has plenty of rough ground to cover before a nice descent back to the car park. The black route is a 7.5-km (or 11.5-km loop if you do the extension) trail that combines the areas outstanding natural terrain of granite, and limestone, and adds enough wooden reinforcements to keep everything flowing, with some brilliantly fun descents including piggybacking on the blue trail's final section to make a combined total of 4km of downhill to end on. Carbisdale has a 2-km blue run that's mostly singletrack, including the brilliant Hissing Sid section where a series of switchbacks will vie for your attention against the stunning backdrop (though you'll want to keep your eyes on the track if you're hitting them fast). The red trail is essentially the same run as the blue, though it has a 2 km added section at the top of the hill that adds some descent and more uphill, and makes the trail 4.5 km in total.

Downhill You won't find any DH-specific tracks at either Balblair or Carbisdale, but both feature some gentle descents that novice downhillers will definitely enjoy. It's not made for the downhill enthusiast.

Freeride Like the DH tracks, there's nothing freeride-specific here. However, there are a few jumps dotted around the trails, just remember that this is predominantly natural-feel singletrack on offer.

Easy The Balblair Blue is great for every rider, no matter what ability level.

Hard The Black route at Balblair has all the makings of a technically difficult, but perfect day out, with approximately one third being natural rock riding, one third hard-packed singletrack and the remaining third being northshore-style additions to the trails that have been painted with a special 'grippy' paint. Worth a journey just to try that out!

Not to miss Trying out the black run. Rik Allsop is renowned for his work.

Remember to avoid Leaving the camera at home – the views across the waters are absolutely stunning.

Nearest Bike/Hire shop Square Wheels in Strathpeffer (T01997 421000, squarewheels.biz), around 40 km to the south.

Local accommodation Monach House in Bonar Bridge is a local B&B and bike friendly – T01863 766147.

Eating There's nothing on site since the closure of Carbisdale Castle but Handmade Crafts and Café in Bonar Bridge is worth a visit. The Balblair Whisky distillery is in Edderton a few kilometres further east from Bonar Bridge.

ⓘ **More info** There are downloadable maps for both Carbisdale and Balblair (as well as how to link between the two) at forestry.gov.uk.

> Lowdown

☺ **Locals do**
Know and love their perfect, natural terrain.

☹ **Locals don't**
Worry too much about crowds – this is about as empty as trail centres get.

✔ **Pros**
Great views and some fun singletrack.

✘ **Cons**
It's a very long way from everywhere else. The trails aren't the longest in the world.

⊗ ⊕ ⊗ ⊕ ⊗ ⊕ ⊗ ⊕ ⊕
⊕ ⊕ ⊕

Train station Newtonmore

Nearest city Inverness

Sat Nav PH20 1BU

Opening times The trails are open 24/7 365 days a year and are free to ride. You will have to pay to park though – £1 for an hour, £2 for three hours and £3 for the day.

Stone slab ahead!

Location Laggan Wolftrax is around 3 km west of Laggan village and is just off the A9 main route that concocts Inverness to the south, and cuts past the Highland centre of Aviemore. When driving from the south, head north on the A9 towards Inverness and turn off at Dalwhinnie onto the A889 towards Laggan Bridge. Turn left onto the A86 towards Spean Bridge and you'll find the Laggan Wolf Trax café and parking (Called BaseCamp) about 1.5 km up the road on the left hand side.

Facilities/Overview Situated on the west side of the impressive Cairngorm Mountains, Wolf Trax (named after the legendary Wolf of Badenoch) is a brilliant all-in-one centre with a bike shop and café at the base, and trails to suit all riders from absolute beginners all the way through to elite riders. The black route here features no chicken lines and joins up with the red route for the last section. The red route is testing but fun for most riders, so there's no danger of being too far out of your element. The blue and green routes are perfect for novices, while a skills area and bikepark complete the package. Laggan might only offer one route of each colour grade but those routes are absolute perfection, and the reason why so many riders visit. It's a beautiful part of the world, and a perfect base from which to explore the peaceful countryside and spot a range of wildlife from golden eagle or Osprey to red deer stags and pine martin from the numerous, unofficial XC routes spreading off into the surrounding Grampian hills.

XC The official trails start with a 5 km green route, built for all riders to get out of the forest and enjoy the scenery. What used to be the old blue route has now been re-graded as an orange route as it has a bikepark-style descent with sweeping bends, jumps and plenty of obstacles. All of these are rollable though so expect to see all types of rider here. The red route is a 15 km loop with plenty of rock gardens and northshore additions. It is also home to several granite rides (similar to The Slab in Dalbeattie) and has plenty of areas where you can jump into the Black Trail for a test on some of the obstacles there, before ending in a brilliant raised boardwalk descent (the Wolf Run). That same Black Trail is 6.5 km of intense riding with lots of rock to negotiate, big jumps, hefty drops and some serious slabs. Remember, there are no chicken lines so try the red and use the 'opt-in' lines before you hit the black for the first time! For those looking for a really long XC ramble, as BaseCamp about hitting the 42-km Corrieyairack Pass. The company can organise a bus for you to the start of the trail so you can leave your car at the BaseCamp car park.

Downhill There's nothing in Laggan that shouts downhill-specific, but if you get yourself onto a cross-country bike, the black route will challenge even the best DH riders, as it contains lots of technical rock features. Plus BaseCamp also run an uplift service so you ride the red or black runs all day.

Freeride The bike park is the main home for freeriders and is perfect for those looking to get in the air! There are also plenty of smaller jumps to improve your riding.

FORESTRY COMMISSION

FORESTRY COMMISSION

FORESTRY COMMISSION

Easy The green trail here is purpose-built singletrack and great for beginners, families and young children.

Hard If you want a tough ride than the black trail is your only choice. Anything you don't clear first time round you can conquer on our second run after lunch, if you still want some more look for the uplift bus and go around again.

Not to miss Air's Rock – try out the steep black optional rock-roll on the red route.

Remember to avoid Riding the black route if you're not technically proficient as it is quite hard.

Nearest Bike/Hire shop BaseCamp MTB (T01528 544 786 or T01479 870 050) are based at the Laggan Wofltrax trails, have a good workshop and hire top of the range bikes.

Local accommodation

Nearby Laggan has a couple of options here. Why not try the Rumblie for B&B (T01528 544766) or if you are looking for a self-catered cottage try Ravenswood Holiday Cottage (T07813 956463), which is only 10 km from Laggan.

Eating The BaseCamp MTB Café is stocked full of home-made soups, cakes and hearty meals, as well as stocking quick snacks for hungry pit-stops. Nearby Laggan is the nearest town with two pubs/hotels serving food – try the Monadhliath Hotel (T01528 544276) on the Dalwhinnie road, which offers bar meals and a restaurant.

ⓘ **More info** The Forestry Commission has a dedicated page to Laggan Wolftrax with a downloadable trails map – scotland.forestry. gov.uk/visit/laggan-wolftrax. Also check out the BaseCamp website at basecampmtb.com and Dmbins.com has info on Laggan Wolftrax.

BASECAMP

BASE CAMP

❯ Lowdown

⊕ Locals do
Incorporate all the trails into one loop: ask in the shop and they'll show you how to do it.

⊖ Locals don't
Ride long travel machines here, they're overkill for the trails.

✔ Pros
Nice, peaceful area.

Compact area with lots to be found.

✖ Cons
The trails are only short so you may exhaust the riding in a few days.

FORESTRY COMMISSION

Train station Inverness

Nearest city Inverness

Sat Nav N/A

Opening times Trails are completely free to ride and are open 24/7, 365 days a year.

Location You'll find Learnie Red Rocks are on the famous Black Isle (not actually an island, but a peninsula) near the town of Rosemarkie, itself around 15 km northwest of Inverness. Driving from Inverness, take the A9 heading northeast towards Tore, then take the last exit on the roundabout (at Tore) onto the A832 heading in the direction of Cromarty. Pass through the town of Rosemarkie and the trails are signposted off to the right after around 4 km.

Facilities/Overview Learnie Red Rocks are another waymarked Forestry Commission site and started out years ago when local riders recognised the potential of Learnie Forest. With trails suited for every ability of rider, you can imagine it gets popular. There's a green route, 3 blue routes, a black route, a bike park and dirt jump area. Many of the trickier features have escape lines (or chicken lines as they're known) so you don't have to do the drops or jumps if you don't want to. Good riders should be aware there there isn't a huge amount of vertical drop, and while there are plenty of features, this isn't a downhill venue.

XC The green-graded Home trail is 500 m of easy singletrack back to the car park. It's a great ride to give yourself

FORESTRY COMMISSION

a taste of mountain biking. There are now 16 km of trails here, though all in short loops. The green-graded Home run is 500 m of easy singletrack back to the car park. The blue-graded Callachy Hill Climb is an easy route to the top of the hill, while the Callachy Downhill is a 1.3-km blue back down again. The two other blue-graded trails – Muirhead Climb (1.1 km) and Firth View (2.5 km) are all gentle climbs with fun, flowing descents that learners and intermediates will love. The black-graded Learnie Hill is 3.6 km of fun riding, with plenty of steep, technical rock sections. The jump between easy and difficult runs is very marked here, so approach with caution.

Downhill There are no specific downhill routes here but the DH riders amongst you will find the Learnie Hill Trail (black run) to have some sections to put a smile on your faces.

Freeride Both beginners and intermediates will find a lot to rider in the bike park at Learnie Red Rocks. The dirt jumps are of a higher standard though, so make sure you know what you're doing before you hit them.

Easy The blue routes here are great for novice riders looking for a challenge.

Hard The black route is full of stone slaps and rooty switchbacks and not for those out for an easy ride.

Not to miss The bike park – it's a great place to brush up on your bike-handling skills, and a great place to try out some jumps!

Remember to avoid Coming here expecting a huge area.

Nearest Bike/Hire shop Mountain Bike Highlands and Islands (T01381 600386) is found in Cromarty only 6.5 km from the trails and offer bike hire, guiding and servicing.

Local accommodation
The Cromarty Arms Inn (T01381 600230) offers bed and breakfast, and a well deserved pint after riding.

Eating There are no facilities on site but there are plenty of shops and amenities in nearby Rosemarkie.

ⓘ **More info** Learnie has a page on the Forestry Commission site – forestry.gov.uk.

> **Lowdown**

⊕ **Locals do**
Know how to make the most from a smallish area.

Keep their gears tuned – the uphills are short but very technical in places.

⊕ **Locals don't**
Ride around the tougher sections.

✔ **Pros**
Really good flowing singletrack.

✘ **Cons**
A good rider could ride every trail in one day.

Train station Stirling/Dunblane
Nearest city Glasgow
Sat nav postcode FK8 3QR

Location The Mains Farm Trails are in between to the Queen Elizabeth Forest Park and the town of Dunblane. When driving north on the M9 towards Stirling, exit at junction 10 onto the A84 and take a left onto the A873. Mains Farm should be signposted from here but for peace of mind, continue to the end of Main Road and take a left onto Kippen Road. Mains Farm will be on your left.

Facilities As this is more of a family resort with a small trail centre built into it, facilities are at a premium. There's a Visitor Centre, a soon-to-be-built café, bike hire and accommodation – in the form of wigwams!

Rough round-up The trails here are merely a 450-m skills track that has been designed to get riders used to conditions and features they would find on forest trails. There are two main routes to the skills trails here – one blue and one red. They both follow the same path just with different sections that tail off for different features that vary in difficulty. The features include

berms, rollers, steps, rock gardens and skinny balance beams. You should note that this is not for the experienced mountain biker and is definitely not worth a long journey. With the accommodation on site, right next to the trails, it's perfect for families and novice riders looking to further their skills.

Conditions These trails are purpose-built so they will be rideable in most weather conditions.

ⓘ **More info** For all info on accommodation prices and a trail map, check out mainsfarmwigwams.com.

Train station Kirkcaldy
Nearest city Edinburgh
Sat nav postcode KY1 3LR

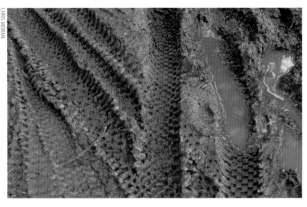

CHRIS MORAN

Location The Middleden Trails can be found in the centre of Kirkcaldy, which itself is just north of Edinburgh. When driving the south, take the A90 north and cross the bridge that links Queensferry to Inverkeithing. Take a right onto the A921 and head towards Kirkcaldy. When you reach the town, continue on the A921 until you reach a roundabout, take the first left onto Dunnikier Way, follow this road for about 2 km and Kirkcaldy High School will be on your right. Take the right just before passing the school and park in the car park for the 5-a-side pitches. The trails are in the woods in the northwest corner of this field.

Facilities/Overview The trails here were built by Fife Coast and Countryside Trust and Middleden MTB Club – a great example of what can happen when two bodies like this work together. There is no Visitor Centre located at the trail head as the trails themselves are located so close to Kirkcaldy that all amenities can be found in the centre of town. You can ride here 24/7, 365 days a year and it costs nothing to do so. It's free to ride, making the routes popular with the local community.

Terrain As this is a forest area, you'll find that the trails can be rooty and muddy – perfect for any rider wanting to test themselves against the elements of a forest.

XC There's plenty here for the XC rider, starting with the Forest Trail – a perfect green-graded route for the family or novice rider. It's a gentle trail that takes you through some beautiful forest, and will get you hungry for more. There are two blue trails; 'Pistol Whip' is a great piece of singletrack that's great for any level of rider, and the other is 'Barrell Roll', a similar run through the forest but with an added water feature before taking you back up the main path. The red trails are home to many features that will keep all riders smiling. Most notably, the 'Trigger Trail' is a technical run with drop-offs, roots and some great descents through the forest.

Downhill There are no specific downhill tracks here but the Trigger Trail should satisfy most downhill riders. If you're only after pure DH runs, then you might want to try a different venue.

Freeride This is no haven for the freerider but there are 3 jumps to hit, in their dedicated freeride area. There's also a pump track that's great for honing your bike handling skills, and testing your ability to keep momentum. If you're a die-hard freerider then these facilities might not be the best for you, but as an introduction into freeriding, they're perfect. The club are looking to work on some extra northshore pieces of the forest, so keep your eyes peeled for them!

Conditions Don't expect the forest to drain or dry out quickly after bad weather, it is a forest after all. That said, the Middleden MTB Club take pride in these trails and work on them a lot, so they are rideable in most weather conditions.

ⓘ **More info** Middleden MTB Club have their own dedicated website (middledenmtb.co.uk) and it holds as much information as you could want, as well as trail maps.

⊗ ⊗ ⊗ ⊗ ⊗ ⊗ ⊗ ⊗ ⊗

Train station Keith/Elgin

Nearest city Inverness

Sat Nav IV32 7PE (Ordiquish car park)

Opening times The trails are open all day, all year round and are free to use. There is a charge for the car park but that's the only charge you should incur. It's always best to check the Forestry Commission website as there are frequent trail closures due to logging.

Location The Moray Monster Trails are in a Forestry Commission piece of land which sits within a triangle between the towns of Fochabers, Keith and Mulben, and is roughly 15 km southeast from Elgin, itself almost equidistant between Inverness and Aberdeen on the road that connects the two cities – the A96. There are three car park starts to the trails: Whitewash, Ordiquish and Ben Aigan.

For Whitewash, head to Fochabers and turn onto the A98. Continue up this road for a few hundred metres and you'll see the car park signposted on the right. For Ordiquish, start in Fochabers but head in the opposite direction to Whitewash and take the Ordiquish Road out of town, in the direction of Ordiquish. The car park will be signposted off to the left of this road. And for Ben Aigan car park take the A96 south west out of Fochabers in the direction of Aberdeen. After 6 km take a right onto the A95 and follow this road to Mulben (where there is a crossroads in which the B9103 turns off to the right). Take neither the A95 nor the B road, but instead turn right into the un-named minor road and park at the Ben Aigan car park around 2.5 km up this road.

Facilities/Overview The three car parks have their own trails although there are a few forest roads that link the areas together. Ordiquish car park has the most routes out of all three and is the place to access the Soup Dragon – a 5-km blue-graded loop, and Gordzilla, another 5-km blue-graded route. Both feature good uphill sections with controlled descents that will have novice riders loving singletrack. The Haggis is the other blue-graded route here (and is 6 km long), which starts and finishes at Ordiquish car park, full of smaller jumps to get you into freeriding. If you continue to the top of the hill you'll discover The Gully Monster. It's a devilish, black-graded route with steep switchbacks and a large drop to your left. Don't be fooled by the fact

CHRIS MORAN

JARVIS GOODYEAR

that it starts from the same trail as The Haggis. Just up from the car park is the skills area, which is a perfect place to hone your bike handling skills before tackling some of the features found on the trails.

Whitewash car park is home to the Fochabers rings – a red-graded, 8-km trail XC loop with a 'no pain, no gain' climb before a rewarding descent that will make you want to ride it again and again. You'll also want to take a look at the Fochabers Freeride area at Whitewash that holds a 750-m feature packed loop, northshore trickery and a downhill section packed with jumps and berms.

Reachable by bike from Ordiquish are the trails at Ben Aigan, where The Hammer trail exists – a 7-km red-graded route which boasts stunning views of the Spey Valley. Also up at Ben Aigan are The Mast Blast – a black-graded, 1-km descent that is easier than its grade suggests, and The Bunny Trail – an orange-graded bike park that's perfect for riders wanting some downhill speed. Expert riders only. Ordiquish and Ben Aigan are easily linked, though for riders wishing to also hit Whitewash in the same day will have to ride through Fochabers town to do so.

Next to Elgin is Quarrelwood – a 4-km green trail perfect for the family, and great for those looking for an easy ride.

Easy The green run near Elgin might be easy but head to Ordiquish first, where you'll find The Haggis Trail and discover it's one of the best blues in Scotland.

Hard The Gully Monster is tougher than you'd expect, especially if you've been surprised by Mast Blast's grading.

Not to miss The Ben Aigan Hammer section of purpose-built singletrack. It's why many make a long journey here.

Remember to avoid Being fooled by The Bunny's first section. It gets worse further down the trail.

Nearest Bike/Hire shop For simple supplies, try Bikes & Bowls in Elgin (T01343 549656), or Rafford Cycles (T01309 672811) in Forres for more specialised kit.

Local accommodation Castle Cottage is a local B&B, T01343 820761.

Eating You won't find any food or drink stops on the trails so it's best to take your own supplies. Fochabers is a quaint village with plenty of shops and amenities.

ⓘ **More info** The Forestry Commission site is well worth checking for trail closures and an online trail map – forestry.gov.uk.

> **Lowdown**

😊 **Locals do**
Link the trails and stop off for lunch in Fochabers.

😠 **Locals don't**
Disrespect The (Pink Fluffy) Bunny trail.

✓ **Pros**
Not a busy trail area with lots of riders.

Plenty to ride in such a small area.

✗ **Cons**
Frequent trail closures due to forest operations.

Not as linked as one might imagine.

⊿17 Pitfichie Mountain Cycle Trails

⊘ ⊘ ⊘ ⊘ ⊘

Train station Inverurie
Nearest city Aberdeen
Sat Nav AB51 7SS

Location Just 25 km northwest from Aberdeen and overlooking some spectacular scenery is Pitfichie, another Forestry Commission set up. When driving from Aberdeen, head northwest on the A96 towards Elgin/Inverness. Just before reaching the town of Kintore, take a left onto the B994 heading towards Cottown, then another left onto the B993 towards Kemnay and then Monymusk. Carry on the B993 past Monymusk and the road ends at a T junction with the A944 heading left towards Aberdeen or right towards Alford. Here, do a U-turn and head back along the B993 and take the first left. The car park is about 600 m up this road.

Facilities You won't find any facilities in the forest as it's pretty remote, but if you head back to Monymusk there's a general store for supplies. Otherwise it's best to bring them with you.

Rough round-up Pitfichie is well known for being part of the Scottish Downhill Association race series, and is home to one of the most demanding and challenging DH tracks in the country. Alongside the DH trail is a lot of official and unofficial XC trails that offer adventurous riders the chance to test themselves in some of Scotland's wildest hills.

Terrain Expect rough, wild terrain with lots of heather hiding the rocky sections and big jumps on the DH track.

XC There are only two waymarked routes here; The White Trail, at 15 km, is the easier of the two waymarked routes and starts from the Whitehill car park. The majority of this route is fire road but it will take you around the forest, and around Cairn William and Pitfichie Hill, offering up some incredible views. The red trail here has three routes and they all lead off the White Trail. There's a tricky ascent of Green Hill, then a rocky trial back to the forest road, and then back up to the top of Cairn William. This is the main thrust of trail building, where there is much slab riding and rocky sections to make the ascent as interesting as possible, while the descent includes lots of jumps, the same granite slabs on the way down, and the Devil's Staircase – a rocky section – as well as plenty of bermed corners.

Downhill The downhill trail here starts at the top of Pitfichie Hill and takes on the heather-strewn hill with plenty of twisting, fast turns and big, big jumps. It's well worth the slog uphill to find it. If you're a beginner, don't even think that you might be able to conquer this – it's for riders who can handle themselves. There are lots of unforgiving rock, hefty jumps and full-on drops to contend with. There are a few chicken lines, but this isn't a place to learn. As part of the SDA race series, expect this to be an elite riders hangout.

Freeride There's nothing freeride or dirtjump-specific here, though the Cairn William trail and the DH track have enough jumps and drops to keep freeriders happy.

Conditions There has been a lot of work poured into the trails to keep them interesting, and the natural base – mostly granite bedrock – helps to keep them firm and well-drained. However, this isn't a purpose-built area, so expect it to get boggy in adverse weather.

ⓘ **More info** The Forestry Commission has a dedicated page for Pitfichie – scotland.forestry.gov.uk, also try dmbins.com for any other info.

Central & Northern Scotland Pitfichie Mountain Cycle Trails

⬡ ⬡ ⬡ ⬡ ⬡ ⬡

Train station Corkerhill/Pollokshaws West/Shawlands
Nearest city Glasgow
Sat Nav G43 1AU

Location Pollok Country Park can be found on the south side of Clyde, which is just to the west of Glasgow city centre. The park is easily accessible by bike from most parts of the city, on either Route 7 or 75 of the National Cycle Network, or by heading to Pollokshaws West train station from Glasgow Central. The M77 dissects the park on its southwest edge.

Facilities Pollok Country Park originally boasted about being Europe's largest urban park until the building of the M77 cut the south west section of the park off. It was still voted Britain's best park in 2007 and is home to a variety of facilities including The Pollok House Tearoom and Restaurant, (plus a café in the Burrell House), a herd of Highland Cattle, an orienteering course, picnic areas, woodland gardens, a Go Ape course and stables. It's also home to the Strathclyde Mounted Police and Dog Handling division are also based in the park. Plenty going on then.

Rough round-up There are three routes here to satisfy the hunger of any XC rider – a green trail that will take all novice riders and families on a gentle ride through the woods; a blue trail with steep terrain and a few small jumps here and there to get you airborne, and a red trail that will challenge your skills and give

you a taste of what to expect in the mountains. None of these trails actually offer anything like the terrain you might find if you're heading up to the highlands or to one of the 7Stanes operations. However, for riders who live in the city, the red route offers some challenges, and there are enough jumps and obstacles littered around to make a day here fairly exciting.

Terrain As this is an inner-city park, you should expect to see lots of visitors and lots going on. However, these are

purpose-built trails so you should have the run of them without dog walkers and ramblers spoiling the ride.

ⓘ **More info** Active Scotland (active. visitscotland.com) is a great site to visit before heading out as it holds as much as information as you might need, as well as dmbins.com for those of you needing more detail about the runs themselves. Call Glasgow's cycling information line (T0141 287 9171) for a Fit for Life travel map and cycle route information, or visit cyclingscotland.org.

CHRIS MORAN

Central & Northern Scotland Pollok Country Park

⤓19 The Fire Tower Trail

ⓐ ⓑ ⓒ ⓓ ⓔ ⓕ ⓖ

Train station Garelochhead
Nearest city Glasgow
Sat Nav PA31 8RS (for Lochgilphead town centre)

JOE MCGHEE/MIDARGYLLTRI-CYCLECLUB.CO.UK

Central & Northern Scotland The Fire Tower Trail

Location The Fire Trail is around 60 km west of Glasgow, thought you'll discover that it's over 120 km when venturing there by road. From Glasgow, head out on the A82 towards Loch Lomond, then take a left onto the A83 heading to Inveraray and down to Lochgilphead. There are three starting points for the trails – from the Forestry Commission Car Park at Achnabreac, just off the A816 on the Oban to Lochgilphead road; or park in Kilmichael and ride over the River Add Bridge, then turn right into the forest track; or get to Lochgilphead town centre and ride up Blarbuie Road by the golf course.

Facilities/overview You won't find much at the trails themselves, save for the Achnabreac Forestry Commission car park which is open every day. For supplies, cafés, accommodation and after-riding amenities, ride back down to Lochgilphead, a picturesque town on the banks of Loch Fyne.

Rough round-up You'll find so much to ride here, especially as the hill has been absolutely filled out with incredible features to ride, and has one of the most interesting descents in the UK. The trail takes its name from the Fire Tower at the peak of the hill (it was a forest fire look out), and the ride down takes in a quarry, plenty of jumps, and some brilliant, technical singletrack.

Terrain The Fire Tower Trail really is a mix of everything, with northshore, granite slabs, dusty singletrack and quarry drops all on offer.

XC Starting from Achnabreac (though you can join from Lochgilphead) this 19.5-km route heads up the hill and back again. It's graded red overall but there are many offshoots that encompass green, blue and red graded trails. There's something here for the majority of riders but the remoteness means that it's not particularly suited to beginners. The Twisted Fire Starter is where you'll start out before shooting off to the Fire Tower (a black-graded loop around the hill), then into the Quarry Drop – a steep drop down to forest road – before heading uphill again on Murder Hill ending in a descent down to the Water Splash,

then more singletrack to the Swamp Monster and its northshore, before looping back to the start. Also nearby is the Wee Toon Trail in Cambeltown (also known as the Beinn Ghuilean Trail), a lovely XC ramble with plenty of northshore additions, check out the Forestry Commission site for more info.

Freeride/Downhill You won't find anything that's DH or freeride specific, but the riding here is technical enough for many downhillers to enjoy. The northshore and jumps found on the trails here will keep the freeriders happy as well.

Conditions As the trails are located on the banks of the Loch, it's best to avoid them in high winds or bad weather.

ⓘ **More info** Make sure you check with the Forestry Commission website (scotland.forestry.gov.uk) before travelling as the routes are susceptible to closures, they also have an online trail map.

ⓐ ⓑ ⓒ ⓓ ⓔ ⓕ ⓖ ⓗ

Train station Inverness
Nearest city Inverness
Sat Nav IV3 8LB

Location The Kelpies Trails are in Abriachan Forest, located next to the village of Abriachan, on the west side of Loch Ness, itself around 10 km south west of Inverness. When driving from Inverness, or heading up from the south, take A82 on the west side of the loch, and turn off near the north end towards Abriachan. When in the village, head to the village hall and follow signs to Abriachan Forest Walks, which have a car park and access the start of the trails.

Facilities Abriachan village is a short ride from the trails themselves and is well placed to provide quaint refreshments as there are no facilities at the trails themselves. Otherwise, bring supplies with you for a day here.

Rough round-up The Abriachan story is a hearwarming one – in 1998 the village population (all 130 of them), clubbed together to by the next door forest, and in the years since they have set about re-inventing the town and forest as an ecologically sound, tourist attraction that gives back to their community. It helps of course that they're next to Loch Ness, and recent trail additions by the likes of Rik Allsop (who built much of Mabie Forest and the impressive Drumlanrig trails) have turned this into a fantastic, family-oriented mountain biking destination.

Terrain You'll be stunned by the picture-perfect Highland scenery here and its well-maintained forest next to a brilliantly quaint village. The trails have been built from locally-crushed rock, and have been designed to work in all weathers and through the winter months.

XC There are main trails here – a green, blue, red and a skills park. The green trail is a gentle 3-km family route, which is perfect for showing the kids how to ride in the forest. The blue trail is a 7-km route that will test novice riders with its interesting features along the way. There are 'opt-out' areas to link up with the bike park as well. The red route is a 4-km struggle that has not been given the same surface treatment as the blue and green runs, but it still offers some great rooty, rocky sections with steep climbs and descents. The climb tops out at the impressive Creag Ard summit, with incredible views over Monadh Liath hills and Loch Ness to the south, and the Affric hills with Ben Wyvis and Ben Bhraggie in the north.

Downhill There's nothing that can be classed as downhill-specific but both the blue and red-grade trails have some fun descents.

Freeride The skills area (Kelpies Dare) is where you can try out your skills on the graded obstacles before taking on the trails, or you can just stay there and practice your freeride skills!

Conditions These are all weather, all season trails.

ⓘ **More info** Abriachan has its own village website (abriachan.org.uk) which includes an online trails map.

SIMON HARRY/ABRIACHAN FOREST TRUST

Central & Northern Scotland The Kelpies Trail

Best of the rest

Callendar Estate

Train station Falkirk High
Nearest city Falkirk
Sat Nav FK1 5LX

Location The Callendar Estate can be found right in the middle of Falkirk, a short drive from both Glasgow and Edinburgh. When travelling from Edinburgh, drive northwest on the M9 and leave at junction 5 onto the A9. At the second roundabout take a right onto the B805 and then right at the next roundabout onto Callendar Road. Bear left onto the B8080 and continue on until you reach Glen Brea (B8028). Take a right onto Slamannan Road until you reach a roundabout and turn right onto Lochgreen Road. As the road splits into two, directly in front of you is Canada Wood – where the green trail begins. Park up and start riding!

Facilities The Callendar Estate is a mixture of woods, trails and a 19th Century Chateau. There's no specific Visitor Centre here but the trails are close to Falkirk city centre so all shops and amenities are within riding and driving distance.

Rough round-up You'll quickly find that the Callendar Estate has 17 km of purpose-built singletrack for riders to enjoy. The Canada Trail is the green-graded route that is perfect for the family or novice rider. At 4.1 km, it's a nice half-hour ride with some gentle ups and downs. The Cragieburn Trail (blue) is 3.4 km with a few gentle hills and twisting drops to get the adrenaline going. The red route is

the same as the blue route but with a 2.6 km addition to the end. It has a strenuous climb up Auchengean wood with a nice descent back. Nearby Kilbean Woods holds a blue (2.3 km) and red trail (1 km), both of which take in a steady climb but have some fun features like berms for riders to try out. The red trail has a steep descent and some switchbacks, but shouldn't trouble the more experienced rider. All routes are linked with easy-access bike routes, cutting out the main roads and making family riding safer. It's great for the town of Falkirk, but probably not worth a long journey for.

Conditions As it's all purpose-built singletrack, expect well drained trails that can be ridden in the majority of weather conditions.

ⓘ **More info** For trail maps, latest news and all other info, visit callendarestate.co.uk. It's also worth checking out dmbins.com as they have plenty of info on the area.

Donkey Hill Dirt Track

Train station Bridge of Orchy/ Fort William
Nearest city Glasgow/Inverness
Sat Nav PH49 4HL

Location The Donkey Hill Dirt Track is the neighbour of the Isles of Glencoe Hotel in Ballachulish, a small village on the banks of Loch Leven, around 15 km to the south of Fort William. From the either north or south, the trunk road to Ballachulish is the A82, which cuts straight through the village. The hotel is

just to the northwest of the village, right on the banks of the Loch, as the road heads to next-door Glencoe.

Facilities Donkey Hill has no facilities or amenities itself but Ballachulish is a small, touristy village with plenty of shops and amenities, though there is nothing specifically at the Donkey Hill.

Rough round-up This is a freeride skills practice area suited to beginner and intermediate riders. The local riders built the single-lane BMX-style track with help from pro mountain bikers Greg Minnaar and Sean McCarrol in 2002, and since then have added numerous tabletops, gaps, step ups doubles and hips. Worth a stop by if you're in the area or fancy a different view other than Fort William, but it is mostly for locals.

Conditions This is a purpose-built little track that drains fairly well, though still best avoided after heavy rain.

ⓘ **More info** ridefortwilliam.co.uk has a page on the track.

Duchany Woods

Train station Perth
Nearest city Dundee
Sat Nav PH2 7BH

Location Duchany Woods are just on the western edge of Perth. From the south head towards Perth on the A9, M9 or A90, and exit towards the town centre. Head over the river at West Bridge Street, and up Lochie Brae for 100 m, then take a right into Muirhall

Road and head all the way up here to the to Kinnoull Hill where you'll find the Forestry Commission Jubilee Car Park on the right. From the car park, head up the fire road and the trails should become obvious when you spot the wallride.

Facilities There are no facilities on site aside from the car park, but Perth is a short bike ride away and full of shops and amenities.

Rough round-up Duchany Woods are very popular with the local riding scene. and is constantly being upgraded. It's full of trails, mostly DH and freeride-based, with a variety of wallrides, jumps, gaps and drops. Not particularly worth a long a journey considering the wealth of proper trail centres in Scotland, but for local riders it's a real boon, and for pure downhillers, it makes an interesting day out, particularly the Fanutti Drop, and is a great place to improve your skills if you're an intermediate rider.

Conditions This is an inner city hill (though a quiet one), so expect the area to also have dog walkers and other forest users, though the atmosphere is mostly friendly.

Train station Dunkeld
Nearest city Perth
Sat Nav PH8 0AN

Location Around 20 km north of Perth is the town of Dunkeld. To find the downhill tracks, head along the A9 to Dunkeld and follow signs for The Hermitage (it's National Trust garden site with waterfalls etc). When you get to the Hermitage car park, there's a forest road on the right, take that road and go to the end where there's a gate and a small car park. Hop on the bike there, and go past the gate and take the first right which should take you to the bottom of the trails.

Facilities There's nothing situated at the downhill apart from the track itself, but it's not far from the town centre which is full of shops and amenities. The Hermitage site has a Visitor Centre, but you're better off heading past and in to town.

Rough round-up Since it was discovered in 2001 it's been home to plenty of world-class competitions and is still one of Scotland's best and more fierce downhill tracks. It's a mostly-natural downhill track, with horrific rock gardens and rooty sections that have seen some incredible crashes over the years. Progression Bikes Scotland (progressionbikesscotland.com) run an uplift service for those wanting to get the most out of the track at £25 for the day. Dunkeld is definitely one for the elite riders out there.

ⓘ **More info** There are also a number of waymarked XC routes around Dunkeld (mostly forest road, or waymarked estate land). You can get the 'Discover Atholl Estates – Countryside Trails Dunkeld' booklet from the ranger hut at the Atholl Estate.

Train station Dyce
Nearest city Aberdeen
Sat Nav AB21 0TU

Location Around 6 km north of Aberdeen, and in between the Village of Blackburn and Aberdeen's Dyce Airport, is Kirkhill Forest. Driving from Aberdeen, head out on the A96 towards Elgin/Inverness. Pass the exit for Dyce Airport and carry on up the A96 for around 1.5 km, then take a right into the Kirkhill Forest visitor car park. The trails start from here, or the north car park of the forest, which is accessed by heading further along the A96 towards Blackburn, then turning right onto the B979, and taking a another right off this road just before the train tracks, then first left. The car park is just off to the right of this road.

Facilities There are no facilities at Kirkhill Forest apart from the car park. Plenty of shops and amenities can be found in the nearby village of Blackburn.

Rough round-up Kirkhill Forest is famous for the Kirkhill Mountain Bike Park, a downhill funpark with plenty of jumps, wallrides, switchbacks, and berms. You can hit them all without needing to build more speed, which makes it a perfect place to learn or perfect tricks. Most riders come here for the funpark, which has plans to expand – though there is also a waymarked 12-km blue-graded loop (called the Kirkhill Trail) to the top of the Tyrebagger Hill and back down (it's a fantastic view, and great if you're into plane spotting – it's right on the flightpath to Aberdeen's airport). There are two other short, singletrack loops – the North and South Spurs, as well as plenty of fireroad and unofficial riding to explore.

Conditions The forest is quite popular with other outdoor users, particularly horseriders, though there's enough space for all.

ⓘ **More info** Kirkhill Forest (and Mountain Bike Park), has its own page on the Forestry Commission site – forestry.gov.uk.

326 Loch Ard Forest Trails

Ⓖ Ⓖ Ⓖ Ⓖ Ⓖ Ⓖ

Train station Balloch
Nearest city Glasgow
Sat nav postcode FK8 3SX

Location The Loch Ard Forest Trails are situated in the northwest corner of the Queen Elizabeth Forest Park, itself around 50 km north of Glasgow and just under 50 km from Falkirk. When driving from Falkirk, head west on the M9 and exit at junction 10 onto the A84. Continue on this road until it forks – you want to take the left fork onto the A873 for roughly 13 km. The road will then split into two again, the right turning being the A81, or the road continuing forwards also being the A81 – continue driving west towards the town of Aberfoyle. Take a right onto the A821 (Lochard Road), and the Visitor Centre will be signposted from here.

Facilities For such a small collection of trails, there's a lot of facilities on hand for visitors. There's a Visitor Centre and café in Aberfoyle, and it can act as your hub for the trails, as well as the place to find out as much info about the trails as possible. The trails are free to ride and open all year round

but you will have to pay for parking (only at the Visitor Centre though – you can park for free elsewhere).

Rough round-up When it comes to picturesque views, you can't go wrong with the Queen Elizabeth Forest Park. And that's probably why the trails here have been designed for families, allowing everyone to take in the beauty of the place. There are 5 waymarked trails here all ranging between 3 km and 16 km, with rest stops and sculptures to admire along the way. You won't find anything to trouble the experienced rider but it's a nice place for a family break.

Condition You won't see any forest singletrack here, it's all forest roads. As such, the trails are ridable during and after the majority of weather conditions .

ⓘ **More info** The Forestry Commission has a page dedicated to Loch Ard – scotland.forestry.gov.uk.

327 Tentsmuir Forest

Ⓖ Ⓖ Ⓖ Ⓖ

Train station Dundee
Nearest city Dundee
Sat nav postcode KY16 0DR

Location You'll find Tentsmuir Forest south of Dundee, located right on the east coast of Scotland. When driving from Dundee, head south over the Tay Road Bridge and take your first left towards the town of Tayport, on the B496 (this will turn into the B495). Take a left onto Olgilvy Street, left at the end of the road onto Golf Cresecent, then first right onto Shanwell Road. Follow Shanwell Road and you will reach the northeastern corner of the forest.

Facilities There's no main Visitor Centre here, but the trails are so close to town and the city of Dundee that it's not needed. All shops and amenities can be found very easily and are all within biking distance so taking supplies with you isn't essential. The trails themselves are free to ride but you will have to pay to park – at a cost of £2 per vehicle.

Rough round-up This is by no means a mountain biking haven and is heavily skewed towards providing a place for families to spend time. The trails themselves are very easy and are used by everyone who visits. There are three main routes here which are the same routes as the walking trails. This forest is here to get people out and about, taking in the great scenery. Not worth a long journey though.

Conditions Don't be surprised to discover that the trails here are all purpose-built or forest roads. It will drain well and you will be able to ride it in most weather conditions.

ⓘ **More info** The Forest Commission has a dedicated webpage for Tentsmuir (scotland.forestry.gov.uk) and Tentsmuir Forest has its own webpage too (tentsmuir.org).

Best films
Callum Swift

Callum Swift is a UK film maker behind 'The Uprising' and 'MADE'. Here he gives us his review of the best ever mountain bike films.

Best film ever "Earthed 1 – It really captures the spirit of the sport, plenty of flat out riding by all the top pros. The sountrack fits perfectly with the riding and the shots done on a super 8 camera give it a nice retro feel. Check out Sam Hill and Nathan Rennie rocking to Led Zepplin or when all the Iron Horse lads style it up over the bridge in Bromont.

One for the scenics "It's got to be Roam. There's the stunning cinematography, it's shot on film with beautiful settings, the best riders, the best locations, big film crew, great sountrack....what more could you want? It really makes you want to ride your bike whenever you watch it. Check the bit in Morocco – such a unique location. Or where Jordy Lunn jumps the river gap in Moab. And don't get me started on the cable cam in whistler with Darren Berreclough through all the northshore.

Best downhill film Between the Tape. It's got incredible cinematography and editing. Clay Porter's documentary style is interesting and the gladiatorial voiceover adds drama to the whole thing. The rider sections are all amazing, especially the Athertons section with some amazing cable cam shots. The best shot is of Sam Hill coming into the finish of the World Champs – Clay manages to track him through the crowd perfectly and it looks insane.

Best for watching again and again Illusionary Lines. The sountrack is superb and the split screen race shots with the timer running are an interesting addition. Check out Kovarik ripping up Scuol during the opening credits with his typical destroyer style. Some of his whips are insane.

Best for showcasing Europe Earthed 3. I had to include this for a guide to riding in Europe! It covers the World Cups brilliantly and has some awesome rider sections and a good sountrack. The Megavalanche section is a must see for anyone wanting to do the event. When someone crashes on the single track of the Megavalanche the camera follows his bike from a helicopter as it tumbles about a kilometre down the mountain. Pretty bad news.

273

Facility breakdown

	XC	DH	4X	DJ	Northshore	Freeride	Bike hire	Bike shop	Bike wash	Uplift	Map	Waymarked	Family	Visitor Centre	Accomodation	Cafe/food	FC
Southwest England																	
50 Acre Woods	✓	✓															
Asham Woods		✓			✓	✓											
Ashton Court (The Timberland Trail)	✓					✓	✓				✓	✓	✓	✓		✓	
Aveton Gifford DJs				✓													
Bath BMX Track				✓													
Bradford Hollow	✓			✓													
Blandford UK Bike Park		✓		✓	✓	✓				✓	✓	✓	✓		✓	✓	
Brunel Pump Track						✓											
Bucklands Ring		✓	✓	✓		✓											
Buriton Chalk Pits	✓	✓		✓													
Canford Heath and Pit DH	✓	✓				✓											
Cann Wood Trails		✓				✓											✓
Combe Sydenham	✓	✓				✓						✓		✓	✓		
Dartmoor National Park	✓	✓								✓	✓	✓	✓		✓		
Decoy BMX				✓													
Forest of Dean	✓	✓		✓		✓	✓	✓	✓		✓	✓	✓	✓		✓	
Haldon Forest Park	✓	✓			✓	✓					✓	✓	✓				✓
Ferndown DJs				✓													
Hidden Valley DJs	✓	✓		✓													
Hook DJs				✓													
Hundred Acre Wood	✓											✓	✓				✓
Island Trails				✓													
JLC Trails				✓													
Lanhydrock Cycle Hub	✓			✓		✓	✓			✓						✓	
Leckhampton	✓	✓				✓				✓							
Leigh Woods	✓	✓				✓							✓				✓
Nationwide DJs	✓			✓								✓	✓				
Patchway BMX DJs				✓													
Maddacleave Woods	✓	✓				✓				✓	✓	✓				✓	

	XC	DH	4X	DJ	Northshore	Freeride	Bike hire	Bike shop	Bike wash	Uplift	Map	Waymarked	Family	Visitor Centre	Accomodation	Cafe/food	FC
Mineral Tramways Project	✓	✓		✓		✓	✓	✓	✓		✓	✓	✓	✓	✓	✓	
Poldice Valley Trails	✓	✓		✓		✓											
Portland Bill Quarries	✓			✓													
Portsdown Hill	✓	✓															
Puddletown Woods	✓	✓											✓			✓	
Queen Elizabeth Country Park	✓	✓									✓	✓	✓	✓		✓	
Randwick DH	✓	✓															
Red Hill Extreme	✓		✓	✓						✓						✓	
Rogate		✓		✓		✓											✓
Sandford DJs and DH	✓	✓		✓													
Sheet DJs				✓													
Stockwood Bike Park			✓		✓												
Stoke Heights	✓	✓															✓
Stoughton Trails	✓	✓															
Stoke Woods	✓	✓		✓		✓										✓	✓
The Track	✓		✓	✓	✓	✓	✓	✓	✓		✓	✓	✓	✓		✓	
Triscombe DH		✓								✓							
Watchmoor Wood Bike Park	✓				✓	✓	✓				✓	✓	✓	✓		✓	
Woodbury Common	✓											✓	✓				

London & Southeast England

	XC	DH	4X	DJ	Northshore	Freeride	Bike hire	Bike shop	Bike wash	Uplift	Map	Waymarked	Family	Visitor Centre	Accomodation	Cafe/food	FC
Aston Hill	✓	✓	✓			✓					✓		✓	✓		✓	✓
A10 DJs				✓													
Bengeo Bumps and Waterford Quarry DJs				✓													
Bedgebury Forest and Freeride Area	✓		✓	✓		✓	✓	✓			✓	✓	✓	✓		✓	✓
Blean Woods	✓																
Bluebell Hill	✓	✓											✓				
Braintree BMX				✓													
Brockwell Park BMX Track				✓												✓	
Broxbourne Woods	✓																
Bushy Park	✓			✓													
Chicksands Bike Park	✓	✓	✓	✓		✓					✓	✓	✓			✓	

Facility breakdown

	XC	DH	4X	DJ	Northshore	Freeride	Bike hire	Bike shop	Bike wash	Uplift	Map	Waymarked	Family	Visitor Centre	Ac comodation	Cafe/food	FC
Crowborough – The Bull Track	✓	✓		✓	✓	✓										✓	
Danbury Common		✓	✓	✓		✓											
Devils Drop DJs	✓			✓													
Devils Dyke DH and XC	✓	✓											✓			✓	
Devils Dyke Nonsuch DJs				✓													
Donkey Island DJs				✓													
Enfield DJs				✓	✓												
Epping Forest	✓						✓				✓		✓	✓		✓	
Friston Forest	✓				✓	✓						✓					✓
Gunnersbury DJs				✓													
Hadleigh Farm	✓											✓	✓	✓		✓	
Hainault Forest & Redbridge	✓					✓						✓	✓	✓		✓	
Harrow Skatepark and DJs				✓		✓											
Hayes Hawks BMX Track				✓													
Highgate DJs				✓													
Holmes Place DJs	✓			✓													
Hurtwood Trails	✓			✓													
Ingrebourne Hill	✓	✓				✓						✓					✓
Ipswich BMX Track				✓													
Kuoni Trails				✓													
Leith Hill	✓	✓		✓													
Lee Valley																	
Limpsfield DJs	✓	✓		✓													
Look Out Gulley	✓	✓		✓													
Lordship Loop						✓											
M3 DJs	✓			✓													
Mereworth Woods	✓	✓			✓												
PORC (Penshurst Off Road Club) aka Viceroy's Wood	✓	✓	✓	✓					✓		✓	✓	✓	✓		✓	
Normandy Hill DH	✓	✓															
Peaslake	✓	✓															
Peckham BMX Track and Burgess Park BMX						✓											
Redlands		✓										✓	✓				

	XC	DH	4X	DJ	Northshore	Freeride	Bike hire	Bike shop	Bike wash	Uplift	Map	Waymarked	Family	Visitor Centre	Accomodation	Cafe/food	FC
Shoreham DJs				✓													
Shorne Wood Country Park and DJs	✓											✓					
Sidley Woods				✓													
Slindon Quarry	✓			✓													
Swinley Forest	✓	✓				✓	✓	✓	✓		✓	✓	✓			✓	
Sloughbottom Park				✓													
Teddington DJs	✓			✓													
Thetford Forest	✓						✓	✓	✓		✓	✓	✓	✓		✓	✓
Tilgate Forest and St Leonards Forest	✓	✓		✓													
Track 40	✓	✓				✓											
Tring Park	✓	✓		✓								✓	✓				
Warley DJs				✓													
Wendover Woods	✓											✓	✓			✓	✓
Whiteways	✓											✓	✓			✓	✓
Wild Park	✓	✓		✓													
Willen Lake BMX Track				✓													
Wisley Trails				✓													
Woburn Sands	✓	✓		✓	✓	✓					✓	✓	✓				

The Midlands

	XC	DH	4X	DJ	Northshore	Freeride	Bike hire	Bike shop	Bike wash	Uplift	Map	Waymarked	Family	Visitor Centre	Accomodation	Cafe/food	FC
Birmingham BMX			✓	✓													
Bringewood		✓								✓							
Brackley DH	✓	✓				✓											
Cauldwell Woods DJs	✓			✓													
Cannock Chase	✓	✓			✓	✓	✓	✓	✓		✓	✓	✓	✓		✓	
Deeping BMX			✓	✓													
Eastridge Woods	✓	✓				✓						✓	✓				
Hopton Castle	✓	✓				✓				✓	✓	✓	✓				
Keele Woods and DJs	✓	✓		✓													
Leamington Spa 4X Track and DJs			✓	✓													
Ribblesford DH	✓	✓									✓						
Rutland Water Cycle Way	✓					✓	✓	✓			✓	✓	✓	✓		✓	

	XC	DH	4X	DJ	Northshore	Freeride	Bike hire	Bike shop	Bike wash	Uplift	Map	Waymarked	Family	Visitor Centre	Accomodation	Cafe/food	FC
Sherwood Pines Forest	✓	✓	✓	✓	✓	✓	✓	✓	✓		✓	✓	✓	✓		✓	
Swithland Woods	✓																
Tiny BMX Track			✓	✓													
Tipkinder Park			✓	✓													

The North

	XC	DH	4X	DJ	Northshore	Freeride	Bike hire	Bike shop	Bike wash	Uplift	Map	Waymarked	Family	Visitor Centre	Accomodation	Cafe/food	FC
Carlton Bank DH and XC	✓	✓									✓					✓	
Broomley Trails DJs				✓													
Calverley Woods	✓	✓															
Chesterfield BMX/4X Track			✓	✓													
Chevin Forest Park	✓	✓															
Chester-le-Street spots		✓		✓													
Chopwell	✓	✓		✓		✓					✓	✓	✓				✓
Delamere Forest	✓	✓		✓	✓				✓		✓	✓	✓	✓		✓	✓
Dalby Forest	✓	✓	✓		✓	✓	✓	✓	✓		✓	✓	✓	✓	✓	✓	
Devils Cascade DJs				✓													
Elland Park Wood	✓	✓															
Gisburn Forest	✓	✓				✓						✓					✓
Great Ayton Quarry DJs	✓			✓		✓											
Guisborough Forest	✓	✓										✓	✓	✓			✓
Hartlepool 4X			✓	✓										✓			
Hookstone Woods DJs				✓													
Hamsterley Forest	✓	✓	✓	✓	✓	✓	✓	✓	✓	✓	✓	✓	✓	✓		✓	✓
Hulme Park DJs				✓													
Hurstwood Trails	✓	✓				✓											
Ilkley Moor	✓	✓				✓											
Kielder Water & Forest Park	✓	✓	✓		✓	✓	✓	✓			✓	✓	✓	✓	✓	✓	✓
Ladybower Reservoir	✓	✓							✓		✓		✓	✓		✓	
Lee Mill Quarry	✓	✓									✓	✓	✓				
Little Switzerland	✓	✓									✓	✓	✓	✓		✓	
Longridge Fell	✓	✓															
Manchester Road DJs				✓													

	XC	DH	4X	DJ	Northshore	Freeride	Bike hire	Bike shop	Bike wash	Uplift	Map	Waymarked	Family	Visitor Centre	Ac comodation	Cafe/food	FC
Meltham Skills Trails	✓					✓											
Midgley Woods		✓				✓											
Park Bridge 4X		✓	✓														
Ramsden Lane DH		✓								✓							
Rawcliffe Pump Track				✓													
Roman Lakes Leisure Park	✓										✓	✓	✓	✓		✓	
Silton Forest DH	✓	✓															✓
Setmurthy DH Trails and Cockermouth XC	✓	✓									✓						
Stainburn	✓	✓									✓	✓	✓				✓
Storthes Hall DH		✓				✓											
Temple Newsam		✓	✓			✓											
TNF Grizedale	✓	✓		✓			✓	✓	✓		✓	✓	✓			✓	
Wassenden DH	✓	✓								✓							
Wiswell Wood	✓	✓									✓						
Woodbank DJs	✓			✓													
Whinlatter Forest	✓	✓		✓			✓	✓	✓		✓	✓	✓	✓		✓	✓
Wooler 4X	✓	✓	✓	✓													
Yeadon BMX Track	✓	✓															

Wales

	XC	DH	4X	DJ	Northshore	Freeride	Bike hire	Bike shop	Bike wash	Uplift	Map	Waymarked	Family	Visitor Centre	Ac comodation	Cafe/food	FC
Afan Forest Park	✓	✓		✓			✓	✓		✓	✓	✓	✓	✓		✓	
Abercarn	✓	✓														✓	
Aberhafesp Woods and DH	✓	✓															
Caerphilly DJs				✓		✓											
Bike Park Wales	✓	✓		✓	✓	✓	✓	✓	✓		✓	✓	✓	✓		✓	
Brechfa	✓	✓									✓	✓					✓
Betws Y Coed (Snowdonia East)	✓	✓					✓	✓	✓		✓	✓	✓	✓		✓	
Clarach DH	✓	✓				✓									✓		
Clyne Woods	✓	✓				✓											
Coed Llandegla	✓	✓		✓	✓	✓	✓	✓	✓		✓	✓	✓	✓		✓	
CoCoed	✓										✓		✓	✓	✓	✓	
Coed Y Brenin (Snowdonia West)	✓				✓	✓					✓	✓	✓	✓		✓	

	XC	DH	4X	DJ	Northshore	Freeride	Bike hire	Bike shop	Bike wash	Uplift	Map	Waymarked	Family	Visitor Centre	Accomodation	Cafe/food	FC
Cwm Rhaeadr	✓										✓	✓	✓				✓
Cwmcarn	✓	✓		✓	✓	✓	✓	✓	✓	✓	✓	✓	✓	✓		✓	
Foel Gasnach DH	✓	✓	✓							✓	✓	✓					✓
Gwydwr Forest	✓	✓			✓	✓					✓	✓	✓	✓		✓	
Kilvey Hill		✓				✓				✓							
Henblas/Caersws nr Newton		✓				✓				✓							
Llantrisant Woods DH	✓	✓															✓
Llanwrtyd Wells	✓										✓	✓	✓	✓		✓	
Maindy Road BMX Track			✓	✓													
Moelfre	✓	✓	✓			✓				✓							
Morriston Park Pump Track						✓											
Mountain Ash DH	✓	✓								✓							
Ponciau Banks			✓	✓													
Machynlleth	✓			✓		✓					✓	✓	✓	✓			
Nant yr Arian	✓	✓								✓	✓	✓					
Rheola DH Trail		✓								✓							
Rhyl Marsh Tracks			✓	✓													
Rudry DJs				✓													
Sandjumps				✓													
Snowdonia National Park	✓	✓				✓								✓	✓	✓	
Wentwood DH	✓	✓		✓		✓											✓

Southern Scotland

	XC	DH	4X	DJ	Northshore	Freeride	Bike hire	Bike shop	Bike wash	Uplift	Map	Waymarked	Family	Visitor Centre	Accomodation	Cafe/food	FC
Ae Forest (7Stanes)	✓	✓			✓	✓	✓	✓	✓	✓	✓	✓	✓	✓	✓	✓	✓
Cathkin Braes	✓					✓					✓						
Dalbeattie (7Stanes)	✓				✓	✓					✓	✓	✓	✓		✓	
Drumlanrig Castle	✓	✓			✓	✓	✓	✓	✓	✓	✓	✓	✓	✓		✓	
East Renfrewshire	✓	✓				✓					✓		✓				
Glentress (7Stanes)	✓	✓	✓	✓	✓	✓	✓	✓	✓	✓	✓	✓	✓	✓	✓	✓	✓
Glentrool (7Stanes)	✓				✓	✓					✓	✓	✓	✓		✓	✓
Innerleithen (7Stanes)	✓	✓			✓	✓				✓	✓	✓					✓
The Jedforest Trails	✓										✓		✓			✓	
Kirroughtree (7Stanes)	✓			✓	✓	✓	✓	✓	✓		✓	✓	✓	✓		✓	✓

	XC	DH	4X	DJ	Northshore	Freeride	Bike hire	Bike shop	Bike wash	Uplift	Map	Waymarked	Family	Visitor Centre	Accomodation	Cafe/food	FC
Mabie (7Stanes)	✓		✓	✓		✓	✓	✓	✓		✓	✓	✓	✓		✓	✓
Newcastleton (7Stanes)	✓			✓		✓					✓	✓	✓	✓			✓
Newmilns Bike Park		✓		✓	✓	✓						✓	✓	✓		✓	
Whitelee MTB Trails	✓				✓	✓						✓	✓	✓		✓	

Central & Northern Scotland

	XC	DH	4X	DJ	Northshore	Freeride	Bike hire	Bike shop	Bike wash	Uplift	Map	Waymarked	Family	Visitor Centre	Accomodation	Cafe/food	FC
Aviemore	✓	✓									✓		✓				
Callendar Estate	✓					✓					✓		✓				
Carron Valley Trails	✓	✓		✓							✓	✓	✓				✓
Comrie Croft Bike Trails	✓	✓			✓	✓	✓	✓	✓		✓	✓	✓	✓	✓	✓	
Fort William	✓	✓	✓		✓	✓	✓	✓	✓	✓	✓	✓	✓	✓		✓	
Glencoe	✓	✓				✓				✓	✓		✓			✓	
Golspie Highland Wildcat Trails	✓	✓									✓	✓	✓				
Glenlivet Estate	✓	✓				✓	✓		✓		✓			✓		✓	
Highland Perthshire Trails	✓	✓				✓						✓	✓	✓			
Isle of Arran	✓	✓									✓		✓			✓	
Kyle of Sutherland Trails	✓	✓		✓							✓	✓	✓				✓
Laggan Wolftrax	✓	✓		✓		✓	✓	✓	✓	✓	✓	✓	✓	✓		✓	✓
Learnie Red Rocks	✓			✓	✓	✓					✓	✓	✓				✓
Mains Farm Trails	✓					✓	✓					✓	✓	✓	✓	✓	
Middleden MTB Trails	✓	✓			✓	✓					✓	✓	✓				
Moray Monster Trails	✓	✓	✓		✓	✓					✓	✓	✓				✓
Pitfichie Mountain Cycles Trails	✓	✓									✓	✓					✓
Pollok Country Park	✓										✓	✓	✓			✓	
The Fire Tower Trail	✓			✓	✓						✓	✓	✓				✓
The Kelpies Trails	✓	✓	✓	✓							✓	✓	✓			✓	
Donkey Hill Dirt Track				✓		✓											
Duchany Woods		✓		✓		✓											
Dunkeld DH	✓	✓								✓							
Loch Ard Forest Trails	✓											✓	✓	✓	✓	✓	
Tentsmuir Forest	✓										✓	✓	✓				
Kirkhill Mountain Bike Park	✓		✓		✓	✓	✓				✓	✓	✓				✓

Acknowledgements

Extra special thanks to Kel Verbiest in helping with the update of this book.

In no particular order I'd like to thank Stacey at The Track, all at MBR Magazine, Andy Heading, Andy Lloyd, Steve Williams, Clive Davies & all at the Forestry Commission, the amazing crew at BGB (Susie Westwood especially!), Danny Milner in the UK, Ian and Dom at DMR Bikes, Gary Ewing & Mat Clark, Gary Williamson, Ian Linton, Jack Beckerson, James Chetwoode, Jamie Rodda, Janet Baxter, Louis Rogers, Pete Derret, Pete Tiley, Phil Young, Rob at Esher Shore, Richard Norgate, Scottish Woodlands, Snowdonia Guides, Steve Behr, The Santa Cruz Syndicate, Tiago Santana, Tore Meirik, Jacob Gibbins, Ali and Ash at Trail Addiction, the Bike Academy, Stuart Tee, Neil Cane, Toby and Jim at the Mountainbike Adventure.

An extra special thanks to: Nick Bayliss at Royal Racing – you're a legend mate. Dan Milner in Chamonix, France (or in cyberspace at danmilner. com), the super snappers Victor Lucas, James McKnight and Steve Jones, Rachel Atherton in Wales, Steve Peat, Sam Dale and Josh Bryceland in England – thanks for taking time out of winning the UCI to help me put this together, the guys at Dirt (Mike and Billy), Callum Swift rom The Uprising, Sam Reynolds and Blake Samson at DMR Bikes and Nike 6.0 and those amazing people that sent in shots and info on the more remote trails. Namely, Dugal D Ross, Greg and Gary Williamson, Andrew Denham, Paul England, Richard Norgate, Jimmy Doyle, Rene Weinberg, Allessandro Marengo, Kenneth Smith, Loic Delteil, Jack Beckerson, Dennis Stratmann, Paul Wurzinger, La Raya Creacions, Alicia Anton, Bruce Taylor, Morven Munro and Andy Boyle. Tim Bell, Jethro Loader, Steve Palmer, Paul Blackburn, Amanda Goller, Roger Knight at the Bike Barn, Malte Iden, Leanne Shipley, Mike at Mountain Bike Brighton, Billy Cheetham in Leamington, John Storey, Steve Cahill, Pauline Sanderson, Julian Williamson, Philippa Clark, Spike at Sqegg, Dan Hendrick, Vicky Chilcott, Rich at Cyclewise Training, Tim Sellors, Peter D'Aguilar, Sam Lattaway, James Colborn, Graham O'Hanlon, Matt Addison, Lyndsey Cheetham, Gail Graham, Julia Strathdee, Ben and Jason Wain, Mike Westphal at Viceroy's Wood, Pete at Roman Lakes, Adrian Taylor, Hilary Carpenter, The Woolybacks! Darren Edwards at Cannop, David Cole at Quench, Stephen Boyd, Arron McGregor, Antony de Hevingham, Tom at Southwales Downhill, Andy Soper, Stephen Garside, Gill Bell, Kate Murray, Alison Kohler, Alice Jell, Colin Williamson, Jeremy Brown, Simon Baxter, Simon Harry, Karl Pugh, Michael O'Connor, Joe McGhee, Michael Marsden, Kirsty Slater at Carbisdale, Gerrard Tattersfield, Ed Daynes, Lyndsey Carruthers.

We couldn't have made this possible without: Patrick Dawson, Angus Dawson and Leonie Drake at Footprint, Isobel Cameron at the Forestry Commission thanks an absolute million, Rowan Sorrell thanks an unbelievably huge amount, and all the riders and photographers and club members who've helped with info, pictures and maps. You're all legends.

If there's anyone we've forgotten, huge, huge apologies, and I'll make sure we put you in the re-print. Oh and please send any errors and omissions to: mountainbikingbritain@gmail.com.

Index

Index

Index

Credits

Footprint credits

Layout and Production: Angus Dawson
Editorial Assistant: Leonie Drake

Publisher: Patrick Dawson
Managing Editor: Felicity Laughton
Cartography: Kevin Feeney
Advertising: Elizabeth Taylor
Sales and Marketing: Kirsty Holmes

Photography

Front cover: Andy Lloyd/Pedal Hounds (Cwmcarn)
Back cover: Andy Llloyd, Andy MacCandlish,
Justin Sullivan
Inside front cover: Ian Linton (Fort William DH)

Print

Manufactured in India by Thomson Press Ltd
Pulp from sustainable forests

Footprint Feedback

We try as hard as we can to make each Footprint
guide as up to date as possible but, of course,
things always change. If you want to let us know
about your experiences – good, bad or ugly –
then don't delay, go to www.footprintbooks.com
and send in your comments.

Every effort has been made to ensure that the
facts in this guidebook are accurate. However,
travellers should still obtain advice from
consulates, airlines etc about travel and visa
requirements before travelling. The authors and
publishers cannot accept responsibility for any
loss, injury or inconvenience however caused.

Publishing information

Footprint Mountain Biking Britain
2nd edition
© Footprint Handbooks Ltd
November 2014

ISBN 978-1-909268-99-9
CIP DATA: A catalogue record for this book is
available from the British Library

® Footprint Handbooks and the Footprint
mark are a registered trademark of Footprint
Handbooks Ltd

Published by Footprint

6 Riverside Court
Lower Bristol Road
Bath BA2 3DZ, UK
T +44 (0)1225 469141
F +44 (0)1225 469461
footprinttravelguides.com

Distributed in North America by
National Book Network, Inc

OS Ordnance Survey This product includes
mapping data licensed from
Ordnance Survey® with the permission of the
Controller of Her Majesty's Stationery Office.
© Crown Copyright. All rights reserved. Licence
No. 100027877.